SOCIOLOGY IN THE AGE OF THE INTERNET

Allison **Cavanagh**

Open University Press

Open University Press
McGraw-Hill Education
McGraw-Hill House
Shoppenhangers Road
Maidenhead
Berkshire
England
SL6 2QL

email: enquiries@openup.co.uk
world wide web: www.openup.co.uk

and Two Penn Plaza, New York, NY 10121-2289, USA

First published 2007

Copyright © Allison Cavanagh 2007

A catalogue record of this book is available from the British Library

ISBN-13:   9780335217250 (pb)   9780335217267 (hb)
ISBN-10:   0335217257 (pb)   0335217265 (hb)

Typeset by BookEns Limited, Royston, Herts.
Printed in Poland by Oz Graf S.A.
www.polskabook.pl

The *McGraw-Hill* Companies

WITHDRAWN

SOCIOLOGY IN THE AGE OF
THE INTERNET

To my mother, with all my love.

Contents

Series editor's preface

In response to perceived major transformations, social theorists have offered forceful, appealing, but contrasting accounts of the predicament of contemporary western societies and the implications for social life and personal well-being. The speculative and general theses proposed by social theorists must be subject to evaluation in the light of the best available evidence if they are to serve as guides to understanding and modifying social arrangements. The focus of the series is the critical appraisal of general, substantive theories through examination of their applicability to different institutional areas of contemporary societies. Each book introduces key current debates and surveys of existing sociological argument and research about institutional complexes in advanced societies.

Allison Cavanagh's book addresses a technological innovation whose impact upon societies has been enormous and which looks sets to continue: the internet. The book is divided into four parts, which discuss the internet, respectively, as a network, as a form of (communication) media, as a social space and as a technology. This neat division allows the author to explore, in detail, the multidimensional nature of the internet and its impact, as well as the quite diverse debates that it has sparked. The result is a fascinating discussion, which serves both to introduce newcomers to this exciting field of investigation and to carve out a persuasive position within it. Allison Cavanagh opens her account with the claim that 'Studies of the internet often become obsolete between writing and publication.' This is surely true, at one level, given the pace of change in both the technology and the uses that social actors find for it. Analytic frameworks, if solid and insightful, however, do not and need not change at quite the same pace. They have the potential for enduring significance. We believe that *Sociology in the Age of the Internet* has this potential and will remain a central point of reference in both research and teaching for many years to come.

Acknowledgements

With grateful thanks to Nick Crossley, who inspired this book in the first place and whose advice on earlier drafts has improved the work immeasurably. Staff at the Institute of Communications Studies (ICS), University of Leeds, encouraged me in writing this and supported a period of study leave. I should particularly like to thank Robin Brown for helping me to reorganize my commitments and stepping into the breach himself to allow me to complete the work on it. Paul Taylor, Katherine Sarakakis and Richard Howells have helped me keep my spirits up, and Steve Lax particularly helped me ground and clarify my ideas around technology. I should also like to thank students taking my first-year course at ICS, who were supportive and generous with their feedback when I road-tested these materials with them, and who have helped me to keep my enthusiasm for the project alive throughout. Any bloopers are, of course, my own. Special thanks are due to Mark Barrett and Chris Cudmore at McGraw-Hill for their support and encouragement. Thanks also to Dr Maria Touri, who kept me on track by threatening to read it. My mother and my sister, Amanda, have listened, consoled, helped me stay focused, and brought me down to earth when some of my wilder ideas were on their annual migration. Finally, a special debt of gratitude to Alex Dennis, my long-suffering partner, for sitting through the umpteenth 'going on' of the day with saintly patience, offering his considerable expertise in leading me out of a myriad of blind alleys, and whose insights often turned the work in new, and better, directions. Without Alex, no book.

Introduction

Studies of the internet often become obsolete between writing and publication. Most academic work on this topic was in progress when the internet, as we recognize it today, was still 'virtual' in a Deleuzian sense, had not taken shape as a compelling force in modern life. The splurge of scholarship that appeared in print in the last years of the twentieth century was part of an early attempt to theorize and understand a technology that appeared as though from out of the blue, both to scholars and in populist discourse. The development of the internet, as a technology, medium and social space, has well and truly outpaced academic responses to it. Over the past decade, the whole nature and form of the internet has profoundly shifted away from its historical roots in military and academic research communities and towards a commercial and mass form. Whereas empirical studies have in some cases kept pace with these changes, the theoretical bedrock of scholarship into the internet has not. Academics find themselves trying to synthesize research and provide a future agenda for empirical investigation on the back of the hastily composed and now largely anachronistic theoretical frameworks of the early theorists. Scholarship which precedes from the premises established in the founding literature of internet studies will swiftly find itself at an impasse. The internet studied by the 'founding fathers' is buried deep under the accretions of the channels and layers of the modern internet. This vision of the internet, optimistic, communitarian, egalitarian and participatory, still acts as bedrock ideology of the internet, but the structures it supports no longer resemble those of the early days. And yet such is the nature of scholarship that the visions of the future of these early cyber-enthusiasts, within and without the academy, continue to dominate a sociological research agenda into it.

This chapter examines the position of the internet in modern sociology, considering the impact that it has had on sociology as a discipline and the reasons why it occupies an unusual position in modern scholarship. I begin by looking at the reasons why a programmatic response to the internet has proved so hard to generate. Here I argue that interdisciplinarity, whilst a rich vein for innovation in research, has not allowed a clear agenda to develop. This in combination with a widespread 'cult of the new' has promoted a view of the internet which takes as a resource that which should be deconstructed into a topic. I then go on to examine the internet's situation in sociology from the other side of the fence, looking at the various ways in which the advent of the internet has led theorists to call for a fundamental revision of sociological understandings in core areas of social life.

Sociology in the age of the internet

Overload and disciplinary dispersion

In 1989 Vincent Mosco comforted academics and students by observing that 'Computers are studied from almost every perspective imaginable ... It is easy to feel swamped by the sheer amount of material available on the computerisation of society and the global spread of communications media' (1989: 18). Mosco had not seen anything yet. With the rise of the internet this academic information overload has reached massive proportions. As with the information *on* the internet, analyses *of* the internet have multiplied to the point that the sheer volume of new materials is impossible to keep up with. However, the force driving this multiplication is still the same as that identified by Mosco, the distributed nature of discourse within the academy. The internet is a technology which touches upon and influences many aspects of our lives. It is appropriate, then, that it is studied from the perspective of all disciplines. However, for the scholar this presents a variety of challenges. Relevant studies on a given aspect of the internet are likely to be widely distributed within the disciplines. Thus, to take one area alone as an example, if we are interested in the topic of the internet and community, we will find relevant literature in sociology journals; in the work of social geographers; in computer studies; cultural studies; social policy; academic responses to speculative and science fiction, and thus in literary journals; in media studies; psychology; philosophy; business studies. The list is, in fact, potentially universal, with the possible exception of history, for studies are for the most part futuristic in emphasis.

The most obvious problem this presents is to awareness. How is it possible for any individual, howsoever methodical and hard-working, to keep up with this deluge of text? The institutional barriers to interdisciplinary knowledge are formidable and of these not least is that libraries, for the most part our point of access to literatures, are organized around subject-specific topics or disciplines. Thus, finding relevant materials, even in the best stocked of libraries, is a considerable logistical problem. The problem of actually getting your hands on the work in question is, however, less formidable than finding out that the work exists to begin with. Academia is organized into disciplines for a reason. In the early nineteenth century the landscape of academic disciplines was very different. A scholar commencing his (usually his) work at the start of the nineteenth century would be expected to master and understand a wide variety of knowledge, from mathematics, to philosophy, to classical languages and literature, in order to be an educated man. Still he would likely feel an intellectual midget in comparison to the philosophers of the Renaissance, for whom mechanics, anatomy, physics, astrology and natural history were as much a part of his (again his) lexicon as social thought and literature and language and art. The disciplines as we know them came about largely as a result of the explosion and multiplication of knowledge, fuelled by social changes resulting in the greater and finer division of labour, the availability of means of dissemination (mass production of print), and changes in mass and higher education. As Donald Case's (2002) synthesis of literature on information seeking shows, the academic strategies adopted in the search for information where supply exceeds demand, at least in so far as it exceeds our attention span, are focused around simplification and generalization. We selectively 'process' 'inputs', filtering out everything we do not regard as having a high priority. In trying to define that priority we use informal contacts, the 'invisible college' of our friends and colleagues. The greater the amount of information available, the greater the degree of specialization within the field. Thus, for example, in the discipline of history, a Professor of Medieval History may well have expert knowledge of an entire century, whereas a Professor of Modern History may specialize only in a decade or two due to the vast gulf in the amount of preserved sources from the different periods.

Thus specialization comes about, in part, as a response to information overload, but quickly becomes a mechanism of its perpetuation. The greater the degree of specialization between fields the wider the gap opens and the more researchers find that they must constantly 'reinvent the wheel', reproducing studies already performed from a different perspective or in a different institution. Moreover, the wider the gap, the more work must be performed to reconcile the disciplines at the end of the day. Thus in the case of internet studies, which does not have a disciplinary structure and instead is located in every discipline and every academic arena, the possibilities of information multiplication and overload are vast. Ironically enough, Case cites one study which claims that between 1997 and 1999 15,000 websites and 3000 newspaper and magazine articles had been published on the subject of information overload itself (Case 2002: 101).

The real irony, though, is that in the case of the internet this inaccessibility of information, and the need to reconcile and allow cooperation between dispersed information workers was the founding rationale of the technology itself (Terranova 2004: 57–8). The internet was designed to overcome institutional barriers to cooperation and dispersion of information. The modern hyperlink design, unintentionally, also overcomes the division of knowledge. As Herbert Dreyfus points out, the logic of hyperlinks is that of the 'interconnectedness of all elements'. Whereas the social organization of knowledge in the pre-hyperlinked era was that of a 'hierarchy of broader and broader classes (of knowledge) each including the narrower ones beneath it' (2001: 10), hyperlinks can support links between everything and everything else (although, as we will see later, in practice the picture is rather different). Thus the internet provides a perspicuous example of a clash of two mutually elaborating logics, those of specialization and those of connection.

However, noting this gets us no further forward for, after all, how can writing *another* book solve a problem of too much information? What this book is aimed at addressing is not the fact of overload, but in part the causes of it. The multiplicity of disciplinary responses to the internet means that in practice there is a perceived necessity for each area to 'reinvent the wheel'. As Burnett and Marshall have pointed out, one of the key problems in drawing coherent conclusions about the 'impact' of the internet is that studies are using different methods, asking different questions and, therefore, inevitably end up with a wide range of conclusions (2003: 65). This feeds back into mainstream debate as a polarization of positions, and debates about the internet inevitably take on a dichotomous quality, with each claim about its nature or development balanced against a contrary claim.

Disciplinary specific terminology

At the most basic level, this lack of a common intellectual currency means that there are no general agreements as to the kind of phenomena that the internet represents. There are, broadly speaking, three main characterizations of the internet in the literature, as social space, as media or as technology. Of course, in reality the internet is simultaneously all three of these. In separating out the different possible definitions of the internet it is important not to fall into the trap of confusing what Bourdieu *et al.* have referred to as practical and theoretical reason (1991). It is not the case that in everyday practice people go around using the theoretical constructs and schemas which sociologists generate to describe their behaviour. Thus, for everyday users the internet may be simultaneously all these, or none of the above. The point is that when we as sociologists talk about the internet we tend to vacillate between these definitions quite freely, and often without any acknowledgement of which sense is being referred to. This is problematic in so far as it obscures the nature of the internet as an object of enquiry. This can easily be seen if we consider the different kinds of questions prompted by the different definitions.

To see the internet as a social space, as many early theorists did, is to understand the experience of being online as being in another place, literally the agora or 'other place' of political theory. If we understand the internet as a place, then certain implications follow, amongst which, that people's actions can be understood as social behaviour using the same tools we use to understand social behaviour in other settings. This also means that text online is or can be a form of social interaction rather than, say, a form of art. What this foregrounds as relevant to the study of the internet are, then, group dynamics, forms of interaction, the amount of time spent online and the way that the internet as a place intersects or fails to intersect with other social arenas in our lives.

To understand it as a medium, however, shifts this focus. There is already a particular and rich vocabulary of concepts and approaches for understanding media. The relevant questions, following an agenda set by studies of mass media, are those of ownership and control, issues of representation and the nature of the relationship between producers and consumers online. If we are interested in the internet as a medium, then we are concerned with questions such as: what are the dynamics of information flow online? What are the main channels by which representations, information and images move around online? Who can control these and with what consequences? What are the similarities and differences between the internet as a media and other prior or potential media? How far can the internet fulfil the functions which we commonly ascribe to the media? How far does the internet challenge these understandings.

To view the internet as technology involves another shift again. This shift requires us to redescribe our questions in the language of technology. How did the internet come to be the thing that it is? Is it a 'thing' at all? What factors affect diffusion of the technology, and what consequences follow from these dynamics? How far can users of the technology affect its subsequent development, above and beyond a decision to use it or not? How far does the insertion of this new technology alter the nature of the social world? To understand the internet as a technology, unlike a media or a social space, is to understand it as an entity with attributes of a particular nature, which in *some accounts* (see Chapter 10) can imbued with a form of agency in its own right. The sociological imagination does not stretch to conceiving of a social environment as an agent, but technology, as will be argued later, has a different status in social theory and the field of technology studies is organized around the discussion of the potential for technologies to behave as actors and the extent to which they can be understood as autonomous agents.

Thus the way we understand the internet, the kind of environment, channel or thing which we understand it to be, is the first pre-given of sociological enquiry into the internet, directing the kind of questions it is logical to ask. Therefore it is important to be specific about what mental image we are generating when we apply one or other definition. This is rendered even more important by the fact that the internet is regarded as a challenge, on a basic level, to the integrity of these definitions. Whether it is still feasible to discuss a social environment as something apart from media in the age of the connectivity is a hotly debated topic. The trajectory of technology studies over the last few decades has been likewise towards a decomposition of the idea that technology and the social occupy different locations, a position which, as I argue in Part Four, discussion around the internet has rendered more public and more urgent. The idea that the internet challenges the separation of these domains does not exempt us from being specific about our uses of the concepts however. In fact quite the reverse. If we are to argue that the formerly separate domains are converging, it becomes ever more important to be precise about *what* we regard as converging. The problem that the dispersion of the field generates is, therefore, that these definitions of the net lead the observer to ask qualitatively different, although related, sets of questions and thus to understand the 'impact' of the internet in different ways. This means that after over a decade of sustained enquiry there are still no real certainties with regard to the internet and little in the way of scholarly consensus is emerging.

'Nerdwords': the cult of the new

Finally, the dispersion of scholarly efforts to understand the internet have led to a relentless and often inappropriate spawning of neologisms, terms which led David Gauntlett to author the ironic neologism 'nerdwords' (2004). As David Holmes notes, new media technology is subject to 'a bewildering array of attempts to define a kind of "cybergeist" in the form of some conceptual singularity … Typically this entails inventing neologisms which have the minimal reference to comparable terms whilst claiming the maximal reference to a universal condition.' As a result 'lexical fragmentation prevails at the precise juncture where an homogenous speech community is supposed to find renewal' (Holmes 2005: 192).

This often also manifests as a lack of discipline memory. The discourses of novelty which surround the internet have beguiled many theorists into the belief, sometimes erroneous, that new theory is required to account for the internet and new media. Whilst there are clearly areas where the internet requires us to make revisions, this book argues that these are less ubiquitous than a first glance at the literature on new media might lead us to think. That discourses of novelty around the internet lead us to take a 'back to the drawing board' approach to theory demonstrates the most fundamental problem with the dispersion of intellectual endeavour, namely that the lack of a clear disciplinary agenda makes it difficult for researchers to avoid accepting definitions of terms and concepts from outside their own field. In short, much of the discourse around the internet has been foisted onto academics or taken up uncritically in an example of what Bourdieu has termed the force of the preconstructed.

This theme is taken up in more detail by Jonathon Sterne, who highlights the conditions that 'have helped to steer the study of technology toward topics and approaches particularly amenable to business, military, and other applied administrative purposes' (2003: 368). Sterne points to the way that academic and commercial discourses have become blurred together, allowing the wholesale transfer of value systems from one arena to another. The continual evocation of novelty, what Andrew Ross has referred to as a discourse of 'gee-whiz futurism' (1999: 56) is, for Sterne, an example of the import of a 'value system of advertisement into scholarship, where "newness" is itself an index of sociocultural significance and transformative power' (Sterne 2003: 368). This is a two-way process, as

> corporate players in the technology field take up discourses originally intended as wholly academic. The most notable example of this trend can be seen through the travels of the idea of 'online community' … these same concepts of community have been widely adapted by dotcoms in an effort to market their product. Amazon.com and ebay.com are now just as likely to market themselves to advertisers and investors on the basis of their own branded 'communities' of users as they are to market themselves on the basis of the products and services they offer.
>
> (Sterne 2003: 368)

'Under these conditions', argues Sterne,

> the force of the 'preconstructed' – as Pierre Bourdieu has called it – weighs heavily upon anyone who chooses to study technology, since the choice of a technological object of study is already itself shaped by a socially organized field of choices. There are many forces in place that encourage

us to ask certain questions of technologies, to define technology in certain ways to the exclusion of others, and to accept the terms of public debate as the basis for our research programs. At worst, the relevant problems in, issues of, and approaches to technology appear entirely self-evident to us, based on the ways in which we have become accustomed to thinking about technologies as consumers, readers of the press, users, investors . . . or otherwise players in the technological field.

(Sterne 2003: 369)

In the case of the internet and 'new media', these preconstructions are not limited to the forms and capacities of the internet itself, nor even to the ways it is used, but extend out to include the forms of discourse itself. Thus the preconstructions of the field include a discourse of informality and another of collapsing boundaries. The majority of the literature in the field of internet studies, and certainly some of the most influential, is not academic in origin, comprising journalistic accounts, or futuristic visions of corporate big players (Gates *et al.* 1996). The playfulness and informality of discourse is reflected back from multiple points in discourse about the internet, from the strongly satirical commentaries in the mainstream press to the dominance of cybercultural approaches within social theory which emphasize the non-instrumental nature of 'the net'. Moreover this discourse is overwhelmingly futuristic and predictive, within and without the academy. This occurs in part as a result of the grafting on of the internet to academic argument concerning the 'information society', debates which were always more orientated towards policy for the production of the information society in the future than analysis of its forms in the present (Webster 1995). In another respect this discourse is echoed in what has been termed corporate 'vapourware', the hype that accompanies the announcement of a product ahead of its release or development. Internet products and services are always imminent. Social changes accompanying them are likewise always on the verge of appearing. Thus for example in the debate on intellectual property, which will be discussed in Chapter 11, fears and hopes are always directed at future possibilities, with various commentators playing Cassandra, scrying the entrails of the current social, legal and technological forms to predict its future affordances. The fear that the internet will lead to the collapse of traditional community, leaving us in an alienated wasteland of high-tech connections with people we never see is counterbalanced by the hope that e-communities may provide for civic renewal and the re-visitation of a lost 'golden age' of cooperation and support but there is little empirical warrant for accepting either. Whether these possibilities are ever realized in concrete form is a secondary, and often seemingly irrelevant, question.

Thus far it would not appear that academic discourse around the internet is particularly sociologist friendly. Sociology, with its grand theoretical schemas, appears forlornly anachronistic in an academic landscape peopled by theorists emphasizing diversity, multiplicity and difference. Sociology's equally dearly held commitment to the here and now, the empirical and demonstrable, seems less well suited to survive than cultural studies' commitments to virtuality, where this is understood as 'the mediation of relations, their malleability, their artifice, and the constant possibilities of arrangements and rearrangements' (Webster 2005: 451). For this reason, among more institutional others, Webster argues that cultural studies has outpaced sociology in responding to the new dynamics of information. Certainly cultural studies, as a more loosely defined academic arena, has been able to be more prompt in its response. It is significant and rather telling that Roger Burrows, in his response to Frank Webster, makes much of the influence of other disciplines in revitalizing the intellectual tools with which we regard the internet. For Burrows 'in recent years it has been the interface between Sociology and Social and Cultural Geography that has been the most productive in generating viable and durable analyses of ICT's' (2005: 468). However, this is in part because cultural studies' strength derives from its status as a bricolage or magpie 'discipline'. The most influential of cultural studies writers are those whose work fits best with a discourse of enablement rather than constraint and proscription. Foucault (1994), for example, regarded his methods as a toolbox not an agenda. Stuart Hall has likewise been generous in regarding his concepts as open and adaptable (Fiske 1996: 212). However this openness, whilst a clear advantage in developing new theorizing and new hybridities in perspective, does not help us in our current situation, for it gives us no means of understanding when new theory is *actually needed*.

This is precisely where sociology is uniquely placed to provide a solution to the problems of disciplinary dispersion, neologisms and imported definitions. Perhaps the one thing that unites sociology into a discipline, where admittedly, as Webster (2005) acknowledges, it can be ultimately decomposed into a collection of eclectic methods, is the rejection of preconstruction. Although Wittgensteinian philosophy has achieved only a limited influence in mainstream social scholarship few sociologists would disagree with Wittgenstein when he points to the problem that:

> Our civilisation is characterised by the word 'progress'. Progress is its form rather than making progress one of its features. Typically it constructs. It is occupied with building an evermore complicated structure. ... I am not interested in constructing a building so much as in having a perspicuous view of the foundations of possible buildings.
>
> (Wittgenstein 1980: 7)

Certainly we can read Wittgenstein's concern with clarity as an end in itself in C. Wright Mills' jeremiad against grand theory:

> When we consider what a word stands for, we are dealing with its semantic aspects; when we consider it in relation to other words, we are dealing with its syntactic features ... Grand theory is drunk on syntax, blind to semantics. Its practitioners do not truly understand that when we define a word we are merely inviting others to use it as we would like it to be used; that the purpose of definition is to focus argument upon fact, and the proper result of good definition is to transform argument over terms into disagreement about fact, and thus open arguments to further enquiry.
>
> (Mills 2000: 34)

Sociology's consistent concern with definition is rooted in just this problem. As Mauss argued:

> when (a) nomenclature has not been established, the author moves imperceptibly from one order of facts to another, or the same order of facts bears different names in the work of different authors ... A preliminary definition will spare us these deplorable inconsistencies and interminable debates between authors who, on the same subject, are not talking about the same thing.
>
> (Mauss, 'La Priere', reproduced in Bourdieu *et al*. 1991: 98)

This seems to me to be precisely the issue that is on the table when we try to understand the state of scholarship around the modern-day internet, that although we use the same terms we are often not talking about the same thing. To take an example, we could consider the case of the term 'virtual' and the multiple meanings which it has accrued. For some writers 'virtuality' is invoked as the unreal, as in the common sense of 'virtual reality' – almost reality. In this sense the word 'virtual' is a negation of what follows. To say something virtually happened – as in 'the ball was virtually in the net' – is also to say that it did not happen – the ball may have been nearly in the net, but this does not constitute a goal. Virtual has also come to be used as a catch-all term designating 'electronic' or 'on the screen', a terminological shorthand for mediation. In Deleuzian terms, however, the 'virtual' has a quite different and very specific meaning. For Deleuze the 'virtual is not opposed to the real but to the actual. The virtual is fully real in so far as it is virtual' (1994: 208). The virtual is, as Massumi explains, 'the future-past of the present', a term which locates virtuality somewhere between a premonition of the present and the conditions of possibility of the production of that present (Massumi 1993, cited in Roe 2003). These slippages of meaning create an intellectual environment in which it is difficult to be sure whether a writer who refers to 'virtual space', 'virtual banking' or 'virtual libraries' regards these things as a real thing, a fantasy thing, a past thing, a future thing or merely an electrical thing. This can be confusing. In the next chapter, I explore this problem further in relation to another of the information revolution's 'hurray' words (Whyte 2003: 61), networks. Here I examine the 'network metaphor' as this is used in social theory, and show that the vast variety of ways of conceptualizing the idea and operation of networks means that even within a discipline it would be serendipity rather than design if two theorists were talking about the same concept at the same time.

This work then is an attempt to provide a context for these debates, examining the differences and common assumptions of the various approaches, and providing an explication of the roots of debate in order to establish common terms of reference. It aims to evaluate the need for new theory and to show where the framing of a problem has reached a research 'blind alley'. In the rest of this chapter I will be examining the main areas where there have been calls for new theory as a result of new media and the rise of the network metaphor.

Sociology and cultural studies

With the rise of the internet, or more precisely the rise of various forms of the 'virtual', some of social theory and philosophy's most sacred cows have been trotted out for potential slaughter. Nicholas Gane's contribution to a very informative debate which took place in the pages of the journal *Information, Communication and Society* in 2005 is an excellent example of this broad-ranging agenda. Gane takes issue with Castells' argument that the internet merely affixes a further dimension to existing social relations:

> The question this raises is whether online interaction simply *adds on* to existing social relationships or in fact transforms them. I would argue the latter. It would seem to me that internet-related technologies *have* directly altered the patterning of everyday life, including the way we work, access and exchange information, shop, meet people, and maintain and organise existing social ties. These technologies have done more than 'add on' to existing social arrangements; they have radically altered the three main spheres of social life, the spheres of production, consumption and communication. This is why it is possible to talk of a qualitatively new field of sociological analysis that might be called 'the information age'.
>
> (Gane 2005: 475, original emphases)

For Gane, the internet and its related technologies present a challenge not only to our understanding of all existing 'main spheres of social life' but further to the most basic category of social understanding, the privileged position of the human as a discrete entity (2005: 475). There is much to take issue with in Gane's account, not least of which is that the notion that the internet might be a simple 'add on' is dismissed out of hand rather than taken as a point of enquiry. In this Gane exemplifies cultural studies, concern with the emergent properties of culture rather than their phenomenal forms. Gane further exemplifies the concerns of cultural studies in his description of the 'three main spheres of social life' as 'production, consumption and communication'. Although sociology would have little problem in seeing production and communication as amongst the main spheres, the substitution of 'consumption' for other possible spheres – for example, 'social integration', 'identity', 'community' or 'society' – although consistent with a cultural studies agenda for the internet (see above), is from a sociological perspective prematurely pessimistic.

Gane's demands for new theory are, however, a valuable summary of the failings of mainstream social theory viewed from the perspective of cultural studies. In the 'takeover of much Sociology by Cultural Studies, or at least the occupancy by Cultural Studies of territory towards which one might have supposed Sociology had a prior claim' (Webster 2005: 440), the differing disciplines' approaches to new media and the internet have been more than instrumental. Indeed, in many ways the field of new media is the ground on which this alleged 'clash' of the academies is fought. Of course this is not to see the field as structured by competition between sociology and cultural studies. This would be overly simplistic and would also overstate the differences between cultural studies and sociology. It is to say that the demands for new theory are largely framed in terms of the concerns of cultural studies. This is clear when we consider that the main arenas in which it is argued that the internet requires a rethink of core concepts are those of community, power and identity. I will deal with each of these in turn.

Community

The issue of community in the digital age is positioned at the intersection between geography, communication and culture. The two main debates in the area, for sociology, have been focused around questions of the internet's relationship with offline life and offline communities, and the intersections between physical and electronic space.

The first of these resolves into the questions of how we can understand the nature of online communities and how far these communities can serve the same socially integrative role as traditional communities. By and large these studies posit a division between virtual and real community, and try to understand the impacts of one upon the other. The majority of studies have considered this in terms of the internet's impact upon traditional communities, rather than the impact of offline life on online community formation, although this approach is also exemplified in studies of area or community internets. The dominance of the impacts approach reveals one of the central assumptions of this body of literature, namely that community formation online is driven by a logic of its own, a logic tied into the technical affordances of the internet itself or to the logic of modernity which the internet expresses. From the point of view of sociology this is rather unhelpful as a sociological 'hunch' would lead practitioners to see impact as running the other way, namely towards an examination of the way offline communities organize online ones, and indeed this is what is most commonly found in studies of the two (see Part Three).

However, studies of online/offline community are more problematic in another key respect, namely that the research evidence to date is more or less evenly split between two opposing points of view: first, that the internet, and mass media more generally, lead to a decline in offline communities and, second, that they actually enhance offline life. The attempts to resolve this baffling impasse in evidence and interpretation have precipitated attempts to re-conceptualize what is meant by community in sociological circles. These issues in turn resolve down to questions such as whether a community is constituted from multiple weak ties or requires a lesser number of strong ties; what the role of communication can be understood to be in relation to community; and what factor takes a primary role in establishing that a community exists, whether the primary basis of community is values, or practices, or co-presence, or shared history or shared mentality.

The second debate, that of the 'impact' of communications infrastructures on the physical spaces in which we live, is concerned with understanding how physical spaces are represented in the electronic. Thus Burrows and Ellison (2004) consider the way that geographical areas are represented online, through mapping, databases and electronic materials. This concern is situated within the context of an attempt to understand how informational capital, as an organizational form of modern life, brings about a reconstruction of physical space, how the spaces of 'flows' and 'places', in Castells' terms (1996) interrelate. In this, however, the space of flows, the electronic spaces, are usually seen as dominant in so far as they are understood to be manifestations of the political and social power of informational capital. Thus, essentially this approach represents a variation of the community impacts approach albeit on a macro level. However, the latter concern articulates and foregrounds changed conceptions of power and inequality as a more central problematic than the social/community impacts approach.

Power

Power and inequality are also key areas in which sociological theory has been said to require an overhaul as a result of the advent and rise of the internet. Over the past decade sociologists have been called upon to reconsider their attachment to traditional, occupational or structural definitions of class in favour of more technologically and media-centric ones. Richard Florida's analysis of the rise of the 'creative class' (2004), Kroker and Weinstein's theory of the 'virtual class' (1994), Scott Lash's theories of information underclasses and overclasses (2002), Mark Poster's virtual classes (1998), Hardt and Negri's multitude (2004), and Manuel Castells's network classes (1997) all have new communications technologies as a central reference point. Social class has come to be predicated on the wider notion of inclusion and access, where access is understood as ability to use and exploit new media.

Thus Lash, for example, argues that, under the new informational order, exploitation is no longer a useful way of understanding the operation of power as it is less central to the operation of power dynamics than exclusion. For Lash, an understanding of exclusion as the locus of power is developed into a tripartite model of social structure. This takes the form of a large mid-section of the 'included', a power elite, the 'self-excluded' overclass who are those whose identification as a global elite allows them to self-exclude from their national/local space and self-include at the global level, and an underclass of the forcibly excluded, those who lack the resources to make personal connections and include/exclude from national or local cultures (Lash 2002: 5). In this and similar accounts inclusion/exclusion is a matter of connection to the social whole through the ability to make unrestricted choices. Power is thus understood within this perspective as the ability to realize the self through personal selection. This understanding is played out at a number of levels. The micro approaches are the most common levels of discussion, where the internet is regarded as reproducing exclusion through poverty, here appearing as not possessing the technological means of access or, taking a broader definition, not possessing enough 'know-how' to self-include. At medium levels, sociologists have been much concerned with the ability of particular groups and social movements to effectively access resources. Thus arguments concerning the use of the internet by women, for example, often devolve down to the question of access considered here as know-how. Feminist writers have therefore become concerned with the extent to which women find information technologies exclusionary (Herring

1996; Plant 1997; Hawthorne and Klein 1999). At a broader level yet access/power is also framed as a political question and as a matter of national/state power. The regulation of internet content by nation states, as in the attempts by many countries, including China, Indonesia and Israel, to prevent their subjects accessing the internet as a whole, frames the power of nations as the ability to self-include/exclude.

However the use of exclusion/inclusion raises particular issues when used as the basis for understanding class. To understand social and global stratification as a question of inclusion/exclusion is to take a rather different approach to power to that previously accepted in sociology. Superficially these discussions may remind us of theories of class which are founded in ideas of social or cultural capital. The game of inclusion or exclusion appears at first glance to resolve into the question of resources which can be marshalled by the individual, whether these are the social capital resources, crudely oversimplified into who you know, or cultural capital resources, which open the gates of a given field. Thus it ostensibly parallels theories of class such as those proposed by Bourdieu, where class situation is seen as reproduced through cultural capital, through the possession of non-material resources which allow the individual to gain entry to a particular field and maximize his/her position within it.

However, this similarity is a shallow surface reading at best. Whereas cultural and social capital theories of class seek to understand the determinants of class position, the social inclusion/exclusion narrative takes a more voluntaristic line, seeing class as mutable. The ability to include/exclude oneself is seen as situationally specific and locally determined, which tends to fly in the face of a substantial body of correlations between indexes which refer to class and life chances more generally. In this sense there is little analytical difference between this approach and meritocratic discourses which abolish the determining power of class altogether.

More interestingly, whereas in Bourdieu's account the dynamics of inclusion are hard-edged, subject to gradations and clear insider distinctions between social groups, social inclusion narratives see inclusion/exclusion as dichotomies. As Perelman has pointed out, 'the flowery rhetoric of the information age rekindles Adam Smith's tattered vision of social harmonies' (1998: 4), a social harmony based on collaboration and cooperation between the ranks of the included. Discussion of class in the information age therefore tends to assume a parity and a level of equality between the informationally privileged, and this is a direct legacy from the earlier information society theories. Daniel Bell, for example, notoriously made little distinction in his analysis of the rise of information workers between those at the top of the information hierarchy – for example, scientists, educators, policy analysts – and those lower down, such as postmen and secretaries (Webster 1995: 42–4). This is not an oversight but an operating assumption that derives from the development of information society theories as a direct rebuke to Marx.

In the immediate post-war period the USA entered a period of economic and social calm, founded on its monopoly of world resources and control of international security. This was heralded by theorists such as Bell as a new age, an end to social antagonism. That these optimistic predictions failed to survive the social unrest of the 1960s has not prevented their revival and since the 1970s we have seen the rise to dominance of various theories which hold similar premises. Of these, theories of the information society occupy a central place and, in the wake of the mass adoption of the internet in the West, scholars have returned to the questions raised by these bodies of theory. Essentially theories of the information society depend on the idea that the widespread diffusion of new information technologies serves to bring about an end to class conflict through bringing about an end to the working class. Dyer-Witheford (1999) has identified the main premises of the argument that the information society leads to a farewell to the working class. First, it is argued that the nature of work is transformed such that the division between management and labour, between the bourgeois and the proletariat, is no longer relevant. In the 'knowledge economy' all workers have a share in knowledge, the knowledge relevant to their work, and therefore all have a share in the means of production and the product in so far as knowledge is both the thing produced and the means of producing it. A corollary of this is the expected elimination of poor working conditions. As the economy comes to be founded on service industries, so the experience of work moves from harsh manual labour to less alienating information work. In the information society, everyone is a white-collar worker.

Moreover, the nature of information itself, argue some theorists, adds a new element to the mix. Information, unlike money, is a non-rivalrous resource, which is to say that it is not depleted with use. My possession and use of information does not prevent yours, unlike in the case of other resources. Moreover, the cost of production of information, unlike the costs of material goods, is minimal in so far as the cost of disseminating it is minimal (Perelman 1998). The logical end point of the transition to the information society is, therefore, the dissolution of the notion of property. Information, held in common by all ranks in the workplace or widely distributed throughout a post-industrial hierarchy, becomes a common possession and with it the basis of class tension is lost. However, the thesis does not end with the experience of work. Information society theorists also argue that these sweeping economic changes would be accompanied by the dissolution of mass urban life and its consequent alienation. In the information society, the experience of the mass urban society is transformed through the individualizing tendencies of late capitalism, leading to the collapse of traditional 'grand narrative' sources of identity such as race, religion and, of course, class. It is the dissolution of the working class that thus puts an end to social conflict. The advent of the information society then renders class struggle irrelevant as 'everything once signified by the red flag – the classless society, nonalienated work, the dissolution of property – will be achieved simply by the operation of the technology that capital is itself so frenetically developing' (Dyer-Witheford 1999: 27). Thus the view of power that is characteristic in this field is a rather flat one in which, lacking the support of grand meta-narratives, broad categories which confer social power are deconstructed into individual relations. In particular this emphasizes the role of identity, which itself is also under attack within the academy in the face of changes allegedly wrought by new communications technologies.

Identity

Identity is central to new technologies of communication, for it is a common trope of the literature that new media bring about fundamental transformations in the way our sense of our self is developed and in the role that identity plays in social interactions and social situations. For theorists of the network society, the self is a 'reflexive project' (Giddens 1991), an artefact developed from heterogeneous resources by the individual as a result of the choices they make. Modernity, for theorists such as Giddens, Beck (1992) and Castells (1996, 1997), rests on the decline of traditional cultural resources, narratives and authority as ways to organize society and identity. For Giddens the collapse of traditional sources of self requires the individual constantly to develop and redevelop their 'self', eternally querying 'Who am I?' For Beck this liberation from restrictive identities allows the self to be multiply penetrated by market forces. In the absence of a prescribed cultural identity, self is developed with reference to ephemeral and unstable institutions and practices. Therefore the only patterns which people experience in common are biographical entry and exit points into market-dominated institutions. For Castells (1997), the impersonal forces of the market are again central, in so far as they are the generating principle behind self. Selves develop with reference to the 'net', they are challenges to 'globalization and cosmopolitanism on behalf of cultural singularity and people's control over their lives and environment' (Castells 1997: 2). They are, therefore, driven by the 'net' in so far as they are a political expression of opposition to it. Castells goes on to describe three formal types of selves or identities: the legitimizing, those which derive from and legitimize dominant forms and institutions of power in society; resistance identities, those which oppose dominant forms and institutions but which seek inclusion into the 'net' and therefore also legitimate power; and project identities, those which resist institutions and forms of power through rejecting their terms. These identities will characteristically involve a contestation of meaning and be part of an attempt by a social group to redefine their place in society (Castells 1997: 8).

The trajectory of theory here is towards the idea that modernity induces conditions of fragmentation and therefore of liberation. It is odd, then, to observe that the same conditions of transformation, loss of community, loss of large-scale meta-narratives such as class and race, has historically led the sociological imagination in the opposite direction. For William Kornhauser, writing in the 1950s, it was clear that: 'People are available for mass behaviour when they lack attachments to proximate objects. When people are divorced from their community or work they are free to unite in new ways' (1959: 60). Where existing strong ties of community and identity broke down, sociologists of the 1950s and 1960s saw the spectre of conformism, ideology, authoritarianism and the mass society. Now, describing the same conditions, we look to the emergence of individualism, voluntarism, the self as the *raison d'être* of modernity and the transcendent will as its *primum mobile*. Such a sea change as this has been explained through techno-centric and media-centric accounts which look to the dominant forms of media. Thus the mass society of the 1950s is understood as the outcome of the dominance of the mass media of broadcasting, and the individualism of the modern era that of the individualizing tendencies of the internet, narrowcasting and satellite television. These approaches enshrine a form of media or technological determinism at the heart of our explanations of these changes, something which, as we will see later, is profoundly problematic.

However, the understanding of the self as a reflexive project, as something that emerges from the confrontation between the individual and impersonal forces of modernity, also provides the background to the development of ideas of the self by cybercultural theorists. For cyberculture the technical affordances of the internet alter the character of identity construction in so far as it transforms a personally experienced imperative towards reflexive identity construction into the postmodern realm of identity play. Thus Sherry Turkle argues that the online self is constructed not given. To be online is to be 'inventing ourselves as we go along', having a fluid and multiple self (Turkle 1995: 10–12). In Turkle's account, as in similar accounts by Hayles (1999) and Stone (1996), the self is a random construct organized around mutation and transformation, and there is no stable subject to act as an arbiter of a real or essential self. For cyberculture theorists, network identities make little sense as they still depend on the idea of a stable subject, a stable identity which shadows the transcendent will of the user as it moves in and between online areas and offline life. The self as it appears in these accounts is liberated from even the limited social determination ascribed to the offline world of the network society. It is a voluntaristic construct, directed by the will of the user and the characteristics of the technology.

This understanding of the self has considerable implications for socio-logical approaches to power. The multiple and fluid self cannot draw on stable definitions of power and status. Rather, power is formed new in each situation and each aspect of each situation. Having power in one area of life does not provide a means of translating that power into another, different, social situation. Power online is argued to be both inherently diffuse and to take precedence over more common cultural scripts of influence. Thus, for example, online a teenager can set himself up as a cultural commentator and gain power in this sense. Bloggers, people who keep online 'weblogs' or 'blogs', are seen to be challenging the international corporate domination of news media.

This multiplicity and fragmentation feeds back into conceptions of power. For Lash, for example, as earlier for Lyotard (1984), the internet is a perspicuous example of the need to revise the understanding of power as situated in discourse in favour of power as information outside discourse. Discourses, or in Lyotard's terms meta-narratives, can no longer be used to understand how knowledge is generated, since internet information is not constrained within them. Thus new knowledge practices and new ways of generating knowledge do not allow for the use of social discourses in mediating that knowledge. Playful knowledge surfing as a standard way of gathering information online (Dreyfus 2001: 10–12) serves to level out all types and forms of information in so far as it decontextualizes it. Any given piece of information can be linked to any other in the practices of playful surfing. In so far as neither the producer nor the consumer is imbricated within the social at the point of production/consumption, grand narratives cannot be brought into play. Hence in Lash's account the levelling effect of the internet, the extent to which it allows the individual to transcend his/her circumstances and invent a new self, is taken to a greater intensity.

In this sense power, when divorced from social status through the anonymity of online life, is understood as a function of persuasion and representation (Yoon 1996). This serves to foreground the role of the symbolic within social life but often, as Webster (2005) and Wynn and Katz (1997) have pointed out, at the expense of attributing too great a role to the individual will, seeing the consciously formulated goals of the individual as both determining and transcendent of local circumstances. The relativism of this approach, however, does not extend to the internet itself. In these accounts the electronic sphere of the internet is often granted a form of determining agency in forming the individual, whose experiences online are regarded as at least on a par with, and more often more real than, those in the material world.

Summary

Thus attempts to provide theories which are capable of encompassing and explaining the internet have led to calls for a revision of sociological ideas of solidarity, power, identity and the self. Very little of this new theorizing is directly prompted by the internet itself, since the majority of theorists whose work has been drafted in to help explain this new phenomenon predate the internet by decades. However, the internet, as a 'hot' topic, serves as a proving ground in which these theories and their advocates struggle for academic mastery. Characteristically in the first blush of enthusiasm for the internet the lines of academic debate were unclear, however now, after over a decade of sustained scholarship, the core debates and areas are clearly visible. Yet the study of the internet as a social phenomenon is still incoherent, a theoretical miscellany which bewilders the newcomer.

This book attempts to ground the debates by examining them within the context of the disciplinary concerns of sociology. It is an attempt to 'set out a stall' and to provide an agenda for the sociological investigation of the internet. The chapters overview the areas of media, solidarity and technology, providing a means of linking new debates back to their parent discourses and situating sociological approaches to the internet within the body of socio-logical thought more generally. The danger here is that this work will be seen as an attempt to argue that the internet is not revolutionary, that there is 'nothing new under the sun' from sociology's point of view, and therefore that there is no need to examine either the internet or sociological theory with a view to revising long-held problematics. To do so would be merely a form of misplaced nostalgia. It is certainly the case that very productive and potentially revolutionizing questions can be asked in relation to the internet, but this book argues that these are not, by and large, the questions that *have been* asked.

In Part One I explore the development of the 'network' metaphor in the social sciences. Chapters 1 and 2 examine the idea of networks as these have been developed in the social sciences from the anthropological social network approaches developed in Britain in the 1960s, which focused on the forms of ties within social entities, through the more heterogeneous networks studied within the actor-network paradigm, and onwards to the political and economic networks of the network society. Chapter 3 then goes on to look at emerging theories in network studies and in particular the new impetus to the development of network theories provided in the writings of Deleuze and Guattari, whose work has been used as a theory of new communicative networks. This chapter argues that the adoption of the network metaphor within sociology offers new opportunities for revitalizing our understanding of many arenas but that the uncritical adoption of networks is not without its problems. Chapter 4 goes on to a consideration of the way that the internet acts as a network, what sort of network it can be said to be and the way that the internet has developed as a network in real space. The actually existing internet, I argue, often bears little semblance to the forms predicted by new social theories.

Part Two looks at the internet as it appears through the lens of media studies, the way that the discourses of media construct the internet as an object of enquiry. In this the idea of a public sphere, and the sense in which the internet is argued to act as one, is central. In Chapter 5 I outline the main approaches to the public sphere through an examination of the work of Habermas, and then go on to examine the ways that Habermas's theories have been applied to the internet. I here argue that there is a fundamental gap in these approaches between the utopian or dystopian futuristic theoretical contributions and empirical evidence currently available and attempts to reconcile evidence and theory. This part addresses the kinds of questions which are foregrounded when we regard the internet as a potential public sphere, and considers the way this constrains the sociological imagination with regard to the topic.

However, contemporary studies of communications and media are strongly divided between the politically inflected studies of the media as providers of information and studies of media as entertainment. The latter figures in political theories as the dark shadow of media manipulation and debasement, the red-haired stepchild of the information revolution. Entertainment is here figured as a synonym for 'dumbing down', the erosion of the public sphere as an arena of reason by mass passivity and commercial 'sofa-culture'. In 1966 Harold Mendelsohn railed against 'the ascriptive language that is used by layman and scientists alike ... the language about entertainment emanating from these sources is equally highly negative, disparaging, and admonishing. In short entertainment is relegated to those rubrics that are ordinarily reserved for the 'evils of society' (cited in Case 2002: 103). The remnants of this understanding can still be detected in the modern academy in the over-determination of the appropriate topic of media studies as 'the public sphere'. It is clear that in restrictively delineating the proper topic of debate about media roles to the political and politico-informational, media scholars have tended to treat as a *resource* aspects of the social which should more properly be regarded as a *topic*. Part Three picks up on some of these themes, looking at issues of social cohesion, identity and integration, themes which are central to our ability to posit an informational culture or a vigorous public sphere, but which are de-emphasised in media studies approaches. In this arena the disciplines of sociology, cultural studies and social geography have had the greatest impact and it is these contributions which will be examined.

The final part looks at the overall context of debates around the internet through an examination of the development of the sociology of technology in recent years. The sociology of technology prior to academic interest in the internet and new communications technologies was rather Balkanized within the academy, constituting a particular strain of enquiry which had become decoupled from that of the mainstream. Part Four argues that interest in the internet has moved this area of the discipline to centre stage in sociological thought more generally, and revitalized debate in this arena. As a consequence new theories, and new readings of older contributions, are being developed in order to account for new communications technologies. This raises questions as to whether technologies can be understood in quite such monolithic terms as they characteristically have been, and whether new theories are required to account for communications technologies in comparison to technologies more generally. This chapter argues that the reconstruction of the sociology of technology which is taking place in reaction to the fusion of new theory around the internet has invigorated the field, in particular deconstructing the organizing framework of agency and determinism which has previously dominated attempts to understand technologies, but that this has often occurred less by redundancy than fiat. In these two chapters I offer a possible line of fruitful enquiry and consider the way that one core debate concerning the internet, that of intellectual property, can be understood from within it.

Part **One**
The **rise** *of the* **network metaphor**

1 Approaches *to* networks

The American spoof newspaper, *The Onion*, in a spin-off volume entitled 'Our dumb century' carried the news of the sinking of the *Titanic* in 1912 under the headline 'World's biggest metaphor hits iceberg'. The *Titanic* has been a metaphor for man's industry; historical progress; optimism or hubris; for man's relationship to nature; for the English class system; for the whole way of life of a society at the birth of the twentieth century. In recent years, though, the internet has taken over as the world's hardest-working metaphor. In academic texts, popular literature, media reportage and fictional representations the internet appears as a metaphor for postmodernity, spirituality, social cohesiveness, the globe, international politics, the self, the body, and even the psyche. From human top to toe, from the most intimate to the most seemingly remote, the internet has been used as a way of explaining and modelling our new understandings of ourselves and the world around us and the resonance of the metaphor is in many ways grounded in the growing public profile of the 'new' science of networks. The network metaphor in social science, biology, politics, technology and economics is rapidly developing as a new way of conceptualizing the workings of the material and social world. The idea of a network has, argue Hardt and Negri, become a key isomorphism, a common form with differing content, of the times. Just as for the social theorist Michel Foucault (1977) the isomorphisms of the nineteenth century were the panoptical institutions of the prison, the school, the hospital and the workplace, so in our time the network has taken over as the common form of our institutions and imagination. 'Today' argue the authors,

> we see networks everywhere we look – military organizations, social movements, business formations, migration patterns, communications systems, physiological structures, linguistic relations, neural transmitters, and even personal relationships. It is not that networks were not around before or that the structure of the brain has changed. It is that the network has become a common form that tends to define our ways of understanding the world and acting in it.

(Hardt and Negri 2004: 142)

Networks today, then, act as an organizing framework in which all institutions, knowledge and relationships are ordered. As John Law notes, 'we've reached the point where every man, woman, child and dog seems to be talking about networks' (2000: 5).

Of course the metaphors we use as scientists do not merely reflect our understandings, they act to constitute them. In the past few years it has become commonplace to refer to the body as a network of parts, and much medical research is framed by the attempt to understand how the body communicates with its parts. As Gareth Morgan (1997) notes, there are a number of ways in which we can understand as complex a social, physical and informational entity as a firm, as an ecology perhaps, or as an organism, or a brain, a machine or a prison but the initial metaphor used draws our attention to some aspects of the entity whilst simultaneously disguising or occluding others. As one commentator puts it:

> Scientific metaphors are not merely linguistic ornaments that can be discarded in favour of literal description ... metaphors are essential to the conception, development and maintenance of scientific theories in a variety of ways: they provide the linguistic context in which the models that constitute the basis for scientific explanation are suggested and described; they supply new terms for the theoretical vocabulary, especially where there is a gap in the lexicon; and they direct scientists towards new avenues of enquiry.
>
> (Lewis 1996, cited in Lopez 2003: 11)

Metaphors act as a set of resources which scientists, and of course non-scientists, use to develop strategies of enquiry and ways of thinking. They are the root of epistemological strategy in real life and in science. When we use a metaphor – for example, 'life is a journey' – then there are certain logical entailments, for example that one has a destination, can make progress, that a journey is individual, that we follow our own paths, and so on. The metaphor encourages us to view our experiences in certain delimited ways, as goal-orientated, as about movement. It gives us a language to comprehend our experience, but also constrains us to particular understandings. The image of life as a journey, for example, does not capture the feelings of aimlessness or lack of purpose which some sociologists have seen as characteristic of modern society (e.g. Furedi 2005). The idea of a destination entails that failure to progress towards it is a set-back. Thus the metaphor accents some aspects of social life, but occludes others.

The common sense of metaphors takes on a different character when we think about how metaphors are used in science. Work in the sociology of science has highlighted the importance of the way that metaphors migrate between different disciplinary domains in academic enquiry. Lopez (2003: 15–16) typifies the processes as either transformation or transfer of a metaphor. A *transformation* has occurred when a metaphor has been entirely appropriated within a new discursive domain such that its alien origins are not readily apparent. Lopez (2003: 16) uses the idea of circulation as an example of this transformation. When we refer to the circulation of currency, the origins of the metaphor in anatomy are not readily evident. The metaphor, however, directs us to understand the economy as the movement of money. From this the idea of, for example, 'trickle down' economics, otherwise known as Reaganomics, where wealth is understood to be like a fluid and therefore to trickle down from the wealthy to the poor, becomes cognitively resonant with our understandings of the way the world works. Water, we know from experience, finds its own level, gravity dictates that its level is the bottom. When we add to this an understanding of social structure as a vertical hierarchy, with the wealthy at the top, then trickle down gels with our own common sense.

However, the process by which a metaphor comes to be transformed, entirely appropriated, can become stalled at *transfer*, where a metaphor remains discrete from the body of knowledge in which it has been adopted. Lopez (2003: 20–42) again gives us a useful example, that of Durkheim's organismic metaphor of society as a body, with limbs and organs. This metaphor is the root of the functionalist perspective in sociology, based around the idea of society as a organism, in which all parts serve a function and without which the continuation of society is not possible. However, whilst the metaphor of a social body has achieved a wide currency within social sciences, it is not the case that functionalist sociology views its objects *as* a body but merely *as like* one, and thus the metaphor has been adopted or transferred but has not been transformed or nativized.

The adoption of a new metaphor from one disciplinary domain to another is significant in so far as it has become a sociological truism that this is often at the root of epistemological transformation within a discipline (Kuhn 1962; Maasen and Weingart 2000). This truism is concretely realized in the case of networks. As Duncan Watts points out, a mutual investment in networks as a research agenda has united researchers in the physical and social sciences, and has brought together mathematicians and sociologists, psychologists and biologists in the search for understanding. Networks are regarded as the new super-science (Barabasi 2003; Watts 2004), a leading contender for the basis of a long hoped for 'theory of everything'.

In the case of networks, however, the migration of the metaphor has been made problematic in so far as there is little general agreement as to what a network actually is, what it is about a network that makes it not a group, or an ecology, or a system. As Watts observes: 'In a way, nothing could be simpler than a network. Stripped to its bare bones a network is nothing more than a collection of objects connected to each other in some fashion. On the other hand, the sheer generality of the term *network* makes it slippery to pin down precisely' (Watts 2004: 27; original emphasis). Where a concept is as ambiguous as this, as I have argued above, scholarship in the area becomes precarious, since scholars may be using the same concepts but they are unlikely to be talking about precisely the same thing. When Barney writes of identity that it is

> constructed as a complex pastiche of relationships, choices and acts, enacted in a variety of parallel and overlapping contexts. Rather than being a fixed, natural and unchanging condition corresponding to a stable situation and set of attributes, postmodern identity is artificial, fluid, contingent, multi-faceted and mutable. It is, one might say, a lot like a network.
>
> (Barney 2004: 151)

what notion of networks is being employed here, and how does it differ from both prior concepts, for example postmodernity, and also from other conceptions of networks themselves?

Where the idea of networks is employed without a rigorous nomenclature then it is likely, as Latour, coming to networks from a different perspective, argues, that terminological imprecision in the use of the idea of a networks renders the term ambiguous and confusing (2005: 129). In this case using the concept of 'networks' flattens the distinction between 'technical networks', social network entities and networks as a method of uncovering social life. Thus for Manuel Castells, for example:

> A network is a set of interconnected nodes ... [a form of organization that has] ... inherent flexibility and adaptability, critical features in order to survive and prosper in a fast-changing environment. This is why networks are proliferating in all domains of the economy and society ... However ... [networks] ... have had considerable difficulty in coordinating functions, in focusing resources on specific goals ... For most of human history ... networks were outperformed as tools of instrumentality by organizations able to muster resources around centrally defined goals ... Now ... the internet, enables networks to deploy their flexibility and adaptability ... an unprecedented combination of flexibility and task performance, or coordinated decision-making and decentralised execution ... which provide a superior organizational form for human action.
>
> (Castells 2001: 1–2)

However, as John Urry's argues in his critique of Castells:

> the term 'network' is expected to do too much theoretical work in the argument. Almost all the phenomena are seen through the single and undifferentiated prism of 'network'. This concept glosses over very different networked phenomena. They can range from hierarchical networks such as McDonald's to heterarchic extremely inchoate 'road protest movements', from spatially contiguous networks meeting everyday to those organised around imagined 'cultures at a distance', from those based upon strong ties to those based on very important and extensive 'weak ties', and from those that are pretty well purely 'social' to those that are fundamentally 'materially' structured. These are all networks, but they are exceptionally different in their functioning one from the other.
>
> (Urry 2003: 11–12)

The problem is not, as we will see later, unique to Castells but derives from the multidisciplinary origins of network analysis combined with its recent rapid rise to popularity in scientific, social and cultural discourse, a popularity which is, as I argue below, not independent of the rise of the internet as a symbol of the times. The remainder of Part One describes a typography of the different conceptions of network in circulation within sociology at the moment, before moving on to an examination of the way that the internet as a metaphor has inflected understandings of networks, promoting some features over others.

2 Network methodologies

The earliest attempts to use networks as a sociological concept stem back to the 1930s (Scott 2000: 7), but did not win many converts and failed to establish a properly developed methodology. These problems were taken up in the 1960s with the writing of anthropologists working out of Manchester University in England. For the Manchester researchers, networks were the concrete form of social structure. Drawing on Radcliffe-Brown, they focused their attention on the roles and forms of connection between people as a way of understanding the structural forms of society. For Radcliffe-Brown:

> In the study of social structure, the concrete reality with which we are concerned is the set of actually existing relations, at a given moment of time, which link together certain human beings. It is on this that we can make direct observations . . . But it is not this that we attempt to describe in its particularity. Science is not concerned with the particular, the unique, but only with the general . . . what we need for scientific purposes is an account of the forms of the structure.
>
> (Radcliffe-Brown 1940: 224)

The forms of the social, the networks of connection and the structure such networks take was, for Radcliffe-Brown, a constant. Although the particular forms of the social life are dynamic over time, the structural form, the spatial configuration of relationships is relatively static.

That anthropology should be concerned not with the particular occupants of roles or connections but with the configuration of these generally was a major breakthrough in developing the network approach for, as these ideas were later adopted by Nadel, Barnes and Bott, the separation of the forms and the content made it possible directly to compare and describe the formal features of these structures. For Siegfried Nadel (1957) the possibilities of this approach could be realized in the form of a mathematical and universal description of structure. Nadel placed the idea of 'role' centre stage in his analysis, believing that the social network approach offered the opportunity to describe a social system in terms of a hierarchically interlocking structure of roles. This in itself could, he believed, overcome a central problem of social theory at this point, namely the conceptual difficulties of identifying and separating out a society or social grouping as distinct from other entities within a similar locality. Radcliffe-Brown saw the problem as a methodological one, how to chart and delineate the universal.

> It is rarely that we find a community that is absolutely isolated, having no outside contact. At the present moment of history, the network of social relations spreads over the whole world, without any absolute solution of continuity anywhere. This gives rise to a difficulty which I do not think that sociologists have really faced, the difficulty of defining what is meant by the term 'a society'. They do commonly talk of societies as if they were distinguishable, discrete entities ... Is the British Empire a society, or a collection of societies? Is a Chinese village a society, or merely a fragment of the Republic of China?
>
> (Radcliffe-Brown 1940: 224)

The problem then is to select a unit of analysis, and Nadel saw that reducing the social to the network meant that the nature of the unit of analysis need not then be specified in advance of the study but could be allowed to emerge through empirical investigation, the nature and boundaries of the social group could be *discovered* rather than forming the basis of the enquiry, essential in the large-scale studies which the Manchester anthropologists were then undertaking (Mitchell 1974: 280).

Nadel's vision of social networks as a universal *method* of discovering the social was only partly realized in the work of subsequent anthropologists. Clive Mitchell, one of the Manchester group, described social networks in terms of a 'personal order'. The personal order is the pattern of links between an individual and others, and the links which these others themselves have. This is hardly novel, being little more than a restatement of mathematical graph theory, which looks at graphs (defined as nodes connected by links) and the formal properties which emerge from them (Barabasi 2003: 10–13). What *is* more novel is Mitchell's specification of the building blocks of such networks. Networks are developed out of interactions, either communicative or instrumental. Whilst in practice these are ideal types and any individual interaction would involve elements of both, the importance of the distinction between communicative interactions and instrumental interactions will be seen later.

Although Mitchell's work advanced some elements of Nadel's vision of the new science of social networks, this was selectively achieved and, as John Scott argues, Mitchell's omissions paved the way for the untimely truncation of social network research in Britain at least. Mitchell developed Nadel's programme of a mathematical and formal anthropology of networks in so far as he rigorously adhered to the formal properties of relations and ties, and resisted reducing relationships down further than the fact of the tie. Mitchell's networks were ones in which 'kinship, friendship and neighbourliness were combined into a single, multistranded relationship that it was inappropriate to break down into its constituent parts' (Scott 2000: 31). Mitchell popularized a number of concepts for understanding the operation of networks. In particular he focused attention on 'reciprocity', the extent to which the tie, and its obligations, is acknowledged by both parties;

'intensity', the strength of the tie, where a strong tie would usually involve multiple overlapping obligations as the tie is present in a number of situations, and 'durability', the temporal length of the tie (Scott, 2000: 31–2). In other respects, however, Mitchell's realization was limited. Although Mitchell argued that in principle the total network of a society was 'the general ever-ramifying, ever-reticulating set of linkages that stretches within and beyond the confines of any community' (Mitchell 1969, cited in Scott 2000: 30), in practice it was necessary to confine the analysis to 'partial networks', the selection of particular aspects of the total network for the purposes of analysis. The requirement to select elements was pressed upon the researchers by the paucity of analytical tools available. This argument parallels that of Weber who argues that sociological analyses should redescribe all complex social phenomena in terms of the actions of their participants – although in practice it is rarely possible to achieve this because of the complexity of the phenomenon in question (Lukes 1968). Total analysis of this nature, thus, although long a methodological ideal, is impractical in real research situations. Whilst this point is uncontroversial in sociology in general, Mitchell's strategic response to the problem proved more problematic. Mitchell and his colleagues operationalized the concept of partial networks to focus upon the structures of interpersonal relations to the exclusion of those of institutional relations. This, argues Scott, meant that the model of the Manchester anthropologists 'tended towards a residual definition of the social network: network analysis concerns only the interpersonal sphere that is left behind after formal economic, political and other roles are extracted' (Scott 2000: 32). As a result social network analysis in Britain came to be understood as a specialized method for examining interpersonal relations (Scott 2000), one which was difficult to use in the field, impractically resource heavy and was, as a result, largely overlooked.

The core features of social network analysis's networks are therefore (see Table 2.1), first, that they act to constrain the behaviour and actions of individuals within them. Second, networks are in principle universal, the commitment to the study of ego-centred networks being a methodological necessity rather than an ontological principle. Third, networks do not affect the identity of the individual components of them, people are linked in formations, but retain an individual purpose and identity. Fourth, networks are formed voluntarily through the interactions of actors, but their patterns are culturally specific. Thus, for example, the definition of immediate and remote kin differs from society to society, and with it the patterning of interaction and obligation between kin. In the modern West where the nuclear family is the norm, relations of interdependency and obligation between cousins are rarer than in societies where the family unit is more extended. From this follows the fifth point, namely that networks are not reducible to the intentions of the actors who constitute them. Although agency remains in the nodes of the network, these nodes are culturally patterned. Finally, social network analysis retains a commitment to networks as a method of studying structure, rather than positing, as in the case of other theories, that they are a structure in their own right.

Table 2.1 Theories of networks

Approach	Extent of network	Network action	Network comprises	Components' relationship to whole	External forces patterning network	Agency/meaning resides in	Perspicuous example
Social network analysis	Universal	Constrain action	Personal connections	Retain identity	Patterned by culture	Remains in nodes	Kinship
American social network analysis	Particular	Enable action	Personal connections	Retain identity	Patterned by choice	Remains in nodes	Club membership
Actor-network theory	Particular	As coherent entity	People, texts, objects, etc.	Lose identity	Goal/success or failure	Comes from goal	Classroom
Castells	Particular	As coherent entity	Locations, functions, technologies, micro-networks	Retain identity to an extent	Global power relations	Comes from goal	The United Nations, the G8
Hardt and Negri	Universal	Amplify/enable action	People, motives, orientations	Retain identity to an extent	Global power relations	Comes from links	Riots
Deleuze and Guattari	Particular	Facilitate flows	Network relationships	Identity is fluid	Patterned by flows	Comes from network	Traffic
Internet theory (post-structuralist)	Universal	Enable action	Personal connections	Identity is fluid	Patterned by connections	Comes from network	Fansites
Internet architecture	Universal	Facilitate flows	Protocols, servers, computers, code, data, fibre-optics	Co-evolution of parts	Efficiency/goal	Comes from goal	Intranet/conduit
Social internet	Particular	Amplify/enable action	People, motives, texts, organizations	Retain identity to an extent	Patterned by connections	Comes from network	File sharing

In the USA, social network analysis achieved a higher status and greater uptake and interest. In the process, however, this involved a revision of the core metaphor, from the structural network metaphor of the Manchester school, to a more spatial, geographical metaphor. The work of Mark Granovetter popularized the use of social network concepts and set the agenda for American research in the area emphasizing the communicative aspects of networks. Granovetter's work *Getting a Job* (1974) examined the social networks formed and drawn upon by individuals in their search for employment. His findings, that the most important sources of information on job opportunities were not individuals to whom the job seeker was closely tied, e.g. family and close friends, but acquaintances and colleagues, led him to formulate his thesis on the 'strength of weak ties'. Strong ties, argues Granovetter, may be more important to the individual in forming relationships, facilitating social cohesion and so forth, but in terms of moving information around they are of less use. Within a group of people who share strong ties it is likely that any information known by one party is also known to the rest. Because these relationships are overlapping, and those with strong ties associate together in many different social circumstances, they would all possess the same knowledge. In seeking a new job, the individual is obliged to move outside this network, to search for new information, and this means drawing on 'weak' ties, associations which are sporadic and unique and which do not form part of the informational gestalt of the group.

In examining networks as a means of informational diffusion, Granovetter moved away from the Manchester model in four respects. First, the focus on the strength of the tie moves away from the temporal models of Mitchell and his colleagues. Where the Manchester anthropologists were concerned with the way forms of social networks endure over time, Granovetter's model is more a 'just-in-time' one where aspects of a network are activated and deactivated according to need. Weak ties are a resource, but one which would not feature in the formal description of an individual's 'personal order' in Mitchell's terms. Second, the communicative model is one in which social ties are facilitative rather than constraining. Where the Manchester anthropologists had sought to understand the way that social networks operate to structure social action, the US researchers understood them to be more an architecture through which the individual will was realized. Third, the communicative basis of networks led Granovetter and his followers to reject the British distinction between organizational networks and interpersonal ones (Scott 2000: 33–6), allowing social network analysis a potentially greater role in sociology than the narrow niche to which it was confined in Britain. Finally, the communicative model eclipsed some of the prior concerns of British social network analysis, in particular concepts around the 'reciprocity' and 'durability' of a network, in favour of the single variable 'strength' or 'intensity'. Thus the American model offered a simplification of social network concepts, but one which increased the theoretical range of the method.

American social network analysis, then, envisages networks as particular, rather than universal. Although, for Nadel, the limits of networks were a methodological shortcoming rather than a description of the nature of networks, the innovations of Granovetter and others see networks as inherently limited, a form of social capital which enables action. American social network analysis, however, preserves its British counterpart's commitment to individual components retaining their individual pre-existing identity after becoming part of the network. Thus it also preserves the understanding that agency resides in the nodes, rather than in links or the network as a whole.

Actor-network theory

As the above discussion shows, American social network theory provides a bridge between anthropological social network theory and the second body of research to be considered here, actor-network theory. Actor-network theory (ANT) (which will be examined again in a different light in Part Four) shares American social network theory's concern with the social as a series of conduits, bridges and linkages which allow the movement of information, resources and ideas around society.

Actor-network theory precedes from a rather different theoretical problematic than its anthropological precursors. Whereas social network theory begins by trying to understand the forms and varieties of social structure, ANT's problematic is an investigation of the nature of power in society, the way actions, beliefs and opinions are formed and developed. For ANT a central starting position is a critique of traditional understandings of power within sociology. For actor-network theorists power has traditionally been understood within sociology as an explanatory variable – when we want to understand how a thing comes to be we search for the source of social power which has enabled this to occur. Thus we could explain the dominance of Microsoft as a software supplier with reference to Microsoft's ability to control and direct the world market for software. For ANT this is unacceptable; power cannot be the cause of power. Rather it is a property that emerges from interaction. When we seek to explain Microsoft's dominance in ANT's terms, we cannot reason circularly that this is an effect of power stored up in the past like a battery, but must seek to understand how that power is developed *in the present.* Thus for ANT power, society, the social order, is something that is always in process, always being developed, furthered, challenged, in the present tense. This puts ANT at odds with the concerns of the anthropologists, who sought to understand how structure, society, binds and forms action today. For ANT this concern is misguided; as Latour epigrammatically puts it 'Society is not what holds us together, it is what is held together' (Latour 1986: 276).

Thus ANT's networks are similar to American 'communicative' networks in a second respect, namely that they are temporally situated rather than eternal. They are assemblages which are activated, deactivated, dynamically created and re-created, rather than eternal cultural forms. For this reason, ANT cannot engage in the comparison of networks, since these are not amenable to comparison in this way. Actor-network theory studies are inherently single case studies, which, moreover, are not intended to be generalizable. John Law (1992) and Bruno Latour (2005, 2004) have both, separately, addressed the terminological confusion around ANT, pointing out specifically that ANT is not, and never had attempted to be, a theory in the sociological sense. Rather ANT is a set of procedures for investigating the social world, a methodology rather than a method or a theory in so far as it constitutes a set of interventions to reduce and analyse complex social phenomena which are bounded and supported by certain epistemological commitments.

Of these, one of the core commitments, which distinguishes ANT from earlier views of networks, is to 'radical relationality', the principle that there is no necessary a priori significance or properties attached to a given object, person or idea. This principle is most clearly expressed in ANT's commitment to regarding natural and social objects on a level of equality. For ANT there is no necessary difference between the social and the natural (see Callon 1986). Networks are understood to comprise an assemblage of objects, of which people are only one element. Thus Callon's analysis of experiments performed at St Brieuc Bay, where a group of researchers sought to establish different methods of clam fishing in order to solve the problem of dwindling stocks of clams in the area, brings together the actions, motivations and effects of the network created by the researchers, the fishermen, and the clams, upon whom the livelihood of the fishermen depends, and whose behaviour is the subject of studies performed by the researchers. For ANT the social is 'nothing other than patterned networks of heterogeneous materials' (Law 1992: 2). Human social relations rarely take the form of

> interaction between unmediated human bodies [therefore] ... If human beings form a social network it is not because they interact with other human beings. It is because they interact with human beings and endless other materials too. And, just as human beings ... prefer to interact in certain ways rather than in others – so too do the other materials that make up the heterogeneous networks of the social.
>
> (Law 1992: 3)

Objects, then, participate in social relations, helping to structure and define them. For example, a telephone conversation held on a mobile phone is structured by the technology as much as by the two parties to the conversation. Mobile phones 'prefer' not to go through underground tunnels for example, they also 'prefer' to not show the face of either speaker. The human ear 'prefers' to hear sound without loud background noise, employers prefer to have their roving employees contactable. All these preferences work to constitute the form of the interaction and thus the form of the network that results when phones, employers, employees and tunnels are brought together.

The corollary of radical relationality is that the level of equality between the parts of the network, the relative power to determine the interaction, is not fixed ahead of time. Actors, technologies and procedures do not possess fixed attributes which allow them to bring power to play in the situation. All points in a network are potentially equal in terms of their determining power, the ability to determine the shape of the interaction and of the network is produced *by the network*, by the interaction of its parts. In the mobile phone example, an employee, who is otherwise powerless, can thwart an employer's desire to maintain contact with her by mobile by invoking the phone's 'dis-preference' for tunnels. In another scenario, the phone's preference for working very well when not in tunnels can thwart the employee's preference for having an evening off at the cinema, to embarrassing effect. The particular configuration of the network at the time in ANT terms produces the power relations within it.

A second corollary of this point is that ANT networks are not merely a linking up of stable parts but involve a transformation of these parts. When groups of actors, things and procedures are linked up into a network they become simplified into the network itself, what ANT refers to as punctualizing. As Law explains:

> All phenomena are the effect or the product of heterogeneous networks. But in practice we do not cope with endless network ramification. Indeed much of the time we are not in a position to detect network complexities. So what is happening? The answer is that if a network acts as a single block, then it disappears to be replaced by the action itself and the seemingly simple author of that action.
>
> (Law 1992: 5)

When a network pattern is naturalized or punctualized it disappears from view as a network and reappears as a unity, as an actor in its own right. What this involves is a transformation of the parts of the network such that they work as a unity, they are 'locked in' to certain roles. This process of locking in is referred to as 'interessement', the process by which actors are enrolled into the network. Callon describes it in these terms:

> Each entity enlisted by the problematization [the original definition of the situation] can submit to being integrated into the initial plan, or inversely, refuse the transaction by defining its identity, its goals, projects, orientations, motivations, or interests in another manner ... Interressement is the group of actions by which an entity attempts to impose and stabilize the identity of the other actors.
>
> (Callon 1986: 207–8)

In the process of forming a network, the identity of the elements from which the network is comprised is subservient to the problematization, the overriding definition of the situation. Thus when a network is formed its elements are not stable nodes and dynamic links, as in social network theory, but are dynamically defined by the network. What emerges then is a network that behaves as thing. Perhaps the metaphor of network here is under strain for a more applicable metaphor would be a melting pot, where elements lose their former identities and acquire a new one from the recipe followed.

This brings us to a problem with the ANT of networks, an area where ANT is notoriously rather vague and potentially contradictory in its account of network development, namely the question of the initial problematization. Actor-network theory has a tendency to speak of the dynamics of network creation, the processes of problematization, interessement, enrolment, mobilization and dissidence (Callon 1986) as though the network was the creation of a specific actor. In the quote from Callon above, we find him referring to 'attempts to impose ... identity', the 'initial plan', the submission of other participants. Monteiro points to 'tendencies in ANT to (over) emphasize relatively goal-directed actions' which, whilst not intrinsic to ANT, are all too often displayed in practice in ANT studies (Monteiro 2004: 130). Latour also recognized the 'managerial, engineering, Machiavellian, demiurgic character of ANT' (Latour 1999, cited in Monteiro 2004: 132) in some studies. This appears at odds with actor-network theorists' own avowed positions that power in networks is co-created along with the network itself. For Latour the initial force of a particular problematization cannot explain the perpetuation and diffusion of that problematization. In a translation model the question is not how the problematization is moved on but how and why each step in the diffusion takes the initial problematization and passes it on. '[T]he initial force of the first in the chain is no more important than that of the second, or the fortieth, or of the four hundredth person. Consequently it is clear that the energy cannot be hoarded or capitalised' (Latour 1986: 267). Thus the view of the network as created by the goal-orientated action of one individual or group *in order to* achieve a given goal is fundamentally at odds with the precepts of ANT. Whether one takes the position that this contradiction constitutes an implementation failure, a gap between precepts and execution, or not, will determine one's view of the validity of ANT as a method.

A mere implementation failure is of less consequence than an apparent incongruity, especially where a great deal of theoretical work rides on the difference. The problem can be expressed in the following terms. As Kenneth Burke (1945) points out, all *social* action presupposes a grammar without which it cannot be discussed at all. In order to describe a social action, rather than a behaviour or reflex, we need to have an actor, a social situation, ends/goals, and the means to achieve them. These concepts, whether explicit or implicit are a necessary prerequisite for describing a social action, and without them placeholder terms have to be introduced. For ANT this condition involves it in a form of conceptual 'bootstrapping' for it is required to make use of concepts from outside its own theoretical system in order to critique these concepts to begin with. Actor-network theory cannot adequately account for intentionality and instrumentality for these are understood to emerge with the network itself. In sociological terms any social action requires a goal, but in ANT terms goals are produced through activity, and so we are left with a circular position that activity produces goals and goals activity. In order then to account for a *'primum mobile'* ANT is required to import intentionality from elsewhere. If intentionality is attributed to the network as a whole, ahead of specific network formations, then the concept of a network and another concept, that of social structure, are interchangeable. It is then unclear why we need to talk of networks at all since we already have a way of describing the phenomena – as structure. If intentionality resides in the connections, then intersubjectivity would be a more valid redescription. If, as seems to be the case in the 'Machiavellian' strain of ANT, intentionality is attributed to the nodes, then we inevitably find ourselves referring to a master node as a theoretical shorthand for agency. Thus if we hold to the view that the identity of components in a network are formed by a master node it is unclear why we need ANT to tell us this, and if we abandon this, viewing identity as a property of the network itself, we find ourselves back searching for the source of this identity. The problem then is one of finding a Euclidean position, being forced to use intentionality as a conceptual shorthand in order to formulate the basis of an empirical enquiry into the origins of intentionality. Thus ANT networks can be considered as goal orientated to the extent that they cannot methodologically be rendered without this.

The final feature of ANT networks, which differentiates them from other forms of social networks are that they are exclusive rather than universal. Although social network theory's networks were understood to be empirically distinct social systems, with social network theory as the *method* to be used in *uncovering the boundaries* of these systems, in practice networks have been found to be less amenable to the imposition of boundaries than the researchers hoped. Most students will be familiar with the issue of the 'six degrees of separation' through the game played by linking film actors to the actor Kevin Bacon. Where an actor has acted in a film with Kevin Bacon they are one degree removed and they have a Bacon number of one. Where they have acted in a film with someone who has acted in a film with Bacon, then they have a Bacon number of two, and so on. The game, invented by movie-buff students in the USA, is a variation on an equally tongue-in-cheek though less fun game played by mathematicians, who link to the prolific mathematician Paul Erdos through co-authors (Barabasi 2003: 47). The games, however, have the same principle, namely that potentially anyone can be linked to anyone else, provided one has a given definition of 'link'. What this flags up is that social networks as they are described in the terms of reference of social network theory are *in principle* particular and *in practice* universal. What we are viewing is potentially one giant network to which we are all to a closer or more distant degree joined. Actor-network theory's networks are similarly situated. In principle they are exclusionary in so far as the constitution of a network depends on differentiating those elements which are part of one network from another. As Callon explains, the process of interessement is the process of defining the identity of the enrolled participants in such a way as to build devices which attach the participant to your group but detach and isolate him/her/it from other groups who would seek to define its identity otherwise and in oppositional terms (1986: 208). Thus it is a set of procedures for removing an object/actor from one network, conditioning it to work within yours and preventing the appropriation of the element by rival networks/problematizations. What this means is that, in principle, networks are discrete entities, with albeit dynamic but functioning boundaries. However, as we will see later, whilst this is theoretically the case, in practice change in any one network tends to impact on the composition and functioning of numerous and diversely located others.

Thus ANT's networks are particular, rather than universal, operating through exclusion as in the case of US network studies. Similarly, ANT networks share their goal-orientated nature with US network studies. Actor-network theory networks, however, unlike either British or American social networks, are composed not only of people and personal connections, but of texts, objects and heterogeneous materials, which are both relational, in so far as objects do not possess fixed properties, and mutational – objects are transformed rather than linked. As a result, agency is seen to reside in the initial goal which prompted network formation rather than nodes, links or networks as a whole.

3 *The* network society

We now move on to look at a different set of interests in networks, those that focus their analysis on the macro or global level. This is a vast area of study and it is beyond the remit of this chapter to discuss all approaches so therefore I will be looking at three theorists, Manuel Castells and the collaboration of Hardt and Negri, as perspicuous examples of different approaches. Finally this chapter will look at a major influence on theorizing new networks in the work of Giles Deleuze and Felix Guattari. What these treatments of networks share, and where they substantially differ from prior theories of networks, is a commitment to understanding networks as a *new form of social order*, rather than, as in the previous examples, a method for *uncovering the existing social order*. For both Castells and Hardt and Negri the network is a new form of order which emerges from human association when that is enacted on a global stage.

Castells: power as ozone

One of the core problems with the notion of the network society is that the etymology of the term is rather vague. The idea of a network society developed out of theories of the information society and in many ways the terms are synonymous (Webster 1995). As a result, it is often difficult to unearth what exactly is meant by 'network' in a network society. As Darin Barney (2004) points out, the idea of networks can be used as a self-validating concept. Networks are the forms of the social in a network society, and a network society is a society characterized by networks. The work of Manuel Castells is the most justly famous of these rather dizzying dissections, and unfortunately does rather typify the trend, for Castells is notoriously reluctant to state terms, defining an informational society as 'the subject matter covered in this book' (Castells 2000: 21). In Castells' work 'the net' is used as a shorthand for the global network society, the structure of interconnections and interdependencies which characterize modern political, economic and cultural life on a global canvas. It is unclear how far such a definition overlaps with or elaborates upon the definitions of networks used by other social theorists and sociologists. However Castells does make use of a more concrete term, 'flows', which seems more comparable to the structures and relationships covered by the term 'networks' in other works.

Yet even with this term we are not much closer to a workable definition since Castells' analysis of the network society is one in which core concepts tend to be bipolar and mutually elaborative. Thus flows are understood to be the structure that exists in the space of flows, which is in turn defined as that which opposes the 'historically rooted spatial organization of our common experience: *the space of places*' (Castells 2000: 408–9, original emphasis). Places are, according to Castells, '*a locale whose form, function and meaning are self-contained within the boundaries of physical contiguity*' (2000: 453, original emphasis). 'Place-ness' is a function of the meaning ascribed to a location as this meaning has persisted over time. 'It is precisely because their physical/symbolic qualities make them different that they are places' (Castells 2000: 457). 'Place-ness' is also that which is eroded by the space of flows. The ability of a locale to maintain a set of meanings, be be self-sufficient and self-determining is limited by the abstraction of power into the realm of flows and networks. Thus far, then, definitions are rather thin on the ground. Flows are the opposite of places, places are that which are eroded by flows.

Castells does, however, specify certain characteristics which can be used to *describe* (he is adamant that that does not mean *define* – Castells 2000: 442) the space of flows, if not the flows themselves. The space of flows is described by the presence of three layers of support. In the first instance there is the material support, the circuit of electronic exchanges. This is the technological and material infrastructure of the space of flows, consisting of telecommunications, transport infrastructures and information technology.

Second, there are the nodes or 'locations of strategically important functions' (Castells 2000: 443), and hubs or 'exchangers', centres of information and goods transfer which are organized into a dynamic and shifting hierarchy. The nodes and hubs are highly specialized: '[t]he functions to be fulfilled by each network define the characteristics of places that become their privileged nodes ... Each network defines its sites according to the functions and hierarchy of each site, and to the characteristics of the product or service to be processed in the network' (Castells 2000: 444). Castells gives the example of Rochester, Minnesota, which is a central node in health research as a result of the presence of the Mayo clinic. Rochester became established as a core node of medical expertise, drawing clinicians, researchers and patients from around the world, which in turn adds to its centrality in the medical network. Thus the network itself produces the specific hubs and nodes, through a process of accretion, and formats them in relation to its need. It is the networks that 'link up different places and assign to each one ... a role and a weight in a hierarchy of wealth generation, information processing, and power making that ultimately conditions the fate of each locale' (Castells 2000: 445).

The final feature of the space of flows is the organization of the managerial elite. The elite, argues Castells, develop and nurture 'personal micro-networks' which have a disproportionate effect on macro-networks. These micro-networks operate in similar terms and under similar conditions to those described by Granovetter, with the exception that in the new space of flows, such networks operate at the click of a mouse, and on a global scale. Access to these micro-networks is policed by possession of cultural codes to open the doors of power within secluded communities (Castells 2000: 446). This is not radically different from an understanding of the 'old boy network' theory of power, with the exception that Castells understands the network managerial elite as global in scope and composition. Castells draws a picture of a homogenous cultural elite, drawn together around common cultural codes, for whom modern 'gated communities' act as both a metaphor and material embodiment of power. For this global elite the network transcends, or more realistically bypasses both culture and place.

Castells' vision of networks, then, is one in which networks are composed of personal connections, places, technologies and functions. Elements are selectively connected to the network, which is exclusionary and particular rather than universal. The network transcends its elements and comes to operate as an actor in its own right. However, crucially it depends on maintaining the heterogeneity of its parts. In this regard Castells' network looks a great deal like a global division of labour, with differing areas and elements performing complementary but distinct functions (Wallerstein 2004). However, in contrast to the more personal networks of social network analysis, this is a network that operates globally and is thus patterned by global imperatives. The network is therefore goal orientated to the extent that it exists in order to perpetuate and further the interests of the elite

Negri: the power of the hive

For Hardt and Negri, as for Castells, the network form is the dominant form of power in modern society, and one which emerges as a result of the reconfiguration of work relations in post-industrial capitalism. However, here the similarities between the approaches end. Whereas Castells' networks are particular in nature, uniting selective elements and disconnecting the valueless residuum, for Hardt and Negri the network society implies a linking of all points. For Castells the network is monolithic, exclusionary and goal orientated, buttressing existing power relations. Hardt and Negri's networks are, by contrast, plural, inclusive and always contested. Castells' networks behave in his account as actors in their own right, whereas for Hardt and Negri networks, as in American social network analysis, enable action on the part of components. For Hardt and Negri, networks do not override the intentions or agency of actors within them, although they do provide a space, a means and a rationale for formulating other intentions. Whereas Castells' networks are metaphorically closer to institutions, with international agencies or the United Nations (UN) acting as emblematic instances, Hardt and Negri's networks are better realized, perhaps, in the example of a riot where individual behaviour is unconstrained and yet an order emerges which is the product of no individual actor. Thus, where Castells understands network effects as the production of a homogenous system, Hardt and Negri see them as the celebration and apotheosis of difference and polyphony.

Hardt and Negri begin from the observation that the network form is the new form of power in modern society. At the level of national conflict and internal security, the network form has had profound implications. Whereas in previous eras, the ambition of government was the creation, maintenance and expansion of its interests, modern world power is characterized by a different dynamic, that of empire (Hardt and Negri 2000). And whereas in other eras the structure of governance was formed around the idea of a nation with solid defensible boundaries, today nations confront a different type of enemy, a network enemy (Hardt and Negri 2004). In agreement with Castells and other information/network society theorists, Hardt and Negri observe that globalization has brought about a reduction in the sovereignty of the nation state. The nation has less power to regulate flows of goods, people, services and information within and across its borders. As Castells observes, power within and between nations is increasingly abstracted out to supranational institutions (the European Union (EU), the UN, the North Atlantic Treaty Organization (NATO), the International Monetary Fund (IMF), the Group of Eight (G8)) and for many theorists this represents a challenge to the idea of sovereignty. Hardt and Negri argue that whilst the decline in national sovereignty is irrefutable, this does not equate to a decline in sovereignty as such (2000: xi). The new supranational organisms are united in a common logic and this logic is empire. Empire, for the authors, 'can only be conceived as a universal republic, a network of powers and counterpowers structured in a boundless and inclusive architecture' (2000: 166). The logic of empire is the logic of capital, a logic in which there is universal inclusivity in so far as all social and material forms come to be included within it. The logic of capital is a constant expansion and movement outwards. Capital cannot remain still, it must be constantly on the move. As a result 'the capitalist market is one machine that has always run counter to any division between inside and outside. It is thwarted by barriers and exclusions; it thrives instead by including always more within its sphere' (Hardt and Negri 2000: 190:). Moreover, 'when it expands this new sovereignty does not annex or destroy the other powers it faces but on the contrary opens itself to them, including them in the network. What opens is the basis of consensus' (Hardt and Negri 2000: 166). Thus empire operates by a form of opening to difference, difference which is then recuperated within empire, annexed and incorporated into its interests (see also Terranova 2004: 60–3). A trivial example of this can be seen in the way capital appropriates ethnicity through fashion and dress, opening out onto difference as an occasion of consumption.

Under empire, then, legitimate power has no 'face', no inside or centre. It operates as a network through the same processes of summing up and simplification as actor networks. Apparent power is a network effect; we understand world leaders as having power, for example, only because they are the visible face of the hive of empire. And as with legitimate power, so with resistance. Nations find themselves confronting their enemies not as stable unitary entities, but as networks. It is commonplace to talk of terrorist networks, and since 9/11, the day of the terrorist attacks on the USA (11 September 2001), this sense of nations being under attack from a distributed network has become more generalized. The problem that confronts the nation when faced by a network enemy is that prior methods of counter-insurgency are largely ineffective, in so far as they are based on the identification of leaders of insurgency who can then be neutralized through 'decapitating' the movement, removing the leadership through war, assassination, discrediting them, bargaining with them or otherwise persuading them to desist. In the case of the network threat, there is no 'head' to be decapitated and thus the state has to alter the terms of engagement, fighting to obliterate the *environment* which supports the network (Hardt and Negri 2004: 58–62).

This network structure comes to be the generalized form that power takes within society through its institutionalization as a result of the re-centring of capital on immaterial labour. Immaterial labour, labour which produces immaterial goods, i.e. information and services, takes the form of networks based on communication, collaboration and affectivity. Fleeing conflict with organized and militant labour in the West, capital alighted upon and relocated to centres of production in the developing world, bringing about a de-territorialization of production. As a result the skills required of workers become skills of coordination and collaboration (Hardt and Negri 2004: 66). As the form of opposition to capital co-evolves with the forms of capital itself (see Hardt and Negri 2004: 87 and Part Four) collaboration becomes the axis of action and organization, which entrenches and diffuses the network form. The form of the social under empire is the 'multitude', a subjectivity emphasizing commonality and linkage which emerges from the network form (see also Agamben 1993).

The model of networks on which Hardt and Negri draw, then, is in some respects different from those which have gone before. For the authors' networks are organizational forms in the loosest sense of the term. We can begin to speak of a network where there is no central power relation: 'one essential characteristic of the distributed network form is that it has no centre. Its power cannot be understood accurately as flowing from a central source or even as polycentric, but rather as distributed variably, unevenly, and indefinitely' (Hardt and Negri 2004: 54–5). Rather we see groups who determine their own beliefs, actions and agendas, and coordinate between themselves in a democratic manner. Moreover networks are those in which the participants act on what they have in common and do not seek to format or homogenize other elements within the network. Hence networks in Hardt and Negri's account are distributed, characterized by autonomy of units, and heterogeneous as to social composition and goals. For this reason the authors take issue with the position that many insurgent groups are networks in the sense that they mean. Al-Qaeda or the Irish Republican Army (IRA) may appear as networks merely because they are distributed in space but are characterized by a high degree of central authority, a chain of command, and are homogenous in composition to a degree, which is further from this model of networks than, for example, the Mexican Zapatistas or the anti-globalization movement, which are distributed networks of autonomous, multiple parts linked only through opposition to a common enemy.

The network form then appears as a kind of 'swarm intelligence'. When a swarm attacks, the authors argue, there is a tendency to view it as random, unintelligent, anarchic: 'since the network has no center that dictates order ... The network attack appears as something like a swarm of birds or insects in a horror film, a multitude of mindless assailants ... If one looks inside a network, however, one can see that it is indeed organized, rational and creative' (Hardt and Negri 2004: 91). Its organization is based on communication between the parts of the swarm, not on communication from the 'head' to the 'body'. When we observe a swarm acting as an agent, we tend to seek a driving intelligence located in one or more of the nodes. What Negri and Hardt are arguing is that the swarm's intelligence resides in its links.

Earlier I observed the analytical problems which attend the idea of agency-without-an-agent from the point of view of actor-network theory. The problem is potentially no less severe in the case of Hardt and Negri, however the authors attempt to avoid this trap through the invocation of commonality and the nature of the multitude. The multitude is a contradictory assembly, both singular and multiple at the same time. Empire, in fleeing from the organized resistance and value obstacles of the industrial West, provides a shape to the multitude. The dispersed nature of work in the modern post-industrial society foregrounds skills of coordination and communication, things which are part of the common stock of human behaviour, owned and developed by no one and everyone. Through so doing, empire creates a requirement for control of this resource, 'reducing the common to a means of global control, and expropriating the common as private wealth' (Hardt and Negri 2004: 212) which shifts the focus of the struggle between forces in society to this 'common'. As a result of the interpenetration of spheres in social life implied by the movement of empire, everything becomes political. This is the sense in which the authors argue that empire has no constitutive 'outside', in so far as everything is subsumed under its logic. Against this unbounded entity of empire the authors contrast the equally unbounded multitude – 'the spontaneous aggregation of a plurality of actions that do not need to be articulated between themselves' (Laclau 2004: 26). The multitude is a based on the commons of cooperation and linkage. Members 'do not have to become the same or renounce their creativity in order to communicate and cooperate with each other. They remain different in terms of race, sex, sexuality and so forth' (Hardt and Negri 2004: 92). Just as capital operates on the basis of consensus, moving forward through the lowest common denominator, so multitude emphasizes commonality and plurality; it is an empirical organization rather than a theoretical form, for the multitude is something realized in practice, an actuated potentiality.[1] In this sense then, Hardt and Negri's multitude does not require a dimension of meaning outside itself. In order to explain this further we need to examine the work of Deleuze and Guattari.

Deleuze and Guattari

In formulating their concept of networks Hardt and Negri acknowledge a debt to the final two theorists considered here, Gilles Deleuze and Felix Guattari. Deleuze, a French philosopher, began his collaboration with Guattari, a pioneer in psychotherapy and a key figure in the anti-psychiatry movement of the 1960s, in the late 1960s. The theorists were interested in the nature of power and the forms of resistance against it. Foucault, in the preface to *Anti-Oedipus*, has argued that Deleuze and Guattari's work is a manifesto against Fascism, both politically and in terms of the 'Fascism of the head' (Deleuze and Guattari 2004: xv). As a 'philosophy of difference', Deleuze and Guattari's writings are situated with those of Derrida, Foucault and other post-structuralist theories. As part of the attempt to dissolve the structures of state-philosophy, Deleuze and Guattari wrote their major works, *Anti-Oedipus* and *A Thousand Plateaus*, in a deliberately obscure and perplexing style, which has slowed the circulation of the ideas they put forward. It is not my intention here to provide a key to their philosophy, but to introduce some of the main ideas emphasized in their work in order to provide a context for the ways these ideas have been viewed in relation to the internet.

The point of departure for a discussion of the work of Deleuze and Guattari is their notion of the difference between what they term *arboreal structures*, or *tree-order*, and the *rhizome*. Tree-logic is a form of cognition in which information, ideas, people and institutions are ordered hierarchically according to predecessors and roots. When we describe the history of Western philosophy we understand it as a genealogy, each thinker taking ideas from previous theorists and altering them. We could draw this process as a family tree, and this representative 'tracing' is what Deleuze and Guattari have in mind when they refer to arboreal logic, the ordering of the world into a stable hierarchical genealogy of branches and roots. This method of ordering knowledge is so engrained that it appears a natural way of thinking, 'the most classical and well reflected, oldest and weariest kind of thought' (Deleuze and Guattari 1988: 5).

Against this logic they contrast their model of knowledge and perception as a rhizome. The rhizomatic model of knowledge is closer to the network model, but it is a network of a particularly chaotic nature, at least at first view. The principles of the rhizome network are as follows. First, Deleuze and Guattari argue that 'any point of a rhizome can be connected to anything other, and must be. This is very different from the tree or root, which plots a point, fixes an order' (1988: 7). Thus tree-order is an order based on similarity, it connects 'traits of the same nature' (1988: 21) and offers a taxonomy of forms within a category. Rhizomes, on the other hand, connect according to a different logic, a logic of movement. Deleuze and Guattari call upon the notion of 'lines of flight', directions in directionless space which comprise the line of escape from repression which is always available. In psychiatric terms a line of flight may be fantasy; in political terms disengagement. Connection within rhizomes is not a question of forming a link so much as a sprouting off of a new line. It will be immediately clear why the idea of rhizomatic, apparently random, actually purposeful connection has much resonance in the era of hyperlinks. Hubert Dreyfus's example of the difference between 'old library culture' and 'hyperlinked culture' illustrates well the difference between the two forms. Dreyfus sees library culture as orientated towards preservation of texts through the imposition of a system of classification which is stable, hierarchical and defined by specific interests.

Thus, if one wishes to know about lions, one could start with natural history, move to fauna, thence mammals, thence felines, thence wild cats, and on to lions. Alternatively a search could be conducted as fauna>predatory>group> mammals>wild>felines>lions. A hierarchy of branching knowledge is already laid out for the reader, such that our encounter with the information we seek has already socialized us in the legitimate uses of and connections between knowledges. As against this model, Dreyfus contrasts hyperlinked culture, where 'intertextual evolution' is the core aim, classification is secondary to diversification and all possible associations are allowed and enabled (Dreyfus 2001: 11). Hyperlinks 'allow the user to move directly from one data entry to any other, as long as they are related in at least some tenuous fashion' (Dreyfus 2001: 10). It is as if all knowledge were disordered and a new order emerges, not from the decisions of library committees, scholars or other credentialized information experts, to order it in some way, but from the activities of those who use it and make their own connections. Thus rhizomes are inherently heterogeneous, bringing together and juxtaposing elements from all social and intellectual locations.

However, Deleuze and Guattari's heterogeneity is rather different from ANT's. For ANT heterogeneous networks can include anything, but its use-value is primary. Once it is incorporated within the network, it comes to function as part of that network, and disappears from view as a discrete object or agent. In Deleuze and Guattari there are no 'nodes' to disappear from view and, moreover, there is no overall unity to the network which allows this disappearance. 'Unity always operates in an empty dimension supplementary to that of the system considered' (Deleuze and Guattari 1988: 8) but rhizomes never have these supplementary dimensions. 'All multiplicities are flat, in the sense that they fill or occupy all of their dimensions' (Deleuze and Guattari 1988: 9). Thus in rhizomatic networks there is no 'pivot-unity', no point or position against which other points can be contrasted. This is the essence of Hardt and Negri's position on the common nature of the multitude, that there is no external referent to which a position can be referred for arbitration and, as a result, there is no basis of dispute.

However, such a new order is dynamic and ever changing. Deleuze and Guattari argue that, in the tree metaphor, allotted places and channels of transmission are already allocated, the individual simply assumes his/her given place in the hierarchy. Tree-logic is an eternal structure in which the identity of the parts may change over time, but the structure itself and its functioning remain. Rhizomes on the other hand are 'acentred systems, finite networks of automata in which communication runs from any neighbour to any other, the stems and channels do not preexist [*sic*], and all individuals are interchangeable, defined only by their state at a given moment' (Deleuze and Guattari 1988: 17).

Finally the crucial point of departure is that rhizomes are anti-hierarchical and totally inclusive. Just as links can be made to *any neighbour*, any node, so it follows that no particular node is *required* within the rhizome.

> Unlike a structure which is defined by a set of points and positions, with binary relations between the points and biunivocal relationships between the positions, the rhizome is made only of lines ... These lines, or

lineaments, should not be confused lineages of the aborescent type, which are merely localizable linkages between points and positions.

(Deleuze and Guattari 1988: 21)

The rhizome's lines do not serve to link discrete networks, or discrete properties, they are rather a pattern created by movement. 'The rhizome is an acentered, nonhierarchical, nonsignifying system without a General and without an organizing memory or central automation, defined solely by a circulation of states' (Deleuze and Guattari 1988: 21).

The core to understanding Deleuze and Guattari is an appreciation of their view of flows, a concept which is far removed from that used by Castells. Whereas Castells uses flows to denote the movement of goods, information, people, objects and services from node to node in a network, for Deleuze and Guattari flows are primal; the most basic factor of social existence and the primary flow for the authors is that of desire. Flows are neither produced by nor produce the nodes; they pre-exist them. Nodes are 'desiring machines', interruptions in the flow, which channel and direct it. The example they use is that of the breast and the mouth. The breast is an interruption in the flow of milk, that which contains it within the body; the mouth is that which releases the flow of milk and directs it into another body. Machines are therefore like switches and channels, but what they interrupt and how they do so is a function of their coding.

In so arguing, Deleuze and Guattari seem perilously close to the problem raised in relation to ANT and later Negri, above – namely, positing meaning as something that has to be brought in from the outside. Coding is not a space that accompanies the object (see above), but is brought about through proximity to other objects. For the authors history is contingency. No objects or machines have an inherent meaning or pattern of use but, rather, come to be associated with other objects within which use is found for it. Thus 'an organ may have connections that associate it with several different flows; it may waver between several functions, and even take on the *regime* of another organ' (Deleuze and Guattari 2004: 41). How this taking on of a regime occurs is through the process of *overcoding*, which is to be understood as similar to the idea of inscription in ANT or real subsumption in Marx. Overcoding, like subsumption, is a theoretical form of history bypass, allowing us to sever determining links between the object and its prior meanings which are elsewhere regarded as determining (see Chapter 10). To give an example of this, when Deleuze and Guattari are writing of the development of capitalism in Asia, they argue that the reconfiguration of the system does not involve replacing former alliances and relationships with something else, but the overcoding of them: 'The objects, the organs, the persons, and the groups retain at least a part of their intrinsic coding, but these coded flows of the former regime find themselves overcoded by the transcendent unity that appropriates surplus value. The old inscription remains, but it is bricked over by and in the inscription of the State' (Deleuze and Guattari 2004: 213). Perhaps the simplest way to envisage the relationships between elements described by Deleuze and Guattari is, then, in the difference between transformation and contract. The social networks envisaged by the anthropologists with whose work this chapter began are more like a contract network, agreements between discrete parties which form and shape action, but which are a function of the intentions of the actor. For Deleuze and Guattari each interaction between elements is a process of 'becoming'. When a particular plant and a bee live in a symbiotic relationship, then the plant is 'becoming bee' and the bee 'becoming plant'; each takes on the attributes of the other, since it is logically impossible to separate them. Evolution of objects is understood as a mutual elaboration of forms, which is not the same as describing the elements in a network as formatted (actor-network approaches) or created (Castells) by the logic of that network.

What the above analysis flags up is that whilst Deleuze and Guattari's position has a certain resonance for examining the internet, the application of their concepts is profoundly problematic. The problem comes about because Deleuze and Guattari's position had been mistreated as a toolbox, rather than as a philosophical elaboration. Deleuze and Guattari's work has a resonance for those interested in networks largely because features of rhizomes are also ones that networks are understood to have. However, Deleuze and Guattari are not trying to talk about specific social or intellectual forms at all and similarities between rhizomatic structures and networks are largely facile surface appearances. Where the internet *can* be appropriately theorized through the use of Deleuze and Guattari is through the reduction of distance. Deleuze and Guattari's view of history is of objects and ideas being brought into proximity with each other. The use of lasers to remove tattoos, for example, does not come about because tattoo ink has an inherent affiliation with lasers. Rather, laser technology has become increasingly sophisticated at the same time as a sudden fad for tattoos ended with large numbers of people sporting dubious ink-work. Foucault's example of the juxtaposition of the availability of lazar houses and the problem of the mad is another case in point (1971). The internet, as in the example above of hyperlinks, alters this process, providing a new order of knowledge is developed not from an abstract schema or overarching taxonomy but from the way things are in practice ordered, for all things are now *potentially at least* proximate. The internet is therefore the architecture of realizing Kuhnian paradigm shifts in knowledge. It is in Deleuzian terms a smooth space. For Deleuze and Guattari there is a critical distinction between two types of space, smooth or 'nomad' space, an original or primary form in which flows encounter no resistance, and striated spaces, where flows are directed into and through prior existing channels. In the next chapter, I will be considering these two models in relation to the internet.

Note

1. As Shapiro argues, this notion of the multitude as both potential and actuality in Hardt and Negri is problematic in so far as a genuine instance of the multitude constituting itself as an active entity would necessarily involve a paradox since the multitude is a 'becoming' not a 'being' (Shapiro 2004: 300). However, Hardt and Negri's instance that the multitude 'needs a political project to bring it into existence' (2004: 212) in some senses counters this.

4 *The* internet *as a* network

When called upon to describe the internet qua network, social scientists are notoriously rather vague. For Charles Ess the internet is simply 'the mother of all networks' (1996: 1). Burnett and Marshall define the internet as the 'global connection of hundreds of thousands of public and private computer networks by means of … nodes, gateways and computer centres using the TCP/IP protocol' (2003: 206). The internet network is flexible, adaptive, a 'non-hierarchical, rhizomatic global structure' (Morse 1998, cited in Urry 2003: 63), 'webs … without central points, organizational principles, hierarchies' (Plant 1997, cited in Urry 2003: 63). However, beyond the fact that it is distributed, net-like and web-like, social theorists have had little to say about the kind of web or net that the internet is. The internet is taken as the 'gold standard' of network, a 'pivot' image in Deleuzian terms, a known standard from which all other forms of network depart. If description is called for, the cry goes up that the internet is too vast, too complex to describe.

The problem with this is that, as John Law has forcefully argued, an uncritical adoption of a metaphor of networks can represent an equally uncritical reproduction of a dominant ideology. The sociologist Pierre Bourdieu, drawing on Durkheim, has railed against the common overuse in the social sciences of 'prenotions'. Durkheim defined 'prenotions' or preconceptions as 'schematic, summary representations' that acquire their self-evidence from the social functions that they fulfil (Bourdieu *et al.* 1991: 13). For Durkheim these prenotions are socially useful; they allow us to apprehend our world on an instrumental level and to act within it. However, when we approach that same world as *scientists* we must put them aside for 'they are as a veil interposed between the things and ourselves, concealing them from us … *idola* which, resembling ghost-like creatures distort the true appearance of things, but which we nevertheless mistake for the things themselves' (Durkheim, reproduced in Bourdieu *et al.* 1991: 94). Whereas for Durkheim prenotions concerned matters such as law and morality, indispensable social concepts for which man could not await the development of sociology to explain, Bourdieu is more worried about the prenotions that sociologists pick up from other organized social arenas. For Bourdieu, sociologists who cannot make a break with the force of the pre-constructed risk nullifying their credibility as enquirers. Rather than taking the constitution of objects and their relationship to others as a given, we must be constantly aware of the way these are presented to us, ever ready to analyse and dissect them.

It is clear that in the case of the internet, this epistemological vigilance has been lax. In part this may be attributable to the vast diversity of scientific discourse from which our scientific understanding of the internet has developed. However, it is equally in part a corollary of the ideological inflection of discourse around the network or information society, which forms one of the arboreal roots of internet discourse. As Darin Barney has argued, the idea of a network society is one which has become profoundly ideologically unsound. The fact that we live in a network society is used to justify and promote social changes, circumventing potential criticism because it is 'the standard for what is normal, desirable, and for what we can reasonably expect' (Barney 2004: 180). Thus he insists

> The 'Network Society' is not just a descriptive name. It is also an elaborate discourse that, in purporting simply to describe a set of contemporary social dynamics, provides a script that sets out roles, norms, expectations and terms of dialogue. Thinking through the model of the network – nodes, ties, flows – certainly helps us to understand a great deal about, for example, the restructuring of capitalist enterprise and work, the disaggregation of state sovereignty, the rise and operation of new social movements, and emerging practices of community formation. But when an idea such as this is elevated from heuristic device to the status of an all-encompassing social and historical fact, its function shifts significantly.
>
> (Barney 2004: 179–80)

The political status of the internet within this constellation of discourse is specifically addressed in detail by Terranova. The network, she argues, 'is becoming less and less a description of a specific system and more and more a catchword to describe the formation of a single and yet multidimensional informational milieu – linked by the dynamics of information propagation and segmented by diverse modes and channels of circulation' (Terranova 2004: 41). The internet, then, loses its specific character and comes to be a 'general figure for the processes driving the globalization of culture and communication at large' (Terranova 2004: 42). That the internet appears to us as representative, whereas in fact this cannot be upheld on the basis of scale, user numbers or formal properties (Terranova 2004: 42), clearly points to its assimilation within a dominant political trajectory of economic and cultural expansion. Thus the idea of a network comes to sociologists of the internet in part as a prenotion from the realm of politics, one which supersedes established discourse around networks from within the discipline itself.

Moreover it is a prenotion that is highly inflected by commercial discourse. That networks are promoted as the functional organizational forms of capital, as described by Negri, should not blind us to the fact that these forms of organization are primarily forms of control. When we refer to the internet as a network, as Law has argued more generally, we duplicate a managerial logic, 'reproduc[ing] and help[ing] to perform a functional relationship between entities' in which '[a]ll that is solid – including human and non-human distinctions – melts into air in a specific way that subjugates that dissolution to a logic of function' (2000: 5–7). In talking of the internet as a network, we validate an understanding of people as nodes in a specific type of system, a *technical commercial system*. Chapter 11 picks up on some of the implications involved in understanding people's brains as network components with reference to intellectual property rights.

Finally there is a sociological imperative towards the adoption of the network metaphor within the discipline itself. An invocation of networks may perhaps be understood as a return to empiricism in another form. When we look back into the history of the idea of networks in the social sciences, we are forcefully reminded of Radcliffe-Brown's injunction to put aside prenotions of state and community (see Chapter 2, p. 27) and of the roots of the development of social network analysis as a means of discovering the boundaries of the social, rather than using them as a starting point. In much of the literature reviewed above, the invocation of 'network' in relation to a phenomenon acts as a call to trace and describe relationships between entities, as in ANT, as well as in Deleuze and Guattari. Where networks are called upon as an explanatory device, this is usually in the context of an appeal to complexity and the need for further information, rather than a different schema. In this sense the dominance of the network metaphor in sociology is a true return to method as the pivot of sociological enquiry, as against abstracted theory or grand schemas. It is ironic that a metaphor that is so closely tied to the disruption of prenotions should, therefore, itself become one.

It is easy to overlook the fact that the network image has not always been the dominant means of describing the internet. When the internet first came onto scholarly and popular radar in the early 1990s, the two most prevalent images of it in circulation were the now seemingly archaic image of the 'information superhighway' with all the attendant connotations of linear progress between fixed points which that implies, and that of a prototype of virtual reality (Slouka 1995; Chandler 1996; Calcutt 1999). The internet was pictured as an environment, a self-contained world that is reflected in metaphors which we have inherited from that period. Thus 'being online', 'logging on', 'going onto the net' all construct the internet as 'cyberspace', a parallel world that exists alongside our own, which has an existence separate from its users, a place that we go to and which retains its identity as a place after we leave. As I have argued in the Introduction, this understanding of the internet as space is one which achieved the greatest currency in sociology, formatting the internet as an arena properly considered in relation to ideas of community or of the individual in *place* (Hicks 1998). However, as studies of the internet moved from constructing the topic through the already established forms of academic discourse in the various disciplines, to an attempt to treat the internet on its own terms using multidisciplinary tools, this metaphor became increasingly outdated. The subsumption of the internet by the more commercial web dealt the final terminal blow to competing metaphors of the internet, and alternate definitions have largely fallen by the wayside.

Now, as Terranova points out, the internet is more commonly represented as a 'common space of information flows in which the political and cultural stakes of globalization are played out' (2004: 42), a metaphor of systems and links that demonstrates the extent to which the internet has been colonized by political discourses. Thus, as we will see in Part Four, the political legal is a core site for the generation of discourse about, and therefore the shaping of the internet (see also Terranova 2004: 45). For sociologists it now appears gauche to describe the internet as an arena or a space. 'Cyberspace' as a term has been disavowed as one of Gauntlett's neologistic 'nerdwords' (Gauntlett 2004: 3), and the dominant metaphors are those of exchange and circulation. Thus Slevin defines the internet simply as a vast interactive network (2000: 1); Urry as a 'metaphor for social life that is fluid, involving thousands of networks, of people, machines, programmes, texts and images in which quasi-subjects and quasi-objects mix together in new hybrid forms' (2003: 63). For Agger the internet is 'an electric circuit bridging production and consumption' (2004: 17). For Castells it is 'the fabric of our lives', 'likened to both the electrical grid and the electric engine because of its ability to distribute the power of information throughout the entire realm of human activity', 'the technological basis for the organizational form of the information age: the network' (Castells 2001: 1–2).

The problem is that that these depictions of the internet as distributed, non-hierarchical, hybrid and flexible may be conceptually resonant but empirically difficult to substantiate. The internet is neither the simple distributed network envisaged by Baran, nor a vast unfathomed and unknowable dimension of data. Whereas Deleuze and Guattari's smooth space well describes the network form of the internet on day one, the textures, grains and accretions of channels and paths which characterize the internet 'on the ground' today are more than the historical mementos of mass daily use on a global scale over the past 15 years. The internet has become a striated space in Deleuzian grammar.

So what sort of network is the internet 'on the ground' so to speak? Although it is more or less an article of faith in cybercultural theory that the size of the internet and the nature of the network is such as to make its shape and geography unknowable, a number of researchers have made attempts to map the net. One type of map has been developed by researchers interested in the geographical distribution of the internet. These studies, such as that performed by the International Telegraphic Union (see Part Two for discussion), look at the distribution of servers, internet service providers (ISPs) and users worldwide.

However, of greater interest to researchers in information science and physics was the internal shape of the internet, and researchers working at Bell Labs, and at Princeton, were amongst the first to try to map the internet's internal links in an attempt to deduce its overall shape. The bot (small automated programs which perform given tasks) survey conducted by Lawrence and Giles at Princeton particularly is credited with revolutionizing our view of the internet (Barabasi 2003). The researchers' bots brought back a rather different image of the internet to that anticipated by post-structuralist theory. Whereas the internet had been understood to be a mass of disorganized information onto which search engines opened and to which they were the key, the Princeton researchers found that the search engines were only a small part of the story and that the internet itself is highly fragmented.

Barabasi (2003: 167) presents evidence from a group of commercial researchers whose mapping project was a collaboration between the research departments at AltaVista, IBM and Compaq. The project, headed up by Andrei Broder, established a topography of the World Wide Web (rather than the internet per se), in which there are four major informational 'continents'. The core continent is the largely commercial face of the internet, where accessing any one node will allow you to surf to any other, by however many links. This is the home of large commercial sites and the main portals, such as MSNBC, Yahoo!, BBC.co.uk and CNN.com. Against this Broder's team contrast the In-continent and the Out-continent. In graph theory the indegree of a point represents the number of other nodes that connect to that point. The outdegree, by contrast, represents the number of nodes to which it itself is connected. In a 'directed' relationship, a relationship where there is a trajectory of movement from point a to point b, there will not be a symmetry between them. Thus an example of a directed relationship would be role models and celebrities. I may have a relationship with a celebrity on the basis that she is a role model for me, or that I loathe her and class her as an enemy of mine, but the celebrity is unlikely, if asked, to cite me in the same capacity. Likewise, just because I claim person x as my friend does not mean person x will equally claim me (see Scott 2000: 69). Broder's team operationalized this concept in describing their other large land masses. The In-continent will allow you to browse *to* the core, but does not contain links back to the In. The Out is easily reached *from* the core but, like a lobster pot, once in there is no route back. The fourth continent is formed from what the researchers term tendrils or islands. These are isolated pages which are linked to each other but which do not have links to the other three land masses. I will be further discussing the implications of this fragmentation in the next section, but for the moment the key point at hand is whether this fragmented condition should be understood as inherent or contingent, whether this represents the inevitable path of development of the internet or is a localized and temporary condition. Barabasi is clear that the network's fragmentation is insurmountable: 'Is this fragmented structure here to stay? Or will the evolving and growing Web eventually absorb the four continents into a single, fully connected core? The answer is simple: As long as the links remain directed, such homogenization will never occur' (2003: 168–9).

However the caveat that this condition is a corollary of the directed nature of links offers some hope for post-structuralists keen to rescue their model of the internet as homogenous. Terranova (2004: 68) offers the most lucid counterclaim in her argument that the prevalence of web rings operates to thwart this fragmented formation. Web rings work by overcoming the central problem of temporal sequence in determining links between objects. A predecessor has a directed link with its successor, but the successor does not have an equal link back with its 'parent'. Barabasi uses the example of his own book to illustrate the point, an example that will work as well for the book in your own hand as for Barabasi's, when he points out that 'following the references at the end of this book will allow you to find the quoted papers. Yet none of these papers could send you to this book, since they do not cite it' (2003: 169). None of the references at the end of this book could cite it, since it was, by definition, written after their publication. Web rings, however, operate a form of mutuality, they are a technical infrastructure of reciprocity in so far as all pages cite each other in that they are part of the ring. Thus the temporal sequence of construction is disrupted and disturbed, and the links between pages lose their directed nature. However, whilst this possibility exists in theory it is also possible that altering the polarity of links will make little difference, simply becoming absorbed into the existing geography of the internet. Thus, whilst this offers a conceptual challenge to Barabasi's assurance that the directed nature of the web cannot be overcome, it remains to be seen whether this will pan out in practice, or simply lead to the formation of greater numbers of information islands and tendrils. It is certainly true that the tendency to the formation of tendrils and islands has, in the past few years, been intensified. Barabasi (2003: 168) estimated that around 25 per cent of all web documents were located in tendrils or islands, however that percentage seems likely to increase as a result of the development of private nets and password-protected sites (see Chapter 5 in this volume, and Lessig 2002).

The shape of the web, at least, then, is highly fragmented overall but exhibits clustering around centres of gravity formed by the pull of brands and portals. Within the core, the internet is becoming centralised, and the information peripheries have an increasingly precarious relationship to the centre. One way of construing this is that the internet is contracting inwards towards the centre with the less mainstream areas becoming inaccessible and falling into general disrepair. Another interpretation would see the periphery as independent of the core, offering liberatory potential. It is certainly true that the internet is highly heterogeneous in nature *as a network*. Whereas other available models of a network depend on formatting and coding their parts in order to operate as a coherent network, as in the case of actor-network theory's networks where heterogeneous elements come to behave as a singularity, the internet is subject to no such overcoding. This results from a path dependence established at the design stage of the internet. Although it is now received wisdom that the internet was developed as a medium to survive a potential nuclear attack, in reality, Terranova explains, the primary rationale governing internet development is the necessity to overcome the tendency of heterogeneous systems to drift and thus to introduce incompatibilities. The history of technological development is replete with examples of projects where decentralized development led to fundamental problems in bringing the system together. The development of rail transport in Britain was dogged by the use of different gauges of tracks such that passengers were often required to change trains at intervals as their initial train could run only on certain stretches of track. Likewise in the development of the telephone network in the USA, competition between rival enterprises to supply phones meant that people were often on incompatible systems (Fischer 1992). In the case of the internet the need was to allow separate and autonomous development of the infrastructure and content, but to prevent this 'mission drift' the solution is the widespread use of protocols.

> new protocols are usually inserted between systems or added to them, as an ulterior layer, without asking the current system to discard its old components and substitute them immediately with new ones. If an incompatibility emerges it produces a 'trigger for change' requiring new technical and social negotiations. Generally, however, a new protocol or level is introduced that, by operating between or on top of different layers, will allow them all to coexist under a single common framework ... Incompatibility, understood as tension between divergent moments, is not relinquished but brought into the network through a process of horizontal addition and/or vertical subsumption.
>
> (Terranova 2004: 59)

In this way networks are added together without there being any need to homogenize or alter the nature or function of the parts (see Jordan 1999a: 40–1). The new network operations can be performed but the individual components, uncoupled from the network, retain their own properties. Indeed it is on the basis of these properties, and the 'tension' between them and other components, that the network proceeds in the first place.

One of the implications of the protocol/layer approach to understanding the 'internetwork' is that no part of the network thus assembled has any determining power on the formation of the whole. Whereas ANT understands elements as having properties which allow them to be formatted in a restricted range of ways, no part of the 'internetwork', as Terranova describes it, has formal preferences in this way. From this it follows that unlike ANT networks, the internet is not exclusive in terms of its architecture. The principle of open architecture is realized through the ability of protocols to make existing parts of the network behave in different ways without uncoupling it from or threatening the integrity of the whole. A good example of this is the use of bots to make computers and internet users (nodes) into 'zombies', where extortionists take control of private computers in order to mount a massive denial of service attack on a business singled out by them for blackmail. The users may not realize that their equipment and their actions are now being turned to the purposes of organized crime. Their actions are unaffected by the transformation and they therefore remain both innocent web users and are enrolled as players in an international mafia-style protection racket. Any element in the 'inter-network', then, can serve dual or multiple, and conflicting, purposes without any change to its status or nature. This is in contrast to ANT where the process of enrolment requires that the node become separated from potential counterclaimants and made to operate exclusively within one network.

Further in contrast to ANT, though similarly to Castells, the patterning of the nodes, and their relationship to each other, is seen as an emergent property of the network as a whole. Thus Terranova argues that on the internet the particular route taken by information in its journey around the decentralized web is configured by the whole. In so far as the research by information researchers had adequately dispensed with the rather naive notion of an internet where all points are accessible from all others, then the particular route taken by traffic is of consequence. As Terranova explains:

> In a packet-switched network ... there is no single vector or route between A and B. Even as such space is perceived as simultaneous from the point of view of the subjects engaged in receiving and sending messages in real time from all over the world, that does not imply an actual simultaneity ... The route which a message might take has to take into account at all points the overall traffic of the network.
>
> (Terranova 2004: 67)

The overall traffic in the network is constantly in flux, routing around political censorship, local disasters, blockages and new channels. Thus the particular patterning of linkages, information movement and nodes is configured and reconfigured by the overall state of the network. A good example of this was the changes in the pattern of network operation after the destruction of the World Trade Center buildings in the USA in 2001. The internet was overloaded, both by demands for information and as a consequence of the loss of a material network node. Wiggins has shown that the overload of the internet was a consequence of the reconfiguration of network traffic such that it overloaded the central nodes of the network. For Terranova what this means in practice is that the internet on that occasion contracted inwards towards the centre. In order to accommodate network traffic the search engine Google mirrored the main news sites in order to ease the overload, thus reconfiguring the system as a whole, albeit temporarily (Wiggins 2001). However, even such temporary reconfigurations can have long-term effects, as the core point is that in any complex system small inputs can have far-ranging consequences. For Terranova and others the pathways taken by information are not merely conduits but sources of transformation. She argued

> information spreading throughout the open space of the network is not only a vector in search of a target, it is also the potential transformation of the space crossed that always leaves something behind ... Information is not simply transmitted from point A to point B: it propagates and by propagation it affects and modifies its milieu.
>
> (Terranova 2004: 51)

Thus the internet's nodes are configured by the shape of the network as a whole and a path dependency established by properties which emerge from this shape.

The final feature of the internetwork which distinguishes it from other models is that its agency is located at the fringes rather than the centre. In Castells' networks, as in ANT's, agency is an input which configures the network to further its interests; for Hardt and Negri, Deleuze and Guattari agency is an emergent property of the system as a whole. In the internetwork, agency and intelligence reside in the ends, the outputs of the network. The network itself is dumb and the processes by which transformations are achieved are incomplete until the end product is assimilated and ordered at the end of its journey.

Thus, to summarize, the internetwork is heterogeneous, non-exclusive, determined by the overall state of the links rather than the nodes (SNA), path dependent rather than temporally specific, highly autonomous, in so far as nodes and links can multi-task without affecting the whole, and non-goal orientated. The differences between the internet 'on the ground' and the ideology of the internet network are therefore multiple. Against the image of the internet as an inclusive network we must contrast the reality of the information islands and directed continents where all but the highly commercialized core spaces of the internet are located. Against the image of the internet as constantly in flux, a libertarian, anarchic space, we have the relentless accretion of channels which form and modulate discourse. Against the idea of the internet as a smooth space, we have a highly striated one. In the next part I will be examining some of the implications of this.

Part **Two**
The **internet** *as a* **medium**

Introduction *to* Part Two

The last chapter explored the idea that the internet is, in Deleuzian terms, a striated space. It is in the literature of the sociology of the media, cultural studies and communications studies that the implications of striations have best been explored. For theorists of the media, the internet is constructed as a political technology whose locus of power is the challenge it presents to traditional mass media forms and institutions. Ultimately these debates tend to dissolve into debates concerning the media and the public sphere, the role of media in democratic participation.

No sooner had the internet crept onto academic and policy radars than the new medium was being heralded as a potential intervention in addressing the West's 'democratic deficit', the gap between the democratic requirement of public participation and the reality of a largely politically apathetic and oblivious voting population. The understanding that the internet could bring about a revitalization of the ailing public sphere was as well received in oppositional as in established political discourse:

> As soon as the internet started to materialise as a set of relays and links between different computer networks, it produced a widespread and hopeful expectation of a resurgence of the public sphere in a 'cyberdemocratic' mode. A networked multitude, possessing its own means of communication, freed from the tyranny of broadcasting, would rise to challenge the phony public sphere of television and the press.
>
> (Terranova 2004: 135)

This section breaks down the claims and counterclaims around the internet and the public sphere. I start with an examination of the idea of a public sphere in media studies and the sociology of the media. I then move on to look at the key prerequisites of a public sphere and consider the extent to which the internet provides for these. This part provides an overview of the main perspectives on what has been termed information poverty, and argues that policy-based approaches have adopted a formula to calculate this which produces a distorted image of the problem. I then move on to look at major theories around the effects of the internet on civic participation, before concluding with an examination of the nature of interactivity online. The final chapter in this part will sum up these findings through a consideration of the role of media in contemporary society. I will here argue that there is a fundamental anachronism in the way in which the internet has been positioned in scholarly discourse as a successor to the journalistic 'fourth estate'. Rather, I argue, it is a necessary media in a context which is sensitive to both grounded media practices and historical configurations of power.

The public sphere

First, then, we need to be clear about some terms, for the idea of a public sphere is far from transparent. No academic account of the development and operation of a public sphere can avoid starting with the work of Jurgen Habermas, for his conception of the public sphere, although widely and variously attacked and critiqued, is the most broad-ranging position statement. In 1974 Habermas outlined the concept as follows:

> By 'the public sphere' we mean first of all a realm of our social life in which something approaching public opinion can be formed. Access is guaranteed to all citizens. A portion of the public sphere comes into being in every conversation in which private individuals assemble to form a public body. They then behave neither like business or professional people transacting private affairs, nor like members of a constitutional order subject to the legal constraints of a state bureaucracy. Citizens behave as a public body when they confer in an unrestricted fashion – that is, with the guarantee of freedom of assembly and association and the freedom to express and publish their opinions – about matters of general interest. In a large public body, this kind of communication requires specific means for transmitting information and influencing those who receive it.
>
> (Habermas 1974, cited in Sparks 1998: 110)

The public sphere, then, is notionally a space, one that exists and mediates between the mass and the power elite, an arena in which power is formed and directed. The requirement for complex societies to delegate functional power, since the scale of societies and the complexity of the issues that they face does not allow the possibility of direct representation, brings about the necessity of a public sphere, where power can be made visible and accountable through communication and scrutiny. In Habermas, the public sphere is a 'between' space in another sense also, it is between the private world of the mass and the public world of power. That is to say, it exists where its members assemble and debate neither exclusively as representatives of their own interests nor as the 'talking heads' of procedures of established power.

Habermas delineates two ideal types of social action, the instrumental or purposive and the communicative. Instrumental action is governed strictly by the means–ends relationship, it is a rational form of action which is focused on a formal calculation of the efficiency of an act in relation to an end. Communicative action, by contrast, 'is a form of linguistic interaction oriented towards the achievement of mutual understanding and agreement' (Crossley 2002: 155). This can itself take two forms, either the normconformative action, where 'agents conform to the shared expectations which apply to whatever types of interaction they are involved in' (Crossley 2002: 155) or discourse, where agents reflect critically on norms and assumptions through rational argument, where rational argument is understood to mean that the reliability of the argument proposed can be assessed with reference to the truth and credibility of the statements rather than the status held by the proposer.

For Habermas the essence of the public sphere is that it is an arena in which the activities of the state can be discussed and subjected to rational debate, the public use of reason. Habermas identified a prototype public sphere in the bourgeois platform which emerged in the fusion of public spaces of assembly in the form of salons and coffee houses and the rise of the new periodical press in the late seventeenth and early eighteenth centuries. As a result of favourable political conditions, in particular the loosening of political control of the press, Habermas argued that the period saw a brief blossoming of a new political force in the conversations and debates taking place in the salons, conversations for which the ballooning production of cheap pamphlets and periodicals provided an information lingua franca, a common point of departure. However, this was short-lived. The rapid collapse of the public sphere was brought about through the rise of mass, commercial media and the return of state censorship. This removed both the ability of citizens to openly participate without fear of censure, a stipulation essential to satisfy truth claims, and of citizens to participate at all due to commercialization. As a result

> [t]he communicative network of a public made up of rationally debating private citizens ... collapsed: the public opinion once emergent from it has partly decomposed into the informal opinions of private citizens without a public and partly become concentrated into formal opinions of publicistically effective institutions. Caught in the vortex of *publicity that is staged for show or manipulation* the public of nonorganized private people is laid claim to not by public communication but by the communication of publicly manifested opinions.
>
> (Habermas 1989: 247–8, original emphasis)

Habermas's depiction of the public sphere has been subject to a number of general criticisms. Writers have argued that Habermas overestimates the significance of this configuration of information and influence in relation to other social and political movements of the period, and thus overstates its success in bringing about social change (Thompson 1995: 71–2). It is generally agreed that this prototype of public sphere was far too limited, restrictive and elitist to qualify for the august role for which Habermas has auditioned it (e.g. Curran 1991; Fraser 1992). Thus one leading writer on historical and contemporary public spheres argues that 'Habermas's account of the historical dynamic of the bourgeois public sphere is wrong, and that the record is of the patchy and contradictory realisation of a concept whose full potential is very much greater' (Sparks 1998: 112). Theorists have also taken issue with the unitary nature of the public sphere as described and required by Habermas, arguing that the bourgeois public sphere he describes is only one of many potentially competing public spheres (Ornebring and Jonsson 2004).

From the point of view of media studies the most damning aspect of Habermas's model is his description of the terms of its collapse. Habermas understands the prototype public sphere as collapsing back into image management and sham public-ness reminiscent of the feudal era, where power was exercised as a spectacle (Foucault 1977; Habermas 1989). For media theorists such as John Thompson this brings into question the notions of publicity and the 'public' that Habermas employs. For Thompson, Habermas is wrong in equating the showy public ceremonials of the feudal era with the 'sophisticated new media techniques [that] are employed to endow public authority with the kind of aura and prestige which was once bestowed on royal figures' (1995: 74). Additionally, Thompson argues that Habermas draws too heavily on the understanding of the audience as a passive mass, after the style of the Frankfurt school, in his description of the collapse of the public sphere. For media theorists this aspect of Habermas's work is contradictory and unhelpful, positing the bourgeois public sphere members as enlightened rational discussants who actively interpret their symbolic world, and the mass audience as flaccid sluggards slumped inertly before an empty goldfish-bowl world surpassing their comprehension.

The terms of this criticism, however, reveal one of the central biases of media studies, towards an overemphasis of the role of the media in social life. Habermas's understanding of the erosion of the public sphere and the transformation of the audience does not emanate from an uncritical adoption of an alien concept from the Frankfurt school. Rather Habermas understands massification as the outcome of the division of information media from the spaces of discussion that rendered the texts intelligible and promoted them from media spectacles to the raw materials of political action. McGuigan, one of the few media theorists to express incredulity at the conflation of the media and the public sphere, argues that 'we cannot possibly mean that a global public sphere is simply the product of the global circulation of media messages' (1998: 96). However, the media-centric appropriation of Habermas by communications scholars does precisely that and takes little account of the fact that the public sphere as described by Habermas was less an outcome of the availability of information than of the juxtaposition of the circulation of information, uncensored public spaces, and the conceptual and practical space opened up by the separation between state and civil society.

The latter is of the greatest practical significance in the operation of a reflective public sphere. The 'colonization of the lifeworld', the increasing penetration of the state and economic spheres into more and more areas of life, including arenas of social life that are primarily concerned with social integration and meaning, means that the gap between social institutions is closing. With the rise of the welfare state, for example, governmental institutions now permeate more aspects of our lives. At the same time the expansion of the economic sector is also an expansion into the lifeworld, wherein more and more of the affective, integrating, meaning-bearing relationships are inflected with the rational cost–benefit calculations of the economic sphere. The over-writing of the narratives and scripts of social integration and existential meaning of the lifeworld by the system, in addition to the increasing bureaucratization and specialization that accompany this, means that we are constantly confronted by a fragmented and incomprehensible social world, at the same time that values we believed were stable are being erased (Crossley 2002: 158). As a result there is, in addition to the erosion of public spaces of debate and the substitution of a free and politically aware press for a mass media of spectacle and gossip, an erosion of the *capacity* for critical reflection. There is no Archimedean position outside of the system from which to reflect upon it, no gap between the institutions of one domain and those of another. It is *this* that Habermas argues is at the root of the transformation of the audience from critical thinkers to lacklustre dimwits, not the provision of information per se. As a consequence the public sphere, as it has been developed by media scholars is rather one-dimensional.

It is against this background that claims that the internet offers the possibility of a resurgence of the public sphere need to be evaluated. It can be argued that the internet, as an inherently interactive media, has re-injected much of the lost sociality to the model. Much in this argument depends on the nature of being an 'audience' online, which is seen as a qualitatively different order of experience to being an audience for mass-media products. The internet is understood as populated by, and possibly producing, the rational, argumentative, media-savvy citizens that are the backbone of an energetic public sphere. In order to examine this further we need first to describe and consider the formal features of a public sphere before we can decide whether these claims are in fact warranted.

5 Elements *of a* public sphere

In his discussion of whether there can be argued to be a global public sphere in the modern world, Colin Sparks, although highly critical of the Habermassian vision of the public sphere, isolates two aspects of Habermas's original model which must be addressed in any discussion. At its most basic, a public sphere, in order to be considered as such, must meet two criteria, namely that 'access [is] guaranteed to all' and that 'citizens have a right to confer in an unrestricted fashion' (Sparks 1998: 112). This chapter considers these elements in turn. In the first section, I will examine the debate over access to the internet, arguing that the current terms of the debate have been atheoretical and technologically deterministic in their approach. I examine the definitions of information poverty implied by these models and offer some alternative perspectives which emphasize the social nature of the audience. Following on from this I move on to consider the nature of the online audience as this is developed in the most influential models of online media, and position these in relation to their theoretical precursors in order to examine their implications.

Access

The debate concerning the level of accessibility of the internet will be familiar to any student who has conducted a cursory preliminary survey of the literature, for it has formed the backbone of scholarship into the social impact of the internet over the past decade, and appears as the debate over information poverty. As I have noted in the Introduction to this volume, this debate is shaped by the dynamics of the inclusion/exclusion model of social power which has overwritten discourses of class in mainstream sociology (Furedi 2004a). Information poverty has become one of the core questions for the study of the internet amidst fears that its popularity is exacerbating or actually creating an information underclass whose exclusion from the benefits of the new informational order will be long lasting or permanent. Whilst it is generally agreed that the composition of this digital underclass will closely mirror that of the economic underclass, the precise mechanisms producing this are under debate.

In general it is clear that access to the internet in the West is stratified by economic situation, education and race. According to estimates from the US Census Bureau in 2003, 30.7 per cent of US households with an income of less than $25,000 per annum had internet access, rising to 57.3 per cent for those in the $25,000–49,999 bracket and 92.2 per cent for those with $100,000 or more (Day *et al.* 2005). A Pew Internet and American Life study, based on a telephone survey of 2001 households, found that of those who had not graduated high school, only 29 per cent had internet access at home, as compared with 61 per cent of high school graduates and 89 per cent of college graduates (Fox 2005). The US Census Bureau further estimates that of white households 57 per cent had internet access at home, as against 36 per cent for black households and 36 per cent for Hispanics in 2003 (Day *et al.* 2005).

Other studies have also identified age as a key variable in determining internet adoption. For Negroponte, whilst 'some people worry about the social divide between the information-rich and the information-poor, the haves and have-nots, the First and Third Worlds ... the real cultural divide is going to be generational (1996, cited in Golding 1998: 141). The 2005 Pew study confirms Negroponte's prognosis, showing a sharply declining curve of adoption with age. The Pew researchers found that 84 per cent of those aged 18–29 had access, 80 per cent of those aged 30–49, but only 26 per cent of those aged 65 or older (Fox 2005).

Of course, these figures relate to the distribution of internet access within a country where, in the slogan of the Pew report cited above, 'internet access is the norm, but is not universal'. Considered globally the picture is rather different. Statistics from the International Telegraphic Union show that, at 62.28 users per 100 head of population in 2004, the USA is disproportionately represented in global internet usage, even amongst the wealthiest countries, where the average percentage for countries defined as 'high income' was 53.12 in 2004. Globally the average for low-income countries for the same year was 2.39 per cent, of which Papua New Guinea at 2.91 is representative, 7.53 per cent for lower-middle income countries, in which category China at 7.16 per cent describes the trend, and 16.6 per cent for upper middle, which includes Argentina at 16.1 per cent. Thus the overall distribution shows a strong bias towards the West, with the Americas and Europe having an average of 30.79 and 31.74 percentage of population online respectively, as against Asia with only 8.18 per cent and Africa with 2.63 per cent. This distribution mirrors that of information technologies more generally. As the then Deputy President of South Africa Thabo Mbeki pointed out in 1995, 'half of humanity has never made a telephone call. The reality is that there are more telephone lines in Manhattan, New York, than in Sub-Saharan Africa' (cited in Golding 1998: 145–6). The finding that the distribution of internet access is even more restricted is therefore unsurprising at best.

It is clear then that internet access is far from universal and mainly confined to the more affluent and culturally capital-rich demographics of the more affluent and culturally capital-rich areas of the globe. Of course, as Wilhelm has pointed out, this understanding of information poverty as a function of having/not having internet access is far too simplistic to be of any real analytical use. For Wilhelm 'the signifier *have-not* is appropriated to represent a monolithic and static information and telecommunications underclass, often without an attempt at distinguishing conceptually or theoretically varying degrees of marginality' (2000: 67–9). In contrast Wilhelm develops his periphery-centre model. This model describes a 'segmented underclass ... in which each subdivision is defined as existing at various stages along the periphery of the information society' (Wilhelm 2000: 10). Thus he describes varying degrees of information poverty as existing in a conceptual space formed by distance from the centre of the information society and thus the differential ability of the occupants of these positions to tap into informational resources. Those who exist on the extreme edge of the information society he describes as 'immune to progress'. For this group the barriers to movement inwards are formidable and include economic poverty; the lack of 'antecedent skills' required for participation, including literacy, basic skills in the use of a computer, familiarity with similar technologies; and the presence of attitudes which act as a barrier to entry. The Pew Internet study 'Digital Divisions' corroborates the presence of attitudinal barriers towards use of the internet. When asked why they did not access the internet 32 per cent were simply not interested in the internet, 31 per cent said they could not get access, 6 per cent saw it as too difficult and 5 per cent as too expensive. There were also more idiosyncratic responses including fears of becoming addicted, preference for face-to-face interaction, concerns over privacy and the belief that the technology represents a moral threat (Fox 2005). Moving inward, towards the centre, Wilhelm identifies a second group, those who have 'peripheral access'. These people may access the internet and use a computer at work or at public terminals, and thus they are not blocked from participation by functional or technical illiteracy, but their use of services is restricted by economic concerns and they cannot access the internet from home. Finally there are the 'peripheral users'. This group are characteristically wealthier, do not lack either the means or the motivation to go online and are likely to have personal internet access, but they are distinct from the power elite in so far as they make restricted use of the internet, neither producing new content online, nor making full use of content already available.

By differentiating the strata of the information poor in this way Wilhelm overcomes one of the problems that dogs attempts to understand information poverty, namely the problem of assessing what is *required* in order to participate in relation to an arena of activity which is constantly in motion. When I first started writing this book, a computer with a 56k modem met my internet needs adequately if not spectacularly. Less than a year later the greater demands my telecommuting lifestyle placed on my home necessitated broadband. Within months I was paying more for faster broadband. More and more equipment and faster and faster connections are increasingly required for an internet user to stay *current* and how this translates into minimal standards to *get by* online is always being revised. The Pew report argues that definitions should be revised from on/offline to a tripartite schema of truly offline, loosely online and highly engaged. 'Truly offline' refers to the 22 per cent of US adults who have never used the internet, do not live in a house with access and have no computer. At the other extreme are the 33 per cent of the highly engaged who use the internet every day and have broadband. Finally there are the residual group who are 'loosely online', a group who would correspond to Wilhelm's peripheral users. These are the 40 per cent who:

> may or may not go online regularly, but would probably be able to go online if they really needed to do so. This group includes dial-up users (30% of adults), people who live in internet-connected homes but do not go online themselves (5% of adults), and people who do not currently have access, but have in the past (5% of adults).
>
> (Fox 2005)

What is clear from these definitions is that, at least as far as policy groups are concerned, the technological bar has been emphatically raised. Without high-speed access to the internet, the user is relegated to the hinterland of the information society.

Free space

In segmenting the information poor in this way Wilhelm and the Pew researchers both point to the fact that definitions of information poverty that resolve into access to the physical infrastructure of the web, connections, computers and keyboards are far too techno-centric. In understanding access to the internet as a 'Manichean have/have-not distinction' (Wilhelm 2000: 67–9), the debate around information poverty reproduces both a technologically determinist logic which understands the internet as a unitary object and the logic of inclusion/exclusion, wherein power is understood as a function of access rather than of use. Wilhelm's schema brings into question the too easily accepted conflation of the economic poor and the information poor, and refers the analyst to broader sociological questions. It is immediately apparent that the divisions of the information poor refer less to what means are available to access information, and more to the way that information is used by the citizen. This in turn enjoins us to attempt to understand the nature of the online 'audience'.

In 1975 Childers and Post described America's information poor in these terms. A member of the poor is one who:

> does not know which formal channels to tap into in order to solve his problems ... watches many hours of television daily, seldom reads newspapers and magazines and never reads books ... does not see his problems as information needs ... is not a very active information seeker ... is locked into an informal information network that is deficient in the information that is ordinarily available to the rest of society.
>
> (Cited in Case 2002: 97)

What we have, then, is a hierarchy of informational sources and uses, from the very active media user, who comments on the material through whatever channels are available to him/her as a researcher and information seeker, active in formal and informal networks of discussion and information dissemination, to the passive isolated mass audience member we encountered in our discussion of Habermas. Information poverty, then, is synonymous with the status of audience, whether an audience of the seeing, or the wilfully or unwillingly blind.

Thus the question becomes, how far does the internet represent, for its audiences, a break with traditional *practices* of consumption? At first glance it appears highly counter-intuitive to talk about the internet audience in the same terms as that for other media. Nie and Erbring, for example, can easily take it for granted that '[f]or the most part, the Internet is an individual activity. Unlike TV, which can be treated as background noise, it requires more engagement and attention' (Nie and Erbring 2002: 280).

At a basic level, when we compare the physical activities of online life with those of another major model of audience behaviour, television watching, it seems impossible to disagree. Being online means that the user is forced to act in order to participate. One has to click links, make connections, in short, decide 'where we want to go today'. Surely this is our active, information-seeking 'good' media user in action. This is in contrast to the 'turn on, tune in, switch off' mode associated with television watching, where the user is captured by an undifferentiated flow of images and sounds. On this theme, Raymond Williams points out that television is less about watching *a programme* than of watching *the television*: 'We can be "into" something else before we have summoned the energy to get out of the chair, and many programmes are made with this situation in mind: the grabbing of attention in the early moments; the reiterated promise of exciting thing to come, if we stay' (2003: 94–5). George Gilder likewise understands television in similar terms as part of the 'master–slave architecture' of broadcast centres that pump out product to millions of passive, 'dumb terminals' (Gilder 1994, cited in Holmes 2005: 9). For both theorists television is mass entertainment, a homogenous product consumed by a homogenous audience. In this sense studies of television audiences have drawn on similar imagery to that used by Debord in describing the 'society of the spectacle' (1994). For Debord the key characteristic of the spectacle is not the content of the scene, but the relations that the media form between members of the audience. In Debord's analysis the spectacle absorbs all glances and channels attentions towards one central, unitary source. The audience look only forwards, each interpreting the spectacle in isolation. Communication is therefore one-to-many, with what Debord refers to as sideways glances, or communications between partici-pants, being eliminated. The audience are thus atomized and isolated in the face of the unitary spectacle, which demands only observation. In the 'society of the spectacle' we are interpellated in all arenas of social life as an audience, action is replaced by observation, doing things by watching things. Against this the internet, as an *interactive* medium, appears as a redemptive force, offering the possibility of breaking through the walls which segment the audience from each other, and requiring participation above and beyond passive presence. However, this vision of the audience depends on ascriptions about the behaviour of people online which may or may not be warranted.

The second common argument for the schismatic nature of the online and mass audiences centres on the content of the message. Internet content is understood to be autonomous of mass-media content, independent of its frames and concerns. However, this proposition is harder to sustain. Holmes points out that online content is often highly parasitic upon its offline 'rivals'. Holmes himself uses the example, originally put forward by Gauntlett (2000: 11), of 'ain't-it-cool-news.com', a website which reports on gossip and news from Hollywood. The site has achieved a kind of internet fame, or infamy, through its popularity online and the site author's anti-authoritarian stance towards his materials. But as Holmes points out, 'Ain't it cool news' is not evidence of a split between internet content and mainstream media content in the sense that Gauntlett uses it, for the site is parasitic upon Hollywood, acting as a second-order elaboration of its content (2005: 104–5). In this respect the site is characteristic of much web content, which is, Holmes argues, interesting only in so far as it elaborates upon content produced in other areas of the media sphere.

There is good reason to accept this position in relation to popular entertainment. In 1997 Baym pointed out that the largest Usenet list was one devoted to the discussion of soap operas (rec-arts.tv.soaps) (Baym 1997; also Holmes 2005: 87). However, there is even more reason to accept it in relation to online news. The Pew Center found that up to 74 per cent of users (see above) used their time online to gather news. It is clear from research into the demand for news at the time of intensively reported world events that the demand for internet services rises rapidly. Richard Wiggins' account of the effect of the events of 11 September 2001 on Google (Wiggins 2001), Shaw *et al's* description of the demands placed on the web after the publication of the Starr report of the investigation into the activities of US President Bill Clinton (Shaw *et al.* 2000, cited in Lewis 2003), and Taylor's description of the role of internet reportage in the conflict on Kosovo in 1999 (Taylor 2000) all emphasize the extent to which the internet acts for many people as a means of broadening their knowledge of events to which they were initially exposed through the mass media. Lloyd *et al.*'s (2006) evidence on the relationship between newspapers and online blogs also brings into question the independence of the internet from mass-media concerns. Although the authors found significant differences in the prevalence of given issues in blogs and newspapers, it is clear from their research that entertainment news is the most common blog topic and celebrity gossip produces pronounced informational 'spikes' or surges of blogging. In this sense, then, the internet acts as a medium of second-order elaboration of mass-media content.

That online audiences attempt to elaborate on offline media experiences is not unrelated to a second phenomenon, namely the colonization of the web by mass-media materials and content. That the web should be so colonized is also unsurprising, especially if viewed through the lens of political economy. Inasmuch as the internet is developed exclusively or nearly so through private-sector activity, each 'node' is only viable as far as it is commercially so. Initially, in accordance with McLuhan's dictum, the content of new media tends to be old media. We can see the operation of this rule in relation to online news. He and Zhu (2002) provide a typology of online news delivery from commercial sources in which the most basic is the transmission model, focused on information delivery. The second type of community is the interactive, understood as merely a bridge linking transmission models to the most evolved form, which is highly focused on interactivity, feedback and exchange.

> Of the three models, the first one is the simplest. It just moves the print version online without employing the interactive, nonlinear, multimedia, space and storage features of cyberspace. The second model is the intermediate model, which has tapped into some features of cyberspace. The third is the most advanced model, which fully utilizes and demonstrates the features of cyberspace, and sets up a virtual community by allowing the online newspaper to interact with its readers, and readers with readers.
>
> (Malukan and Zhu 2002: 134–5)

The most striking point about this typology is that it does not describe mutually exclusive coexisting forms but an evolution. In the early days of the internet 'gold rush' news companies rushed online in an effort to 'stake out a turf'. Inevitably this meant reproducing content from one media to another (see Lewis 2003).

That this works to the advantage of large-scale media concerns can be illustrated with reference to the mathematics of networks for, in one sense, it is an example of the 'rich-get richer' mechanism common to all networks. As Barabasi explains, hubs emerge in networks through two mechanisms, growth and preferential attachment. If we assume a network where new nodes are regularly added, and each node attaches to two other nodes then a 'power law' will come into operation in forming the network.

> The expansion of the network means that early nodes have more time than latecomers to acquire links. If a node is the last to arrive, no other node has the opportunity to link to it. Thus growth offers a clear advantage to the senior nodes, making them the richest in links. Seniority, however, is not sufficient to explain the power laws. Hubs require the help of the second law, preferential attachment. Because new nodes prefer to link to the more connected nodes, early links with more nodes links will be selected more often and will grow faster than their younger and less connected peers.
>
> (Barabasi 2003: 87–8)

Thus in the matter of growth it is clear that established 'information merchants' have a clear advantage considered with reference to the internet at the beginning, 'moment zero', a hypothetically level playing field, for they were able to hit the internet with large amounts of pre-existing content, as against their younger rivals who had to develop content as they went along.

This mechanism is familiar to students of media history, as it was one of the reasons why radio networks eventually came to dominate television broadcasting in the USA in the 1950s. Radio networks already had successful shows that could be translated from radio to television, familiar celebrities under contract, and the equipment, capital and links with major advertisers and financiers to exploit the new medium. Start-ups had none of these. Thus in the case of the web, CNN.com or BBC.co.uk could simply reproduce existing content, making it available to the online audience and in so doing stake out their turf in the central 'core continent' of the internet (see Barabasi 2003: 143–78). Moreover, just as in the case of radio and television in the 1940s and 1950s, large media concerns are already rich in the resources required to make and distribute high-quality content, which is to say professional programme makers, marketers, journalists, technicians and equipment. Finally, large media concerns are capital wealthy, enjoying privileged status with potential advertisers and investors, and possessed of complex and specialized financial and procedural routines for handling the risk involved in new product development. Thus, although the mythology of the net is the 'microcosm of the American dream [where] [e]nergetic and inventive young men, in backyards and garden sheds, are the driving force which kickstarts the industry taking America into the information age', in reality 'The suits were there at the beginning' (Golding 1998: 136–7).

However, Barabasi's mathematics will get us only so far. Whilst new 'nodes' may prefer to attach to richer nodes, human nodes will need human motivations. Here the rich-get-richer mechanism requires that internet users, commercial and private, link to these early-flowering mega-nodes and expand and extend their reach. Surely, after all, it is rather pointless for, say, a blogger to link to an article on CNN, for everyone interested in that topic would find the CNN article long before they stumbled upon the blogger's script? True, but this assumes that the appropriate unit of analysis for the web is the private citizen going about his or her personal and idiosyncratic journey; it assumes, in short, precisely what we should investigate. If we do not take Joe Blogger as our model then the picture changes radically. If the majority of web development activity comes about through the private sector (Golding 1998; Herman 1998; McChesney 1998; Robins and Webster 1999) then the activities of commercial users are analytically more to the point. In formal bureaucratic systems the use of information is tied to the ability of the user to substantiate not the accuracy of the material, but the user's warrant for regarding it as accurate. As a result, it is more likely that such users will link to and use information from socially endorsed credited sources than 'outsiders' (Gans 1979; Ericson *et al.* 1987). Thus it is not simply that the early-comers to the internet game gain more links because of their seniority, but also that they can leverage their offline reputations to mould and shape their environment. Given this, it is hard not to accept McChesney's bleak prognosis that '[d]espite the much ballyhooed "openness" of the internet, to the extent it becomes a viable mass medium, it will likely be dominated by the usual corporate subjects' (1998: 41).

The corporate penetration of the internet in turn recapitulates commercial imperatives. As Peter Golding (1998) points out, there are only three major sources of revenue available in the online environment: sale of goods, advertising and access to a network. In an environment constructed through links, multiple access points to information and a promiscuous multiplicity of reproductions, selling subscription-only services is a chief means by which the internet as a new outlet for informational goods can be turned to commercial advantage (see below, p. 73). Barabasi suggests that in 2003 around a quarter of all information held electronically was situated in online 'informational islands' (2003: 168), islands which Terranova likens to the corporate 'black ice' info spaces of Gibson's futuristic cyberpunk virtual realities (2004: 48). These informational islands are cut off from the mainlands of cyberspace, impenetrably defended behind password-protected firewalls. It is these subscription and private land masses which are most likely to proliferate.

What this suggests is that the commercial centre of gravity to the internet can be said to act as a form of informational flypaper, drawing users from the interactive periphery towards the 'mass' centre, further fragmenting the already fragmented and directed internet networks. In this sense the internet, contra the ideology of universal availability of information from any point, is actually characterized by heterogeneity of access levels. The internet, far from acting as an open, energetic medium of debate, is likely to mirror other extant forms of mass communication in so far as people are formed into consuming units who are fed information generated by corporate media.

However, whether this proposition is accepted or rejected is more a function of the ontological commitments of the researcher than of the fate of the internet. Much rests on the distinction between the internet as a technology and as an extension of a social system, capitalism. If we regard the internet as a technology then the dour prognoses of the political economists seem less warranted. The internet, unlike other forms of mass media, does not suffer from the problems of resource scarcity that form the warrant and sufficient reason for market regulation of broadcast media. The scarcity of bandwidth, the fact that only so many terrestrial radio and television stations can broadcast, was the initial spur to the regulation of the mass media in the interests of preserving or establishing a heterogeneous media sphere in which multiple voices and interests would receive representation. It is argued that such warrants have become increasingly outdated in the modern media environment. The rise of satellite broadcasting rendered the question of bandwidth and its limitations largely redundant as satellite and cable provision offers scope for an almost infinite number of channels to exist simultaneously, which in turn warranted market deregulation. The same argument can be put forward in relation to the internet, that as a medium in which bandwidth is not an issue there is no reason to suppose that the commercial web and the interactive net cannot coexist.

If, on the other hand, we view the internet as an extension of a social system, then the technological features are overwritten by social and political imperatives. Robins and Webster point out that ICTs:

> represent – and have long represented – one of the fundamental means by which capital has sought to achieve control over society ... Driving this project has been the concern to impose a rational and efficient order, first in the sphere of production, then across society as a whole. This desire to constitute a coherent order is what we describe as the cybernetic imaginations of capital.
>
> (Webster 1999: 129)

The cybernetic imagination of capitalism is a totalizing venture, one which in its hurry to appropriate all potential sources of value, expands into or opens onto all free spaces, swallowing them up and incorporating them into the logic of capital (Hardt and Negri 2000; Castells 2001). The key means by which this is achieved is through the creation of precisely the scarcity that the internet's *technological* architecture overcomes.

At the heart of the ideology of the market is the proposition that the market works to allocate scarce resources in the most efficient manner. Only those who can derive the greatest benefit from goods will be willing to pay for them and thus societies ensure the circulation of goods to those who can maximise their benefits (Perelman 1998: 105–30). However, as Perelman goes on to argue, this mechanism collapses in the case of information. Information is neither a scarce resource which must be allocated to those who can best use it, nor is it depleted by use. It can be held and used by multiple persons simultaneously and, indeed, the use of information by larger numbers of people means an increase in the flow of information rather than a restriction. As a result, in order to commodify information, capital is required to create a scarcity, something that Perelman argues is achieved through the use of patents and copyrights which create the artificial scarcity and restriction necessary to bringing goods to market. The same principle can be seen at work in the establishment of the private information nets, subscriber-only services and password-protected firewalls which proliferate online. In an environment where information is a commodity, and is anything but scarce, artificial restrictions must be applied. In this sense the social institutions of the internet take precedence over its formal features.

However, both accounts, those that emphasize the political economy of the internet and those that emphasize its formal features, fall victim to a totalistic either/or-ism, either through a species of technological determinism or through an appeal to Marxian and Weberian views of capital and the iron cage of rationalization. These accounts appear as an inclusive range of possible positions only once the proposition that the internet is most appropriately understood as a mass media is accepted. Both the political-economy and technology approaches to medium factor out the social nature of the audience, and in so doing uncritically adopt and overemphasize the internet's separate and unitary nature. The media-centric appropriation of the work of Habermas, as I have argued above (p. 64), fails to take into consideration the third crucial element of the public sphere, the nature and forms of interactivity and audience experience.

Audiences

Earlier, I pointed to the argument that the internet audience behaves differently to the audience for mass media. The compulsion to perform physical actions in order to move through the internet is, at the most basic level, the core distinction between broadcast and online behaviour. However, whilst this distinction operates as a resource in analysis it is seldom if ever constructed itself as a topic. The ability to take this feature for granted in accounts of the online audience tends to rest on one of two premises. The first is the idea, which technological and media-centric views of the internet promulgate, that there is a unitary way of consuming internet content, a particular way of being an audience online. Such a view can only rest on the basis that the technological form or the content induces a specific relationship which then acts to produce behaviours and modes of consumption. Sociologists would, by and large, find this position untenable, seeing it as an analytical evasion and as a species of technological determinism (see Chapter 10 for further discussion). The second basis, which is more ecological in nature, is associated with postmodern theories and exemplified by two approaches which will be considered in turn here, Mark Poster's *second media age* theories and the idea of the *digital citizen*.

The second media age

The second media age theory posits a radical rupture in forms of media between the ages of mass media and the new media logic of individualization and interactivity. In the first media age the form of communication was one-to-many, where a small number of producers faced onto a large number of consumers, and in which there were clearly defined roles of audience as against producers. This means that the audience is interpellated, or hailed as Althusser would put it, as a generalized subject, which is to say addressed as an example of a category and obliged to behave in line with the discursive norms of that category. The first media age is dependent, then, on people entering the media sphere as preconstituted subjects, and identity pre-exists incorporation in the media discourse.

Poster (1995a) argues that the modern media sphere is novel in so far as it is founded on a reversal of the polarity of these positions. In the second media age, the audience is not bifurcated into audience and producers, instead we are all both simultaneously. The ratio of producers to audience is higher, but also the sense of there being clear, distinct roles between the two has collapsed. Communication is inherently more many-to-many. Whereas in the first media age the audience are individualized subjects whose attention is focused hierarchically on a central information source, the second media age is characterized by the proliferation of lateral relations (see above p. 68 for discussion). In Poster's second media age, this dynamic is broken down. The directedness of the gaze towards a central spectacle decomposes into multi-directionality, where the captivating power of the image is replaced by a sidelong and lateral communication between the observers.

Moreover, in the new era people are argued to develop themselves online through interaction with each other, not in relation to a monolithic media-generated 'prêt-à-porter' identity. The distinction for Poster is that whereas mass communication interpellates the subject as a mass, a generalized audience, who can be addressed through generalized discursive forms, the internet is a more individualized media, where messages are directly addressed to the subject. For Castells the 'price to pay for inclusion in the system [the mass media world] is to adapt to its logic, to its language, to its points of entry, to its encoding and decoding' (1996: 374). The movement from the logic of the mass to that of the individual means that neither producer nor consumer is caught up in these adaptive subjectivities.

Thus the crux of Poster's position is that the second media age is characterized by identity formation through social interaction, and this interactivity is of a different order to that of the first media age. For Poster the interactional forms of the second media age are 'thicker', more 'rich'.

> [i]f you look at it on the screen where the conversation is, let's say in the chat-mode in real time, the individuals are absorbed in their conversation and the interactivity is very different but very intense. Especially in the MOO [multi-user object-oriented] form, things go very quickly. You are in that conversation and it takes an incredible amount of attention to maintain the flow of the conversation. So one could argue that it is a more thick, a richer interaction than, say, an interaction of a family at a dinner table, where people are distracted and maybe the television set is on and people are not really paying attention or listening to one another.
>
> (Poster 1995b: 149)

From this perspective the experience of the internet 'audience' and those of the mass audience are clearly radically different.

However, there are a number of serious problems with this account which render it unhelpful in considering the nature of online audiences. In the first instance, Poster appears to want to sustain two mutually exclusive positions: on the one hand, that the internet's uniqueness as an experience for the audience comes from the individualizing nature of the online environment and, on the other, that this individuation leads to the formation of horizontal webs of sense-making. When we consider Debord's position on the relationship of the image and the gaze, it is clear that the internet, by increasing the individual nature of the experience, which it achieves largely through the physical interactivity which has led theorists like Poster to posit it as a radical departure, actually extends the processes of isolation and one-to-many communication which are characteristic of broadcast media. John Holmes expresses this more eloquently: 'if an "audience" is constituted only in an atomised form by mass media, then the difference between the phenomenological world of a broadcast audience member and that of an individual immersed in a so-called "interactive technology" begins to flatten out' (2005: 90).

Second, Poster's argument that the interactivity of the cyber-audience is of a qualitatively different order to everyday interaction flags up a further problem, namely the extent to which cyber-theorists are basing their analyses on an out-of-date model of the internet. Although in the early rush of enthusiasm for the internet it seemed, certainly according to academic writers, that everyone was spending time in multi-user domains (MUDs) and chat rooms, experimenting interactively with identity, that picture is largely alien to internet users less than a decade later. Longitudinal studies by the Pew Institute (see Fox 2005) have found little variation over the past six years in the forms of activities that people engage in online and the relative popularity of these activities. The Pew studies, running from March 2000 to the present day, show that email remains the most consistent activity (91–95 per cent of respondents report that they send email). Following this, searching for news online (between 59 and 74 per cent) is the next highest ranking category. Other categories include instant messaging (39–47 per cent) researching goods and services (72–78 per cent), checking the weather (62–78 per cent), and downloading programmes and audio files. The data gathered show a strong bias towards these less interactive activities. With the exception of email the most interactive categories, creating a blog and chatting in a chat room or an online discussion, both gathered few positive responses. Between 3 and 10 per cent of users reported ever creating a blog, and although chatting in a chat room or online discussion produced more positive responses, the number is steadily falling (from 28 per cent in 2000 to 17 per cent in 2005) (Fox 2005). Therefore it is not after all clear that interactivity is the primary 'selling point' of the internet for its users and they do not appear to be behaving in the interactive, reflexive ways that Poster and other post-structuralists would predict.

However, it would be premature to reject Poster's thesis on these grounds, for by doing so we would sustain and sanction the view of the audience as essentially a unitary homogenous body, in short we again presuppose what we seek to investigate. Although it is clear that the general trend online is towards the interpellation of the audience as a mass audience, this does not preclude the possibility that other forms of audience life exist, albeit not as a majority. In attempting to generalize about internet audiences from survey data, commentators have overlooked the importance of emergent norms. For Raymond Williams (1961), in any empirical instance, culture may be described in terms of the dominant norms, institutions and practices but also features and integrates residual forms, those that belong to a prior era, and emergent forms, those which point the way to a possible future. The interrelationship of residual, dominant and emergent forms in a given way of life is not a simple temporal one, in which the residual will eventually give way to the dominant entirely. Rather these forms of culture all inform the whole, and interact with each other in productive ways.

The cybercitizen

In the case of the internet, some commentators have rejected the general trend in favour of an investigation of the emergent forms of life online – the new cybercitizen. The cybercitizen instantiates a category of subject who is politically active, civically aware and involved, and married to a creed of interactivity and participation. I say instantiates for the portrayal of the cybercitizen does not make recourse to the suggestion that such a style of citizenship is universal or even prevalent. Unlike Habermas's prototype bourgeois public sphere, where the observed limitations on participation were understood as temporary boundaries that could be overcome in the next 'release', the cybercitizenry are *inherently* a bounded group.

The cybercitizen is one to whom the internet and new communications technologies has given a voice and a platform that they would otherwise be denied. The basic model of the cybercitizen was that described by the journalist and cyber-enthusiast Jon Katz. For Katz,

> The Digital Nation constitutes a new social class. Its citizens are young, educated, affluent. They inhabit wired institutions and industries – universities, computer and telecom companies, Wall Street and financial

outfits, the media. They live everywhere, of course, but are most visible in forward-looking, technologically advanced communities … They are predominantly male, although female citizens are joining in enormous – and increasingly equal – numbers. The members of the Digital Nation are not representative of the population as a whole: they are richer, better educated, and disproportionately white. They have disposable income and available time. Their educations are often unconventional and continuous [*sic*], and they have almost unhindered access to much of the world's information. As a result, their values are constantly evolving. Unlike the rigid political ideologies that have ruled America for decades, the ideas of the postpolitical young remain fluid.

(Katz 1997)

Katz's digital citizen is distinguishable by his/her core values, a commitment to libertarian ideals, individuality, materialism, tolerance, anti-authoritarianism, a belief in rational debate, a contempt for mainstream media and mainstream political divisions, and an overriding enthusiasm for interactivity – defined as 'the right to shape and participate in their media'. 'Like it or not,' he argues, 'this Digital Nation possesses all the traits of groups that, throughout history, have eventually taken power. It has the education, the affluence, and the privilege that will create a political force that ultimately must be reckoned with' (Katz 1997).

For Katz, as for those who have followed in his footsteps, the cybercitizen transcends statistical representativeness. They are the core 'movers and shakers' of online political and cultural life. The grab bag of dissonant values which they embrace are the core values of the internet, and of these the overarching commitment to personal expression and development, which is the definition of interactivity as it is here used, is the cornerstone value.

When we translate Katz's concerns from the narrow lexicon of cybersociology into a more general idiom of power and power relations it is clear that there are high theoretical stakes on the table. What Katz is positing is an intellectual vanguard, an intelligentsia who occupy no formal position in social life, but nevertheless behave as free-floating intellectuals. This implies a rather different conception of the operation of the internet as a public sphere from the plebiscitary democratic sphere that is the tacit model more usually invoked. If we understand the power of the internet as a space for discussion as a function of the way it redistributes a voice from formal to informal channels and thus as a redistribution of power to those outside of a formal system of knowledge creation, then cyberspace's power elite begin to appear more as the staff common-room of an intellectual class. What then might we expect of an intellectual class? And what is the composition of such digital overlords?

The outlines of a response are already at hand in the work of theorists from the sociology of knowledge. For theorists such as Mannheim and Shils, an intellectual class occupied a pivotal role in society in so far as they possessed a monopoly over the development of ideas (Islam 1988). Mannheim regarded the intelligentsia as a 'socially unattached' group whose position within the social offers them the opportunity to critique the social order. In modern societies 'intellectual activity is not carried on exclusively by a socially rigidly defined class, such as a priesthood, but rather by a social stratum which is to a large degree unattached to any social class and which is recruited from an increasingly inclusive area of social life' (Mannheim 1936, cited in Turner 1999: 119). For Mannheim this circumvented the central problem of identifying knowledge with its material conditions of production, which appears in sociology and philosophy as the problem of relativism (Turner 1999: 133). Briefly, the situation is stated thus: if all ideas are relative, so is the idea that ideas are relative. There is no philosophical warrant for exempting relativism from relativism's dynamic. Thus the problem becomes how to retain credibility for philosophical endeavour against the background of a deconstruction of all knowledge claims. In the work of the Frankfurt school, where ideas are more closely tied to ideology and the reproduction of the social status quo, this problem takes on a more sinister guise. How can we talk about the enslavement of the masses to a foreign conceptual creed, that of the ruling class, without a theoretical warrant to position ourselves outside of the determining power of that creed or, more prosaically, why can we as intellectuals see what others cannot?

The invocation of the intellectual as a free-floating group provides this warrant in so far as they are understood to be outside of, and structurally independent from, the class system and the mechanisms of material production. Intellectuals, for both Marx and Weber, were associated with the working class, in so far as their social location mirrored that of the oppressed, for they were excluded from ownership of the means of production. For Mannheim, on the other hand, the free intelligentsia were free precisely because they were not a class in the traditional sense of the word. Their diverse composition meant that they were not associated with any particular group, they were outwith the class order (Islam 1988). Thus the value of the intelligentsia lies in their objectivity. Because they are an 'interstitial class', existing between antagonistic groups but affiliated to none, they are able to maintain neutrality and view issues from many perspectives (Turner 1999: 134).

How far, then, can the digital intelligentsia be said to occupy this same position? If we shift the frame from Mannheimian to the post-industrial models of class proposed by theorists such as Poulantzas then a different perspective emerges. Poulantzas, contra Weber, sees mental labour as no less a part of the means of production than the physical labour of the worker (Poulantzas 1978). In an 'information economy', an economic system organized around information and communication rather than material goods, the extent to which intellectual work can be exempted from class positions is questionable. Therefore, the social composition of the digital class may as easily be that of an intellectual proletariat as that of Mannheim's free intellectuals or Poulantzas's petit bourgeois. In Katz's account, of course, they are not. The digital class is a class of the wealthy and privileged, who are already affiliated and positioned within the class order. They are closer in form to Gouldner's (1985) and Bourdieu's (1984) vision of the intellectual as a bourgeois class, reiterating their economic capital through cultural capital, and vice versa. The image of the digital class is therefore not redemptive in the sense that enthusiasts have taken it to be, they are ill suited for the role as a 'revolutionary vanguard'. Rather they appear to represent a simple translation of offline capital into online and this gives little warrant to regard the digital nation as revolutionary. In looking to the digital class as a source for political renewal, theorists have raised social exclusion from a fact to a virtue.

Thus the view from theory is pessimistic. What, however, is the empirical status of the debate? The evidence on whether this digital class can be truly said to exist is sharply divided. Research conducted between 1997 and 1999 found no correlation between internet use and civic engagement (Aspden and Katz 1997; Putnam 2000). Putnam explains:

> We also know that the early users of Internet technology were no less (and no more) civically engaged that anyone else ... once we control for the higher educational levels of Internet users, they are indistinguishable from nonusers when it comes to civic engagement. On the other hand these oft ballyhooed results prove little about the effects of the Net, because of the likelihood that Internet users are self-selected in relevant ways. The absence of any correlation between Internet usage and civic engagement could mean that the Internet attracts reclusive nerds and energises them, but it could also mean that the Net disproportionately attracts civic dynamos and sedates them.
>
> (Putnam 2000: 170–1)

Of course, again, this evidence is directed at understanding the general composition and profile of the online audience, rather than the elite avant-garde of Katz's account. More recent evidence suggests an emergent split in the internet audience based upon levels of access. The majority of the research evidence now available suggests that those who are information-*technology* rich tend to be more interactive in their use of the internet and other media and information services, although this may not necessarily correlate with economic wealth as such. The Pew researchers, for example, found that broadband users were more likely than dial-up users to read news online (82 per cent versus 68 per cent), to read (35 per cent versus 20 per cent) or create a blog (4 per cent versus 11 per cent) (Fox 2005). This can be understood to demonstrate two propositions. First, that in terms of the distinction discussed above, the information-technology poor and the information-behaviour poor are at the moment apparently the selfsame people and, second, that there is a correlation between interactivity as an ethos and a privileged position in the online hierarchy.

For both Poster and Katz, then, the chief feature of the online audience is its participatory self-constitution. Although for Poster this is a generalized feature produced by the environment of cyberspace, and for Katz this is a feature of a specific group whose education and privilege offline allows them to capitalize on the affordances of the online environment, the two commentators are united in their views of the central and determining status of interactive self-creation online in the production of the cyber-subject. Thus the question then becomes: what forms does this interactivity take? What rides on this question is whether we can validly regard the internet as a potential public sphere, whether its members are the active postmodern subjects created by the forms of the interactive environment (Poster), or merely those who already have pre-existing tendencies in this direction and who are given a platform by the internet (Katz). The next chapter therefore investigates the nature of online interactivity.

6 Interactivity: it's got to be jelly 'cos jam don't shake like that

The interactive possibilities of a given medium are critical to any conception that it takes a role in the formation of a public sphere, howsoever limited. For Habermas the interactivity of the bourgeois public sphere of the eighteenth century lay not in the media product but in its social locations of consumption, the coffee houses, which provided a space and interactional frame for discussion. In this regard the media are less the carrier or architecture of a public sphere, so much as an informational 'lingua franca', a common resource which allowed people to coordinate and frame responses to a rapidly changing political world. Thus in Habermas's prototype the informational and interactive elements of the public sphere were both present, although segregated into different structures. The importance of the interactional elements has, as I have noted above, frequently been down-played in mainstream media studies. However, as Sparks points out:

> To confer is to participate in a discussion, to have the rights both of auditor and speaker. Again any analysis needs constantly to return to the question of whether all people in fact have an equal right to participate in both capacities. We cannot use the term 'public sphere' in anywhere near its full sense to describe a situation in which a tiny minority have the right to speak in public and the vast majority are at best consigned to the role of audience, still less when they are, for whatever reason, unable even to follow a debate conducted by others.
>
> (Sparks 1998: 112)

The ability for participants to act both as audiences for and producers of discourse, to fully participate as speaking and listening subjects within the debates, is critical to understanding a space as a public sphere. What, then, are the dynamics of online debate? And how does online interactivity overlap as a category with rational debate?

For many cyber-theorists the question of interactivity and debate is dissolved into the formal and technical features of the internet. The high bandwidth properties of the internet mean that there is no scarcity of medium to host debate, allowing all contributions, and the architecture of the internet itself is such as to 'route around censorship', as John Gilmore famously argued. These two features, abundance and the lack of preset formal channels through which information moves, are the core claims to the internet being an inherently anti-authoritarian medium, and as such uniquely placed to provide for debate and discussion. The implications are that 'anyone can say anything', that the internet gives people a voice but, unlike other media, also lacks any means by which that voice can be suppressed. The argument essentially reduces down to an assertion that in the absence of mechanisms to prevent it, rational debate/interactivity will naturally emerge. This in essence substitutes the features of the medium for the activities of the users. This chapter examines this proposition from the point of view of the behaviour of the audience. Rather than accepting this substitution I here examine the evidence for interactivity with reference to internet content and the environmental constraints on the users.

Interactivity and overload

In their foundational work on informational theory, Claude Shannon and Warren Weaver established a framework for understanding the communications process. Shannon and Weaver's diagrammatic representation of communication as source, transmitter, message, channel and receiver, whilst often criticized, laid out a framework for the development of studies into, particularly mass, communication which emphasized the integrity of the process as a whole (Shannon and Weaver 1963). Whilst Shannon and Weaver's work has been adopted within media and communication studies as a founding narrative of the disciplines and their topics, the almost heretical implications of their analysis have been largely overlooked as they do not now easily fit with the content-based frames which, through the influence of cultural studies, dominate Western media scholarship. In the work of Titsiana Terranova (2004) the 'mathematical theory of communication' is restored to a central position within critical media theory. For Terranova the significance of information theory is that by deconsecrating the meaning of a message as the central point of analysis, the approach allows us to foreground the communicative process. For Shannon and Weaver the mathematics of communication were tied to an instrumental rather than a critical agenda, in so far as they were concerned with the effectiveness of a channel of communication. However, as Terranova argues, when the 'problem of communication is reduced to that of establishing a bridge or a contact between a sender and a receiver ... where all communication is reduced to a drive to clear out a channel for transmission between two points separated by space and united only by the channel' (2004: 15), the implications are radical. Rather than seeing two interlocutors as debaters, on opposite sides, we must understand them instead as on the same side, cooperating in the maintenance of the channel or link between them. In this context Terranova cites Serres's maxim that 'to hold a dialogue is to suppose a third man and to seek to exclude him' (2004: 15). This radically alters our conception of the nature of communication. If the first principle to which we must attend is simply establishing and maintaining a link, and the content transmitted along that channel is only a secondary concern, then the interactional forms of communication appear in rather a different light. Terranova's own example clarifies this, when she argues that in the case of a screened political debate on television:

> can we say that such a debate is won or lost on the basis of a dialectical argument involving the interplay of truth and persuasion? Can we say that politicians are really conveying a persuasive content? Or isn't the main problem that of clearing out a channel through a noisy mediascape, of establishing a contact with the audience out there? In this context, the opponent becomes noise and the public becomes a target of communication: not a rational ensemble of free thinking individuals ... but a collective receiver to which a message can be sent only on condition that the channel is kept free of noise.
>
> (Terranova 2004: 16–17)

Perhaps we could even go further than this, and consider that the other politician is not the noise in this scenario. Rather the two politicians cooperate, as a team, to raise the profile of the debate *at all*. When we consider noise in relation to the busy multi-channel, rapid-fire mediascape, it is clear that politicians, whether on the same ideological side or not, must cooperate in order to gain public attention to the fact of politics, let alone to an election or particular policies.

What we gain from applying these sets of concerns to an analysis of internet discussion is a shift in focus from the content and personalities of the debate towards the environment in which it is held, and this foregrounds two related issues: the questions of interactivity and of information overload. One of the chief virtues of the online environment in promoting rational debate is understood to be the asynchronous nature of interaction. When compared against other conversational forums, for example a conversation in a bar, or a seminar or a live television broadcast, online discussion groups and mailing lists have a clear advantage, as the non-concurrent nature of the interaction allows space for reflection and composition, which is presumed to increase the quality of response. In offline debates we may find ourselves saying 'that's not right' but be unable to explain our 'gut feeling' in detail, or know why we object to a point but be unable to frame it in persuasive discourse. It is common for students in seminars to say 'I read a different view in another book but I can't remember the title just now' or for participants in a bar-room discussion to say 'I can't remember how many it was, but it was a lot.' These statements, though characteristic of spontaneous debaters everywhere, do not fulfil the generally accepted requirements for persuasiveness, and certainly do not approximate to Habermas's ideal speech for they do not provide us, the audience for them, with the means of assessing their truthfulness or otherwise. I may accept your view that it was 'a lot' but if I do so without the numbers it can only be because I trust you, either personally – an affective judgement – or through your role – a status judgement. Neither of these satisfies the requirements of public debate. In an online forum it is argued that the asynchronous debate allows people to take the time out to properly frame their arguments and thus to present statements in a form amenable to the assessment of truth claims.

However, when we consider this argument from the stance of mathematical communication it becomes clear that it is not that simple. The rapid-fire nature of internet forums is a key feature enabling the democratic participation of all parties. Poster's point concerning the 'thickness' of virtual environment interactions may be outdated (see above) but the speed of responses is not. On more popular boards hundreds of responses to a message can be posted within hours and new 'threads' or topics are posted all the time. Thus debaters are faced with the problem of keeping the debate 'on message', i.e. relevant to the topic at hand without censoring others, and the problem of maintaining the profile of the debate. This latter comes about as a function of the interaction between the popularity of the board, the composition of its members and the layout of the interface (Baym 1998). Most forums place threads with new contributions at the top of the list, where they are more likely to be noticed by members, and so it becomes important to maintain the profile of 'your' thread; hence the practice on some message boards of 'bumping' – artificially maintaining the topic at the top of list by posting spurious responses – if that topic is viewed as urgent by group members. Here, to maintain the debate, people will need to make rapid-fire contributions and these inevitably will no more satisfy the criteria for rational debate than the under-prepared seminar student or person in the pub of offline life.

This problem is compounded by group composition. As observed above, there is a strong bias in internet usage towards Western, English-speaking nations. Asynchronicity supposedly enables the global reach of discussion across time zones in so far as the conversation may drop off in Europe as people leave work, or go to bed, but be taken up when the USA wakes up or comes home from work. Clearly the exact dynamics, as Baym (1998) has argued, depend on the composition of the board. However, in theory this means that the 'wired world' at least can interact and discuss. In practice the disproportionate concentration of internet access in the West means that this will only work out in practice on more specialized and less popular boards. In general forums or very popular communities, issues of more local concern will be 'drowned off the airways' once the West logs in.

What this flags up, then, is that information exists not as a property in its own right, but in an oppositional relationship to another phenomenon, noise. Noise is understood as that which interferes with the correct transmission of a message, and it is intimately related to the question of information overload. Generally speaking, scholars have approached this question as a zero-sum debate. Phillip Meyer (2004) argues that the wealth of information consumes, and therefore creates a dearth of, attention. What this presupposes is that attention and information are fixed quantities, and that information can be analytically separated from both attention and non-information. Whilst both of these propositions appear reasonable from the point of view of mainstream media audience studies, neither will necessarily hold up when considered in relation to internet audience studies. What is required is a move away from looking at how audiences attend to a specific and predetermined message to consider the 'photographic negative' image of how audiences define information and noise and handle the dynamics of overload.

One of the key ways in which people handle information overload is to limit their exposure. On the internet, as in other real-life situations, this takes the form of selective retrieval and organization, which in turn requires the imposition of categories and classifications. As the sociologist Charles Perrow points out, the chief utility of libraries is not their comprehensiveness but their systems of classification: 'I require libraries to *hide* most of the literature so that I will not become delirious from the want of time and wit to pursue it all. There is just too much material. The problem is not access, it is the reverse, containment ... Were I now to browse the stacks ... I would drown, or panic, and certainly lose my way' (cited in Case 2002: 94; original emphasis).

Online the most obvious way to handle overload is through the use of a simplified interface, and of these the most commonly used are search engines. However, as Dreyfus points out, search engines as things stand at the moment are not that efficient at retrieving useful information. This can be considered on two axes – recall and precision, where recall is the number of relevant of documents which the search retrieves and precision is the percentage of those documents retrieved which are relevant (Dreyfus 2001: 19–26). Given that search engines do not provide complete coverage of the web – Lawrence and Giles' 1999 study found that search engines only indexed between 7.8 per cent and 15 per cent of the web (cited in Barabasi 2003: 165) – recall is clearly patchy. Precision on the other hand is also a problem, although greater research and development is directed towards solving this problem. Two main types of search engine algorithms are commonly used. The first uses information from bots, in this case identifying keywords to return results. A second model, usually layered onto the first, is popularity engines, which use time spent on a site and user clicks to rank results. Dreyfus estimates that whilst keyword-only engines have only a 10 per cent chance of retrieving useful documents, popularity-based ones have around 20 per cent (2001: 22). This still means that in practice most of the 'hits' generated from a search engine are irrelevant or of little use.

This problem is less a problem of the technical attributes of the internet and more a problem of these attributes as they are coupled with changes in the knowledge base of advanced Western societies. The mythos of the internet as the 'great library of Alexandria', the fount of all known knowledge, obscures the fact that the meaning of knowledge has been subject to radical change in recent years, a matter which some academics have seen as cause for concern (e.g. Furedi 2004b) and others for celebration (e.g. Lyotard 1984). Whether we understand the social transformation of knowledge in terms of a terrifying vision of knowledge subservient to instrumental reason, useful only in so far as it is tied to extraneous goals, or as a postmodern festival of the oppressed throwing off the chains of a centuries old elitism, it remains the case that knowledge has become increasingly tied to a 'just in time' ethos where knowledge of a topic is less valued than knowledge of how to know a topic. When we marry this ethos to national educational policies which emphasize the role of information technologies, then the question of informational organization becomes a more political one. In this example, given that for the majority of web users search engines are *the* primary means of finding out both specific information and also of discovering *what there is to find out* about a broad topic, their role in the knowledge base of modern societies is critical.

Search engines are proffered as a technological solution to the problem of information overload, but it in turn foregrounds a second problem, that of the quality of information supplied. Online search engines enshrine the principle of the commercial organization of information retrieval and this can create problems. In order to remain commercially viable, search engines work on profit models, of which one of the most common is the 'pay-per-click model' – where advertisers bid on keywords and the results are ranked on the basis of the outcome of the auction with the highest bidders results returned first. This, it can be argued, represents a threat to the integrity of the stock of social knowledge. However, this is a lesser concern than attempts to artificially alter the structure of results in search engine returns, which has resulted in the coining of neologisms such as 'spamdexing', referring to the mass submission of web pages to search engines in an attempt to promote a particular institution, or the more political variant 'googlewashing', where a search engine is manipulated into providing a partial 'reading' of an issue through emphasizing only certain views. These are clearly high-stakes manoeuvres in an public relations and commercial war. However, they depend for their effectiveness on the unavailability of alternate perspectives linked to alternate sources of information and upon information overload inducing the often observed tendency to review only the first page of 'hits'. In this sense 'googlewashing' and 'spamdexing' are effective only in the sense, discussed above, that the web audience can be presumed to act in a similar fashion to those of mass media, as consumers of a single unitary information source. Paradoxically, then, the internet's capacity to distribute information and circumvent censorship can limit the information available.

Overload also acts as a force in the restructuring of interactional techniques on a micro level and this can be seen clearly when we move the focus from the wider internet to online forums. The prevalence of these forums online is a substantial warrant for the claim that the internet is both an interactive space and one in which rational debate is the key defining feature. However, even a cursory examination of the evidence on the behaviour of the audience for these forums gives rise to scepticism over the nature of online interactivity and the overlap between this and rational debate. In large measure the audience's response to overload is at the root of this mismatch between technical potential and realized actuality.

If we put aside for the moment the question of whether the mythology of the internet as impermeable to censorship is valid, we are still left with the problem that whilst the internet may or may not route round censorship, people, generally speaking, do not. Since the mid-1940s research into the dynamics of mass communications has consistently emphasized people's selective consumption of media. Generally 'we drift towards information that supports our point of view. In other words we tend towards a usual diet of information that is *mostly* congruent with out beliefs and opinions' (Case

2002: 93; original emphasis). That people tend to gravitate towards media that confirm or reinforce their own attitudes counteracts the hypothetic breadth of opinion that the internet can be understood to channel to people. When these considerations are translated into the frame of online interactive debate we can see that there is a strong tendency for homophonous opinion to emerge. In his study of political discussion boards Wilhelm found that 70 per cent of the messages posted could be considered homophonous in so far as they expressed strong or moderate support for the dominant position of the board as a whole (2000: 86–105). This finding will surprise neither sociologists nor political theorists as it is a variation upon well-documented tendencies towards social centripetalism. The tendency for conflicting views to be marginalized and ultimately 'outsourced' to other forums is in line with Noelle-Neumann's description of the 'spiral of silence'. Briefly, Noelle-Neumann found that the further away from what they perceived as the common opinion people were, the less likely they were to express their views, whereas the closer they perceived themselves to be the more likely they were to express them and be vocal in their support (Noelle-Neumann 1984, cited in Sunstein 2001: 68). Thus, although 'anyone can say anything', in reality it appears that they mostly say similar things.

However, homophily is not the same thing as reciprocity, which brings us to the second problem with online debates, namely the nature of dialogue online. This issue is covered in more detail in Part Three, but here it is important to bring out the qualities of interaction which affect the circulation or quality of information. In the first instance there is the question of 'interactional noise'. Even the most committed cyberspace advocates acknowledge that there are significant interactional problems in online discussions, problems which tend to hinge on the lack of visual and aural cues which serve to narrow the indexical range of utterances and reduce the probability of misunderstandings. This paucity of cues, when taken against the background of overload, represents a difficulty for internet debaters. In some ways it is the offline equivalent of carrying on a potentially inflammatory discussion in a loud room. The possibilities for misunderstandings where responses are rapidly composed and delivered at the click of a mouse, and the likelihood that many responses will simply be ignored, both serve to increase the confrontational possibilities of online debate. However, '(w)hen technology provides *both* speed *and* anonymity, it produces a concoction that can spark hostility and attack' (Tannen 1999: 252, emphasis added) and the semi-anonymous nature of online interaction may be at the root of noted hostility. As Tannen argues, disagreements escalate into confrontations where mechanisms of resolution are absent or weak. In contemporary society the chief means by which reconciliations are achieved is the recovery of the personal: we seek out face-to-face interaction in order to overcome disagreements; getting to know someone is a time-honoured method of diffusing tension. Online, where, if postmodern psychologists and post-structuralist theorists (e.g. Poster, Turkle) are to believed (see Chapter 9), anonymity facilitates identity play and self-reconstruction, there is no 'other' co-present to enable this negotiation. As Tannen points out, for some of the internet users she studied 'email is like writing in a journal; you're alone with your thoughts and your words, safe from the intrusive presence of another person' (1999: 245). This lack of an imagined dialogical other tends to remove the restraints on self-expression which operate in face-to-face environments. We are all familiar with the practice of composing interior and usually defamatory monologues when we are upset. That we do not actually confront our bosses or spouses or friends and unleash our full vitriol is also universal. It may be therapeutic to think it, but less so to say it. Where we lack the restraint of co-presence, we are likely to find it easier to externalize and express these monologues, with desperate consequences. Thus, although the internet is sometimes represented as a palliative to what Benjamin Barber has called 'talk radio and scream television' (1995: 270), the confrontational possibilities of the technology actually appear to be worsened.

Moreover, studies of online debates have found that the tendency towards monologue rather than dialogue is well entrenched. In his analysis of political boards, Wilhelm's data supported 'the conception of online political forms as facilitating self-expression and monologue, without in large measure the "listening", responsiveness and dialogue that would promote communicative action' (2000: 98). In order to be understood as truly interactive, communication must be dialogical. As Rafaeli argues, 'defining interactivity as a variable relies on how much messages are based on the way preceding messages are related to ... earlier ones' (1988: 111). Wilhelm found that this was not the case on the boards he studied. Only a small percentage (one in five) of responses were direct replies to a previous post. This contradicts Sproull and Faraj's study of six online groups where over 50 per cent of messages were replies to prior messages (Sproull and Faraj, cited in Wilhelm 2000: 98). Moreover the majority of posts in Wilhelm's sample were opinion pieces rather than posts which offered or solicited information or clarification. On the basis of this research Wilhelm concludes that online political forums:

> are in general home to an array of overlapping, short-lived conversations, usually among like-minded individuals. Sustained deliberation is rare in these forums, which means that ... they may not be effective sounding boards for solving problems, engaging in collective action, and articulating issues to be addressed by government.
>
> (Wilhelm 2000: 11)

Thus far, then, research into the operation of online forums does not support the position that they *do* act as a medium for public discussion. Indeed, the central tendencies induced by information overload tie the practices of discussion closely to the dynamics of promotional discourse (Wernick 1991) where the primary objective of interpersonal understanding and communicative action is eclipsed in favour of maintaining a link, drowning out signal noise. In this respect online forums appear to offer a form of discourse closer to publicly manifested opinions than to public communication (Habermas 1989: 247–8).

The image that emerges from this, of a fragmented audience drawn together around collective representations and affirmations rather than one of rational debates, challenges the idea that the internet can act as an alternative to other forms of media in the matter of public opinion. The claim that the net, even if independent of mass-media frames and sources, can challenge meanings promulgated in the 'mainstream' or mass needs to be supported by a more sophisticated conceptual apparatus than the simplistic assertion that alternative views or information merely need to be placed in circulation in order to be effective. When Wilhelm argues that '[o]wnership and control of the mass media in the hands of a few corporate powers limits greatly the ability of citizens to articulate policy problems and solutions' (2000: 48), this limitation is a limitation not on the supply of information but on the frames available for the use of such information. In grasping the problem of information and commercialism as a problem of ability to frame, Wilhelm's position is closer to that propounded by Christopher Lasch when he argues that 'Information, usually seen as the precondition of debate is better understood as its by-product. When we get into arguments that focus and engage our attention, we become avid seekers of relevant information. Otherwise we take in information poorly – if we take it in at all' (1995, cited in Case 2002: 39).

Information, then, is not a raw material which can be converted to a resource without context. Some necessary frames, mostly established through argument, are required in order to make sense of it. Without context, information is reduced to factoids, data, images and impressions which may be trivial or important but which cannot be turned to political, social or cultural ends without the establishment of a frame of relevance, or without being tied to the organizational forms of social movements that actively contest meanings and bring issues to the debating table (Habermas 1989; McGuigan 1998).

In the matter of framing, however, there is little doubt that the internet is not the most effective medium. Esther Dyson, an early cyber-enthusiast, was in no doubt that the net 'is asymmetrical in the way it gives power to the powerless. That is, it undermines central authorities, whether they are good or bad, and it helps dispersed forces to act together, whether they are good or bad. In other words, it is a feeble tool for propaganda, but it is perfect for conspiracy' (1997, cited in Wallace 1999: 236). What this flags up, contra Dyson's own ecstatic tone, is that the internet fails as a medium in providing a coherent interpretation which can act in turn as a means of organizing opposition. As Burnett and Marshall have argued: 'The web's production of personalized informational news cannot operate as a guarantor that the material users access is common. The dispersion of sources can lead to a breakdown in national political understanding among the populace' (2003: 169).

What is lacking is the sense of a commonality of perspective online. As the information sphere becomes increasingly fragmented (see above) there is no common informational lingua franca and thus little means of raising awareness of common concerns. As Cass Sunstein (2001) points out, the social dynamics of cyberspace (see Part Three) are such as to produce an information architecture where debates become polarized, and once polarized unfold in entirely separate areas of the web. Sunstein's research found that only 15 per cent of political sites contained links to opposing positions, whereas 60 per cent linked to like-minded sites (Sunstein 2001: 59). The lack of a shared informational architecture is a serious disadvantage to rational debate in so far as it limits the possibilities of collaborative action.

One way to consider this is in relation to the idea of the contestation of disadvantageous media images. Media framing of groups, activities and people is something which is always contested. The media representation of gender and the framing of the feminist movement is one key example. As Susan Douglas and Meredith Michael points out (2004) the framing of feminists as man-haters is a common trope of mass-media discourse, and one which is damaging to feminism's attempts to combat inequality. However, framing is not an imposition but a contestation and pressure groups and organizations contest through supporting different frames, different interpretative schemas. A new frame does not merely provide a different interpretation but also enrols new actors. The feminist challenge to the media image of feminists as man-haters drew upon commonalities of oppression, which foregrounded the similarity of position of women and ethnic minorities, as one example. In this sense frames act to generate support, either through aligning the interests of those who hold compatible views, whether active or latent, or through overcoding a previously damaging frame in the interests of promoting a more compatible one (see Crossley 2002: 127–48 for a more detailed discussion). When we consider this in relation to the internet, there is a clear problem. Frame diffusion, tied as it is to the function of proselytizing, is unlikely to be effective where the audience is self-selected, homophilous and fragmented. Here attempts to reframe issues would be likely to founder, either because they are in essence 'preaching to the converted' or because they are too alien to be incorporated into the particular 'channel's' worldview.

Where the internet can certainly further frame diffusion is through its impact on the mainstream media. It has become common practice for journalists to use the internet as a source of their copy (Cavanagh 2002). Using web sources as a means of discovering and generating newsworthy stories began with the practice of reporting about the internet, with many radio, television and print outlets devoting space to special 'web' slots. In Britain at least, this often took the format of 'news of the weird', whimsical portrayals of odd things people did online (Cavanagh 2002). Now, however, the internet tends to be used less in reportage as a topic and more as a resource. The driving forces behind this are the extent to which the internet has shed its image as a marginal space for 'geeks' and 'nerds' and moved to the centre in terms of legitimacy, and partly the ease with which materials can be gathered from online sources. Meryl Aldridge, in her study of the occupational mythologies of journalists (Aldridge 1998), has pointed out that the rationalization of the news industry has led to a decline in investigative journalism. For journalists there is a need to weight the resources required to report a story against the 'potential drama of the consequences' (Aldridge 1998: 119). For newspeople, working to deadlines, an orientation towards the accessibility of stories is understandable. When rationalization of the industry manifests itself to the journalist as increased demands for productivity, then the question of accessibility is sure to become ever more salient. Here the advantage for the journalist in using the internet as a source for stories becomes obvious. However, the 'source', for a reporter, is an extremely important and integral element of the day-to-day activities in which they engage. Ericson *et al.* have argued that '[s]ources themselves function as reporters in the sense that they prepare accounts already tailor-made for both their own purposes and the journalist's purpose of news communication' and that thus 'news can best be seen as an ongoing communication among journalists and influential sources' (1987: 9). This is perhaps to go too far in assessing the importance of the source. As Gieber (1964) has pointed out, the terms in which information is conveyed from a source to a journalist are likely to differ substantially from the way in which it is used by the journalist. Fenton *et al.* (1998) have also taken issue with accounts which portray journalists as neutral conduits for the views of sources, developing models in which the relationship is understood as far more complex, contradictory and reciprocal. Howsoever the relationship between the source and the journalist is analysed and understood, it is clear that sources play a central role in the public 'provision of knowledge' as this occurs through the work of journalists.

The use of the internet as a source means that to some extent, at least in so far as they are filtered through the discourse of mainstream journalism, public voices reach a different audience to that at which they were originally aimed and as a result undergo a qualitative transformation. As Golding and Middleton have argued, 'media coverage not only moulds public opinion, to all intents and purposes it *is* public opinion, or at least that visible version of it to which politicians and administrators respond' (1979: 19; original emphasis). In using the internet as a source, journalists amplify the voices of those who would not otherwise be part of a public conversation. As Astroff and Nyberg have argued, 'discourse of the people is a discourse *about* not *by* the people' (cited in Critcher 2003: 138; original emphases). The intersection of the mass and the 'marginal' in the practices of journalists may well challenge this and therefore provide substance to the claim that the internet can act as a public sphere. It is not the public sphere which we might have predicted, but is nevertheless more empirically valid.

In summary, then, close up it is harder to sustain the idea of a radical discontinuity of practice and experience between the internet and other forms of media. The individualizing tendencies of both forms of media make it difficult to drive a sufficiently rigorous wedge between them in terms of audience composition. Audience behaviour online seems to gravitate towards forms and content with which we are familiar from other media, as evidenced by the decline in 'interactive' online behaviour. The same large-scale media concerns continue to dominate the core continents of the internet. Internet content is often parasitic upon offline content. Autonomously generated internet debates appear too weak to effect much in the way of influence and the primary impact of these on public consciousness is a result of the take-up and amplification of online debates by mainstream media, demonstrating the continued primacy of mass media. Thus in a sense what we are seeing is the colonization of the internet by its more commercial offspring, the web, and the web has a much greater potential as a medium of one-to-many communication, but is less effective at the many-to-many forms more characteristic of forums, discussion groups and chat.

7 *The* global public sphere *and* forms *of* power

Thus far this analysis of the internet as a medium has done little but confirm the pessimistic visions of media as a relentless commodification of the cultural sphere. Adorno and Horkheimer would surely nod sagely and bitterly, vindicated by the very technology that threatened to topple them. However, in viewing the internet in this way, we are looking at it through the lenses and constructs of media theory as this has been promulgated by media studies. In so doing we are perhaps accepting a frame that is perhaps not capable of accounting for the internet. The debates around the media and the public sphere are dependent on the extent of an overlap between forms of media discourse and forms of collective interest and power. As this chapter will go on to argue, both of these are mutable and historically specific. In order to examine this question further it is necessary to consider a little of the historical back-story of the media.

The form of public debate that is consolidated in a discourse of 'news' is a debate about the nation, for as Gans (1979) points out, all news is about the nation, and it is no surprise that historically we witness the development of a discourse of news which is associated with the rise of the nation as a political unit (Schudson 1978; Briggs and Burke 2002). The rise of the newspaper as a mass medium in the nineteenth century, associated with rising literacy, better techniques of distribution and technological advances in printing (Curran and Seaton 1981; Williams 1998; Briggs and Burke 2002), was also tied to political change. In the advanced industrial nations of the nineteenth century, we see the realization of a civil sphere, an economic sphere of social relations which exists alongside, and rivals, the political sphere, but one which is closely tied to nationalism in the context of political imperialism. Throughout Europe the story of the nineteenth century is the story of the development of the nation state as the unit of political life (Hobsbawm 1975; Anderson 1991; Bayly 2004). Accompanying this, throughout the West, we see the rise of mass participation politics. In the UK this came about through electoral reform, the gradual extension of the franchise in successive stages from 1832, culminating in the total enfranchisement of the male population by 1885 and the eventual enfranchisement of women (1918 and 1928). The development of nationalism and electoral change give the shape to the mass-media sphere of the nineteenth century, a sphere tied to social reform, rationality and individual reformation in the national interest (Hobsbawm 1975). It is this discourse that is behind the Victorian identification of newspapers as an educational medium, and behind the idea that accessing an information sphere was a prerequisite, and entitlement, of citizenship. It is noteworthy that Gladstone's support for electoral reform and extension of the franchise was in part based on his observation that the 'respectable' working classes had proved their mettle through auto-didactical consumption of newspapers (Hampton 2001: 216).

The origins of this discourse are found in the early forms of newspapers, tied as they were to the internal organization of the party system in politics. Newspapers, at the start of the nineteenth century, were, largely, organs of the political parties. Newspapers acted as a means of coordinating opinion *within* the party rather than as a means of *proselytizing* opinion outside it. As politics became more complex in the wake of electoral reform and the enfranchisement of the middle classes, parties needed recourse to a more effective, and more bureaucratic, source of discipline than the newspapers could provide. Newspapers were freed from their role as organs of political opinion but also often unwillingly 'freed' from the financial patronage that attended such a role. The press turned to the newly emergent commercial sectors for patronage, the early basis of commercialization of the media. Thus as the long nineteenth century wore on, we see the newspapers moving away from their dependence on political parties and, excepting a short reinvigora-tion tied to the brief flowering of political activism in the form of working-class movements such as Chartism, towards a largely commercial model. As Perelman (1998) has argued, these changes imply a redefinition of knowl-edge: 'What seems to set the information age apart from earlier epochs is the widespread codification of information; that is, general knowledge is worked into a form that simplifies its transfer from one party to another' (Perelman 1998: 10). Whilst opinion or wisdom has moral and social value, information is purely operational, something that can be reduced to a discrete quantity for ease of transfer and sale. This is precisely what occurs in the nineteenth century. Rationalization enabled by more efficient methods of information gathering and newspaper distribution (Briggs and Burke 2002), and backed by the fragmentation of the political sphere, increased both the availability and the market for factual content. Hampton cites one writer in the *Westminster Review* who complained of this new trend that 'the 'public does not want opinions and arguments, it wants facts, or, what is better, facetoie' (1899, cited in Hampton 2001: 218), an early complaint about dumbing-down.

As we move towards the end of the nineteenth century the orientations of newspapers start to change again. William Stead, editor of the British periodical the *Pall Mall Gazette*, is widely credited with being one of the forerunners of this new sensibility, although Pulitzer, editor of the *New York World* was equally at the forefront in the USA. For Stead and Pulitzer the role of newspapers was to promote what Stead referred to as 'government by journalism', government which took the form of rallying the public, proselytizing opinion and inflaming sensibilities such as to harness the power of the mass, in the case of Stead in the interests of social reform. This, then, is the beginning of the era of newspapers as lobbyists, gathering to themselves a public in whose name they then speak.

What we see over the course of the nineteenth century is the rapid alteration in the nature of the discourse of a public sphere. Where in the early part of the century the public are constituted as cerebral, concerned with the eternal truths of philosophy debated by a small group of the cognoscenti; to the mid-Victorian reader, who is interpellated as 'rational man', a knowledgeable citizen seeking and able to discover the facts of his (usually his) world; to the later Victorian reader, an 'emotional man', the concerned citizen whose energies may be tapped in the interests of promoting change. Thus the forms of discourse interpellate the public as a different species of public in different eras. In light of this it makes little sense to judge the modern public by the standards of an ideal typification of a fictional eternal one

Moreover, the example of the nineteenth century is instructive in other ways. Just as the forms of both the media and the public were historically specific, so were the forms of power onto which the media faced. At the start of the nineteenth century, power rested in the political institutions of the party system. As we move towards the mid-century period, the mid-Victorian period of calm often referred to as the 'Age of Equipoise', the class-based political struggles of the early part of the century gave way, in the face of the final defeat of Chartism, the decline of radicalism and increased prosperity, to a more national form of power. Newspapers, with their dramatically increased reach, came to be national media. Whereas at the start of the nineteenth century the journals of opinion were slow moving, by the late 1870s it became possible to read the London editions of newspapers across the country (Briggs and Burke 2002). That this served as a spur for the development of fact-based news is of less significance than the fact that it also served as the food for the development of a national news culture. At the same time, and not of course coincidentally, we see the rise of the nation state as *the* chief form of power. European internal empires gave way to autonomous nations, and smaller ethnic-based groups became subsumed within its administrative unity (Hobsbawm 1975; Bayly 2004). As a result, the forms of power onto which the media faced were the powers of the nation and the topic of its discourse was national in tone.

As we move into a new political era, theorists have argued that modern media are incapable of providing this overlap between the nature of their forms and content and forms of power. Colin Sparks has expressed this concern well. 'In its contemporary usage,' he points out,

> the public sphere concerns debates about the nature, legitimacy, scope and direction of public power. It assumes, not the democratic right to control power, but the existence of that power as a public matter. That is the fundamental distinction between the property of the monarch, and the bourgeois epoch when it is the property of the people.
>
> (Sparks 1998: 121)

However in the modern era of global media, he argues, this debate has become attenuated and misdirected. For Sparks a global media cannot comprise a global public sphere because the media debates only private and not public power, 'the future of markets, of property, both material and intellectual, of resources, of currencies ... that is the subject of global media' (1998: 121). For as long as there is no global power, no clearly identified form of global governance, this mismatch between the nature of debate and the nature of power will persist. Thus for Sparks the media and by extension the public no longer face onto power in the same manner as the nineteenth-century media did.

For Hardt and Negri, this analysis would make little sense. In the opening salvo of *Empire* they argue that whilst it may be the case that the national is no longer the most relevant unit of analysis for viewing the operation of global power '*[t]he decline in sovereignty of nation-states ... does not mean that sovereignty as such has declined*'. Rather, it has taken a new form, 'national and supranational organisms united under a single logic of rule', that of Empire, where Empire comprises global flows and exchanges (Hardt and Negri 2000: xi–xv, emphasis in original). If we take Hardt and Negri's view of the nature of power, then the alleged mismatch between media forms and content and power is not so pronounced. The global conversation over private power is indeed a facing onto the most significant forms of power in the modern era. This is as true for form as for content. Just as the national media of the nineteenth century took the form of the 'space-binding' media of newspapers (Innis 1986), facing onto the power of the nation through developing the unity of the nation, so the modern internet faces onto distributed power and the open empire of capital. Thus:

> the Internet [is] not simply a specific medium but a kind of active implementation of a design technique able to deal with the openness of systems. The design of the Internet prefigured the constitution of a neo-imperial electronic space, whose main feature is an openness which is also a constitutive tendency to *expansion*.
>
> (Terranova 2004: 3; original emphasis)

Thus it is clear that, when viewed over time, the forms taken by the triad of media, public and power have been subject to rapid and dramatic transformation from era to era. In simply reading off older forms which this relationship took, i.e. journalism as the fourth estate facing onto national interests articulated through national structures, and then looking to see how well the internet matches these, we are perhaps guilty of an anachronism. Given this it becomes imperative to understand why media studies has constructed the public, the media and power as eternal and monolithic forms.

Following Habermas the public sphere is constructed within media and cultural studies as an ideal type. However, unlike Weberian ideal types, the public sphere is not treated as an heuristic device but rather as an 'ideal' ideal type, which is to say it is tied to a utopian discourse which artificially raises the profile of 'the media' at the expense of the social. The way that the public sphere is invoked as an ideal type is as a historical institution, the 'blue remembered hills' of political activism, or as a future state to which we must aspire. What we are left with is either the nostalgic invocation of 'the land of lost content', which draws a bead on modern media through valorizing the past, or an instrumental discourse which posits the public sphere as a future state, which begs only the question as to why the promise has not yet been realized and what we can do about it. Whilst both of these positions serve to tie media to the utopian/dystopian extremes of thought which we observed earlier (see Introduction), neither are valid uses of ideal typifications. For Weber, ideal types were analytical tools which could be used to reflect on the nature of actually existing phenomena, institutions and practices. In focusing on the democratic potential of the media above their current uses and forms, it is clear that sociology has taken on board preconstructions of the role of the media from elsewhere, in this case the media themselves.

The early role played by editors and journalists such as Stead and Pulitzer in sanctifying their own functions as a democratic conduit cues us as sociologists to understand, as Conboy and Schudson have separately argued, the discourse of the 'fourth estate' as an attempt to work on the field in such a way as to increase the value of one's capital within it. In Bourdieu's terms the occupational ideologies of journalism work to promote the field as a whole, successfully as it turns out, for, as Hesmondhalgh (2006) argues, the journalistic field has become an overarching one which distributes the value of capital within other fields. However, the success of the manoeuvre should not blind sociologists to the fact of it. As Conboy (2004) and Schudson (1978) have shown, the development of the ideals on which the media claim their roles as intercessors was historically specific and limited in time. The heady heyday of investigative journalism, and its concomitant passionate commitment to objectivity, were both short-lived products of specific historical circumstances, not eternal truths of journalism. In this sense, by accepting the discourse of the fourth estate, sociologists have focused on the *unusual and exceptional* forms and functions of media rather than the *usual and routine*, and this represents a severe distortion of sociology's remit. It does, however, go some way to explaining why the public, the media and power have been treated in such monolithic terms.

Finally, in questioning this, we find ourselves obliged to sacrifice another of media studies' sacred cows. It is a commonplace of intellectual discourse that the chief role of the media in societies is a political one. As Terranova points out:

> one of the most fundamental assumptions of modern political thought [is that] in which the relationship between the transparency of communication and democracy is foundational. From Diderot and Voltaire to Thomas Payne, modern conceptions of democracy start from the demands of bourgeois revolutionaries for free speech and political representation. A democracy does not just guarantee but is guaranteed by the rights of its citizens to representation in the spheres of both politics and communication.
>
> (Terranova 2004: 131)

What lies behind this is a fear that the 'media' can be used to exert undue influence and that only a free, in the sense of uncensored, media can ward off the spectre of a nation intellectually enslaved through ignorance. This understanding of the media as a space of influence is an idealist position, one which sees media as performing a 'sluice-gate' function. Societies have many competing ideas and different philosophies, and media partially represent these. It is in this sense that the media are supposed to perform the roles of the 'fourth estate', the guardians of free speech and wardens of the public interest. Of course, as Dennis McQuail (2000: 61–90) points out, this conception of the relationship between media and society is only one of many interpretations, but it is the one which is most privileged by media studies accounts. This idealist position selectively appropriates some media functions as topics but uses others as tacit resources. However, from a sociological perspective, it is as valid to consider media as implicated in producing social cohesion through continuity over time and/or space, or in reducing social tension and in promoting lateral connections through entertainment, as purely an arena of political representation. Indeed, beginning our analysis with the politics of representation, the assumption of the media as representational sluice-gates, presupposes the efficacy of the media as agents of social cohesion and promoters of social action in so far as it presupposes a moral order which highlights a politics of consensus as desirable, a society with a means of reintegrating those who are defeated in debate, a common culture which frames and makes sense of the debate, and so on. Whilst these are crucial to the success of a public sphere, they are not treated as integral elements which also need to be investigated when we view the internet as a potential one. Thus the public sphere debate is itself a highly selective one, one which through framing the debate in terms amenable to media content analysis overlooks critical dimensions of the debate. It is to these questions, of the capacity of the internet as a media of cohesion and sociality, to which we now turn.

Part **Three**
The **internet** *as a* **social space**

Introduction *to* **Part Three**

The previous chapter argued that the way that the internet has been constructed in media-centric accounts depends on unexpurgated assumptions about the social role of the media. The chapters in this part address this through an examination of the linked themes of community and identity. Chapter 8 examines the implications of the coming of the internet for sociological understandings of community. Beginning by tracing the development of the concept of community in sociology, this chapter goes on to look at empirical studies of internet life. I begin by analysing the alleged divisions between online and offline communities, before going on to an examination of the dynamics of online communities, with particular reference to forms of internal organization, group solidarity and the relationships between groups. I here argue that identity has come to be an organizing narrative of community as this has been developed by internet scholars. Chapter 9 goes on, therefore, to examine the ways that identity has been theorized within dominant approaches to the internet. I argue that cybercultural approaches exhibit profound inadequacies as a framework for accounting for the dynamics of online interactions in so far as they are demonstrably empirically false, and methodologically flawed. Moreover, as I argue in the final part, accounts of cyber-identity are often guilty of a selective appropriation of prior theory, and one which is characterized by an overly easy acceptance of voluntaristic accounts of the self, which underestimates the constraining and enabling powers of the social.

8 Community

That the coming of the internet has made an impact on the way we view community is a common theme of most general accounts of the internet and society (see Slevin 2000; Castells 2001; Flew 2005). Before we can examine this in detail, however, we need to first understand how it was before and this, unfortunately, is no easy enterprise. Earlier I pointed to the central status accorded to definitions in sociology and never has the issue been as thorny and intractable as in the case of community. Not for nothing did the German sociologist Herman Schmalenbach grumble that '"community" has become a catchword used to designate every possible delusion of the time' (cited in Delanty 2003: 43). Even a brief scan of the literature reveals that one of the few areas of agreement between sociologists of community is that an agreement on an adequate definition is impossible to reach (Bell and Newby 1971; Baym 1998; Delanty 2003). Jenny Preece (2000) offers a list of definitions commonly used today for community, including shared goals, common interests, shared activities and governance, cooperation, satisfaction of mutual needs, enjoyment and pleasure, and location. However, Preece's list, although extensive, is quite overshadowed by George Hillery's, now legendary, 1955 study which identified no less that 94 commonly used definitions of community (Bell and Newby 1971: 27–9). From these Hillery distilled 16 core concepts, including in the list common life, kinship, consciousness of kind, possession of common ends, norms and means, locality, totality of attitudes, social system and individuality. Common usage of the term today includes: geographical location, neighbourhood; membership of interest groups, for example the sociological community; lifestyle, e.g. the rock community; as a shorthand for common forms of social identity, e.g. the gay community, the Asian community; amongst many others. Amidst such a diversity of usages agreement is thin on the ground.

It is not really surprising that community is such a disputed concept. In the first instance the concept has a particularly privileged place in the sociological cannon. As Nisbet has pointed out, the community–society dichotomy is one of the central 'linked antitheses [that] form the very warp of the sociological tradition ... epitomizations of the conflict between tradition and modernism, between the old order made moribund by the industrial and democratic revolutions, and the new order, its outlines still unclear and as often the cause of anxiety as of elation and hope' (Nisbet, cited in Bell and Newby 1971: 25). Community as a concept was at the heart of sociology's project in the nineteenth century to understand social changes wrought by the transition to the new urban-industrial society. Modernity, early sociologists observed, brought about the decline of community through the gradual erosion of its functions and nature, and through the colonization of these by the state and the nation. Hence early sociology takes as its point of departure the attempt to understand the forms and nature of social cohesion in this new, reconfigured world. The seminal work here is that of Ferdinand Toennies (2001), whose analysis of the transition from small-scale, agrarian *Gemeinschaft* community to the large-scale, industrial and urban *Gesellschaft* was a powerful influence on Durkheim and, later, Parsons and Merton. Toennies argued that the composition of society was brought about through changes in the form of association. The central point for Toennies is that the forms of association into which people enter bring about different types of social organization. In the *Gemeinschaft* society relationships are 'primary', close, affective and overlapping; law is informal and derived from consensus, derived itself from custom; the community is realized in a common set of customs and a common sense of place. In the *Gesellschaft* society, by contrast, interpersonal relationships are rational, produced through and maintained by means–ends calculations, supported by formal contracts which derive their power from centralised authority, and in which social cohesion is achieved through public opinion and shifting priorities. In Durkheim's work, as in that of Toennies, modernity involves a movement from one pole towards another, in this case from mechanical solidarity, a sense of community founded on shared beliefs and customs, to organic solidarity, social cohesion brought about through mutual dependence based on specialization and the division of labour. In both accounts community is seen to be eroded by the advance of modernity. People become more socially fragmented and isolated, the social bases of the communal order are broken down. For Durkheim this could produce the pathology of anomie, a sense of normlessness, social isolation and lack of purpose that was at the root of social ills (Durkheim 1952).

This conception of community as a sense of belonging and common purpose is picked up and amplified in the work of the Chicago school. In the accounts of Robert Park, Louis Wirth and Ernest Burgess in the 1920s, the characteristic concern of the Chicago sociologists with the spatial contexts of social action (Abbott 1997) leads to an abiding interest in the composition and forms of community, social cohesion and integration. It is, oddly, this concern for spatiality that leads the Chicago sociologists to de-emphasize the role of location and geography in understanding community. For Park and for Wirth, neighbourhoods were more than physical entities bounded by geographical limits. Rather, the Chicagoans understood space as the synchronic organization of social action. This allowed them to put aside location as the sole identifier of community and instead consider space itself as formed through interactional fields.

This in turn led to an early interest in understanding media's role in social cohesion. The Chicagoans took their lead here from Dewey's now famous assertion that 'Society not only continues to exist by transmission, by communication, but it may fairly be said to exist in transmission, in communication' (Dewey 1916, cited in Foster 1997: 34). As Wirth puts it:

> [a]s long as we identify urbanism with the physical entity of the city, viewing it as rigidly delimited in space ... we are not likely to arrive at any adequate conception of urbanism as a way of life ... The technological developments in transportation and community which virtually mark a new epoch in human history have accentuated the role of cities as dominant elements in our civilisation and have enormously extended the urban mode of living beyond the confines of the city itself.
>
> (Wirth 1938: 4–5)

Robert Park was more explicit concerning the role of media. For Park it was the newspaper that allowed us to 'learn to know our community in the same intimate way we knew them in the country villages' (1923: 278), to act as the means to convert a 'mere geographical expression into a neighbourhood ... a locality with sentiments, traditions and a history of its own' (Park 1926, cited in Abbott 1997: 1155).

The decline of the Chicago school witnessed a retreat from this newly expanded way of treating community. '[L]ocation in a natural area simply became another variable describing the individual' (Abbott 1997: 1155), and the shifting sociological sands drifted over the work of the Chicagoans. It was, therefore, a retrograde step from this richer understanding of community contexts that allowed Parsons to attempt to define community as 'that collectivity the members of which share a common territorial area as that base of operations for daily activities' (Parsons 1951: 91, cited in Delanty 2003: 36). Moreover, it is the backlash against the centrality of location to this new sociology that opens the door, in the 1960s, for McLuhan and his acolytes to present their thesis of community as connection by heterogeneous means as new and radical. Thus Richmond defines community as:

> social systems in which the characteristic forms of social interaction take place through networks of communication maintained by means of telephone, teleprinter, television and high speed aircraft and spacecraft, etc. Such relationships are not dependent upon a territorial base or face-to-face contact, nor do they involve participation in formal organization.
>
> (Richmond 1969, cited in Bell and Newby 1971: 47)

Whilst this would hardly be a credible critique of Chicago sociology's approach to community, it is a devastating attack on the mainstream definitions established after Parsons. Community studies were thereafter forced into retreat along one of two lines. The first is towards the affective root proposed by Weber: 'a social relationship will be called communal in and so far as the orientation of social action ... is based on a subjective feeling of the parties ... that they belong together' (cited in Delanty 2003: 39). The problem here is that community can then only be said to consist in the subjective orientation of an actor towards a social situation. Thus community moves from the more or less involuntary connections between people to the solely voluntary relations into which we enter as free individuals. This in turn then means that the conceptual space covered by the term 'community' can more validly be represented by other terms, lifestyle or subculture being two leading contenders. In these terms community appears only as a resource for the individual in the construction of self-identity. The idea of community as a compelling moral force, as this appears in Durkheim and Toennies, is sheered away.

The second line of retreat is again towards a 'stem' definition. Whereas 'community' as a term once encompassed religious belief, family, culture and profession, referring to ties that exhibited depth and continuity as well as an affective bond (see Bell and Newby 1971), once these areas have been clawed away by other descriptors and concepts sociologists were left with the study of 'the formal properties of social configurations' (Scott 2000: 9), which is to say the form, rather than the content of social relationships. It is this that aligns community studies with actor-network theory (discussed in Part One). This movement is presaged in Margaret Stacey's work from the late 1960s, in which she calls for an abandonment of community as an object of enquiry and a refocus on 'institutions and their interrelations in specific contexts' (Bell and Newby 1971: 49) as the proper subject matter for study. The focus on the local as a site in which specific institutions bring about the interaction of local and national systems removes the need for further discussion of the local/national/global divide but only at the expense of a reduction of the object of enquiry to the interaction of systems.

Thus the development of the concept of community in sociology has been a highly politicized process but this again is hardly surprising. The status of community as a political hot potato, as well as its centrality to sociology, reflects the political loading of the term more generally. 'Community', as Kamenka (1982) has argued, has been the repository of political fears and dreams throughout the ages, and its invocation functions as a form of ideology. Community appears to be something of a 'hooray' word (Whyte 2003: 61) for, as Raymond Williams points out, it is never used unfavourably, whether in mainstream or alternative discourse. For Williams (1961), community evokes the ideal or pure form of the social, uncorrupted by influence and power, a social bond which pre-exists and nullifies the power of the state. This is much the meaning of the term community, as Delanty (2003) points out, when we speak of alternative communities such as the Israeli kibbutzim, or survivalist communities in the USA, groups that are reflexive, artificially constituted communities organized by and through opposition to modernity. It is also often the ideal that online communities attempt self-consciously to foster, whether through the communitarian ethos of groups like the Well (Rheingold 1994) or through the provision of a safe haven which is the purpose of many self-help and similar groups online. These forms of alternative communities are based around a normative understanding of community which exhibits either nostalgic or futuristic tendencies, positing community either as something to be retrieved from the past or, as in Marxist ideologies, as something projected into the future (Delanty 2003). Community in socialist terms is a project in progress, which will reach fruition with the death of the state. The more common sociological and political argument is more conservative, namely that we have witnessed a 'loss of community', that historically real communities thrived in ways that are no longer possible. In much the same manner as the discourse of 'the social' is used to mobilize and legitimate political interests (Rose 1991), so the discourse of 'community' is also a politically loaded site of contestation or reproduction of meaning. It is precisely this politicization of the term, the fact that it has become a repository of 'fears and dreams', ideals and hopes, that ultimately causes Bell and Newby to despair of ever being able to give *the* definition of 'community' (1971: 31).

Thus what the study of online community inherits is a sense of community as a political construct, tied into utopian or dystopian possibilities. This idea often takes the form of a portrait of community as opposed to power, a refuge from the ills of the state or of modernity. Accompanying this, however, is another legacy, a particular view of community as reducible to self-created voluntaristic linkages, which is a severe attenuation of the concept as this was initially used. This partial reading, in combination with the utopian cast of the debate privileges a reading of community as primarily an affective space. As the next chapter will argue, this in turn feeds back into constructions of the self. For the purposes of this chapter it is sufficient to note that the definition of community used in many discussions of the impact of the internet on it is a particular, and from a sociological point of view, partial, reading. As Joseph Lockard notes, the idea '[t]hat cyberspace can even be mistaken for "community" testifies to the attenuated sense of community that prevails in too many quarters of American society' (1997: 224). The same is true in a sense of sociology.

In order to examine the way this discourse of community has been mobilized in relation to the internet I will now move on to an examination of the major themes that have been foregrounded by researchers of online community, beginning with early scholarship on the relationship between online and offline communities. The chapter will then consider the nature of online community and evaluate the major claims to novelty which have been made in relation to it, including propositions concerning internet communities and hierarchies, and the nature and form of solidarity in cyberspace.

Online and offline communities

The study cited most often, and the point of departure for most subsequent work on online community, is Howard Rheingold's 1994 work, *The Virtual Community*. Rheingold's study of the online community 'The Well' set the terms of debate for subsequent work in so far as he posited that virtual communities were communities *in* cyberspace, that they were supported by, and existed solely in, interaction online. This opened up a space for discussion of online community as something unrelated to, and therefore perhaps opposed to, community in real life. This in turn drew on and enshrined a 'sticky' common sense of online and offline life as fundamentally divided and it became logical to discuss online community in terms of its impact on 'real life'. This 'impacts' approach has, then, been core to developing the field of internet community studies. In essence the impacts approach is focused on the effects that internet use may have on ot of social behaviour and interaction, and is concerned with demographics and time use. The published research and the co which emerge are, however, sharply polarized. On the one hand, the Homenet study (Kraut et al. 1998; Kraut and Kiesler 2003) and the work of Nie and Erbring (2002) found that high internet use lessens social involvement in other fields. Nie and Erbring's studies found that internet users had less contact time with family and friends and spent less time in offline social activities than non-users. The Homenet studies argued that internet use was associated with a decline in the size of the user's social circle and that users were more likely to suffer from loneliness and depression. The Pew Project on the Internet and American Life, however, found quite the reverse. These studies established correlations between internet use and improved relationships, especially strong ties, and a slight increase in the size of a user's social circle. White et al. (1999) have argued that internet use leads to a decrease in reported loneliness and isolation, and the University of Southern California Annenberg (USC) Internet Reports (Cole et al. 2004) have consistently shown that internet use does not reduce time spent with family and friends.

The contradictory findings of the different studies thus present a serious problem for assessing the nature of the impact of the internet, if any, on offline social life, and this problem is aggravated by the way that these studies have been used in secondary accounts, with Homenet and Pew both attracting legions of adherents. In part the contradictory results can be traced to methodological difficulties in the research designs. For a start, the studies draw on different data sets and ask quite different questions (see Burnett and Marshall 2003: 67). Moreover, as Castells has pointed out, the researchers drew on quite different constituencies. Whereas the Homenet studies took already active internet users as their subjects, in Kraut et al.'s study subjects were provided with computers in order to observe their online experience. Thus, in explaining the contradiction in findings, Castells points to studies showing that frustration, depression and information overload are linked to early-stage adoption and decrease as familiarity and competence with the technology increase (Castells 2001: 123–4).

More serious, however, is the tendency within this approach to mistake correlation, the co-presence of internet use and civic engagement or disengagement, for causation and also a lack of specification around the direction of cause. As Putnam points out, the forms of negative impact which these studies register cannot logically be traced back to the internet. 'The timing of the internet explosion means that it cannot possibly be causally linked to the crumbling of social connectedness ... Voting, giving, trusting, meeting, visiting and so on had all begun to decline while Bill Gates was still in grade school' (2000: 170). In fact, Putnam suggests, rather than understanding internet community as contributing to the decline of the social, we should better understand it if we saw it as response to that decline. This point is one that seems to unite both the cyber-optimists, of which Putnam is one, and cyber-dystopians. For Mark Slouka, whose work has been a rallying point for the disaffected, the core question of online community is '[w]here does the need come from to inhabit these alternative spaces? ... the answer I keep coming back to is: to escape the problems and issues of the real world' (cited in Wellman and Gulia 1999: 169).

For Wellman and his co-authors the rise of internet communities is also seen as linked to changes in the nature of community in real life, although Wellman would resist the easy identification of these wider changes as a loss of community. Wellman argues that internet communities should be understood not as a response to changes in the offline social, but as an example of them, seeing such groups as 'a technologically supported continuation of a long term shift to communities organized by shared interests rather than shared place or shared ancestry' (Wellman and Gulia 1999: 172). This view is also taken by Castells, who sees the internet as an instrumental space tied to the everyday life of users (Castells 2001: 118). Both Castells' and Wellman's work moves away from the understanding of internet community as a response to modernity, an alternative community founded on opposition to the status quo or as a means of meeting needs not addressed in modern communities, and understands them as a continuation of those social arrangements by other means. Castells and Wellman are the most prominent authors in a concerted sociological endeavour to dispel the dualism between real life and online life that was originally introduced in the work of Rheingold and others (see also Miller and Slater 2000: 5–6). In so doing these authors are reinstating the necessity of the rich contexts of the Chicago tradition. Thus a final major problem with the Homenet/Pew contradiction is the extent to which the studies are dependent on the construction of the internet as a separate domain, distinct from and in competition with other social arenas and other activities. It may be possible for a sociologist to separate internet use from other activities in the laboratory but it is more problematic outside of it.

Understanding these communities as an extension of real life, however, draws on a definition of the internet as a neutral medium rather than as a social space, and this is to sidestep the questions posed by internet communities. A secondary strand of research takes up this issue, namely the characteristics of internet communities in their own right. In this emergent area, internet communities are examined with a view to understanding their internal dynamics, the forms of relationship which they facilitate or foreclose, and it is to this which we now turn.

Types of community

In considering internet communities *sui generis*, a form of association which need not directly map onto other forms of communal activity, the idea of the internet as a truly social space, rather than as a medium of other social spaces, is foregrounded. However, such studies in practice cannot disregard the offline in quite the manner that such an attempt would suggest. Indeed, the level of integration, overlap and replication between offline and online is a core issue for these types of study. The extent to which these communities are structured by offline, external considerations is regarded as a key analytical resource for understanding their dynamics. Early on, Baym's work on fan communities (Baym 1997) ranked external contexts as one of the five main influences on the forms and style of community concerned, the others being: the technical infrastructure of the system, speed of connection, organization of materials; the purpose of the group; the personal characteristics of the users; and the temporal structure of the forum. For Baym, virtual communities are not an artefact or a resource, but a type of association which can take many forms. The five factors she identifies dynamically interact in practice to shape the eventual form. Thus, to take an example, a support group dedicated to helping members overcome an addiction could operate primarily as a means of collating and disseminating information about the addiction, resources for the recovering addict, inspiring stories, and so on. In this sense it would act similarly to a broadcast medium, in the sense of a central message being disseminated to multiple sources. Alternatively, it could act as a support, group in the sense that individuals chat, offer each other practical and emotional support and are 'there for each other' when in crisis. However, if the members are widely dispersed geographically then it is less likely to be able to support that role. The provision of emotional support, to be effective, requires a rapid, if not immediate, response. Thus someone posting in crisis to the support group who was one of a few members in a different time zone to the majority may be unlikely to receive an adequately rapid response. The temporal structure of the group, therefore, also relates back to the demographic characteristics of the members. If the majority are North American office workers, as in the case of the soap opera fan community Baym first studied, then our exemplar support group would operate best to provide emotional support during North American office hours as the majority of users are most likely to be logged in at that time and in that context. The personal characteristics of the members, profession, extra-communal resources and personality will also act to shape the nature of support received, whether advice given is practical help or commiseration, and so on. The purposes for which the community was originally set up are also a key to understanding its eventual form, according to Baym, although it is clear from the above example that such purposes are dynamic and change according to changes in the other four factors.

In studying the nature of online communities the core issue which has been foregrounded by sociologists has been that of heterogeneity versus homogeneity. In large measure this is a reactive research agenda, prompted by fears that the prevalence of online communities is producing a deformation of what it means to be social. As Putnam explains, the fear is that internet communication is subject to a form of cyber-Balkanization, where interaction is single-stranded, connected only in one limited context (Putnam 2000: 178). The fear that internet communities actually represent the dissolution of the concept of 'community' into that of 'interest group' is founded on the anxiety that such 'communities' actually close down the options that they purport to elaborate. Where the promise of the internet is bringing people together, providing the opportunity to explore new interests and gain new knowledge, it is argued that the processes at work in online communities tend to reduce the possibility of exposure to the new. 'Much of the net,' argues Doheny-Farina, 'is a Byzantine amalgamation of fragmented, isolating, solipsistic enclaves of interest based on the collectivity of assent' (1996: 55). For Foster, computer-mediated communication engenders an egoistical self-absorption which occurs as a result of the subject's attempts to limit an informational deluge by selective exposure to information (Foster 1997: 26–7).

The counter-argument to this is that associated with the cybercultural approach popularised in the work of Turkle (1995), Stone (1996) and Poster (1995a) (discussed below). In this approach the cyber-subject is one who has membership of multiple communities in multiple identity guises, and it is the reflexive engagement with them and between them which attenuates tendencies towards solipsism and narcissism. Cybercultural theorists would argue that fears that the net will degenerate into defensive solipsism depend on two presumptions. First, that the internet is understood as a rational goal-orientated space and, second, and more crucially, that the cyber individual possesses a stable self into which he/she can retreat.

In the first instance the idea of a defensive retreat presupposes a necessity for defence and this would certainly be ruled out of Turkle's account since the net is understood as a playful space. Foster's idea that we will seek to retreat from information overload online (Foster 1997) makes little sense unless it is accompanied by a social injunction to achieve mastery of a given portion of cyberspace, and this cybercultural theorists would not recognize. In a playful leisure-orientated space, what you do not know or use is irrelevant, the online experience is developed from what you do use. However, more importantly, the idea of a stable self, a 'me' which organizes relevant and irrelevant materials, desired and disliked experiences, is precisely what is lacking online for these theorists. For Turkle, the web is an architecture of role-playing games, in which the individual cyber-subject has membership of multiple contradictory communities in each of which he/she actively constructs and reconstructs a self. In the process of moving between communities, the subject adopts different positions and personas and through this becomes acculturated to difference and able to handle diversity.

If we leave aside for the moment the question of the legitimacy of the unstable self (see Chapter 11 for discussion), we are still left with several problems with this account. First, there are a number of factors which seem to militate against equal simultaneous occupation of multiple communities, of which one is the centrality of group-specific norms. As Connery (1997) points out, online groups often have codified and well-established norms and procedures for dealing with common group tasks. These often include particular ways of handling posts to forums, what should or should not be included in a header, for example, injunctions to politeness, specific rules as to what politeness is considered to be, rules around levels of anonymity that are to be allowed (Baym 1998) and so forth. These group rules and norms are often codified in the form of frequently asked questions (FAQs) and, as Connery (1997) further notes, the formation of an FAQ is often a sign that a group has matured into a community. If the drafting of FAQs acts as a means of developing group solidarity, it is also a resource for future solidarity in so far as it allows the recognition of existing group members and the socialization of new ones. Being a member of several communities simultaneously obviously involves an ability to internalize and operationalize different and contradictory norms, depending on the group one is in at the time. Of course, occupying different social positions and roles is hardly limited to our experiences online. Offline we also learn to handle different positions and to be able to move between them. However, these contradictory roles are generally kept to a minimum number and are, moreover, roles within an established culture. Where people have to occupy roles within different cultures we regard this as an anomaly and a specific problem for social order, rather than an example of it. There is an abundant literature, academic and otherwise, which speaks of the problems of trying to occupy contradictory cultural roles, particularly as this concerns ideas around multiculturalism. Thus it is difficult to substantiate the cybercultural thesis that contradiction can be a source of social order in this sense.

A further complication here is the extent of personal investment required in order to develop a role and status within a community. Becoming a full participating member of a community requires time and effort, in reading the volume of posts, exchanging information and help, and becoming personally known to the other members. Gaining a high status within an online community is in this respect no different from gaining status in a real-life one, with the exception that, as Haythornwaite has noted, the efforts of the individual are not only directed at achieving a certain type of recognition but also at achieving visibility at all (2002). As Doheny-Farina notes, 'it is a monumental task to develop close relationships while keeping the particulars of the body anonymous' (1996: 65). To achieve this in relation to multiple communities would involve a heroic level of commitment. There is little reason to suppose that the early cyber-enthusiasts studied by Turkle and Poster are representative of the majority today (see also Flew 2005: 66).

Thus, there are good reasons to question whether multiple community occupancy addresses the problems of cyber-Balkanization. Moreover, there is equally a substantial body of evidence to suggest that fragmentation and the creation of public 'sphericules' is accelerating online. Many commentators have observed that community cohesion is often based on opposition to other groups, a them and us approach. Thus Burkhalter observed that in one online community founded on ethnic identity, differences between participants were apparent within the community, only fading into a monolithic stance when the community became involved with another community (Burkhalter 1999).

Finally, many commentators have observed that online communities are subject to fragmentation and specialization. Baym describes the way that the large soap opera community R.A.T.S. came to be specialized into three other smaller communities based on the network on which the soap was broadcast (Baym 1997). Haythornwaite's (2002) work on online learning communities found that although internet links were able to activate latent (potential) ties into weak ties, weak ties themselves tended to fall away in online environments and only strong ties survived, suggesting that established relationships survive online only if they have another media or offline counterpart. Kolko and Reid (1998) also observed that online relationships suffer from a lack of robustness, a factor they attribute to the essentially transitory nature of online interactions. Online identity play, they argue, leads to a lack of investment in any particular persona. Lacking a reason to work out our differences, we are more inclined to abandon a persona and create a new one rather than deal with the consequences of our interactions. Thus internet communities become inherently unstable as people move in and out of them in different guises. In this sense, whether internet communities are understood as an affective space to which we have a strong commitment, or a playful space in which we are free to experiment and log off from the consequences, the result appears to be the same. Online communities are subject to centripetal tendencies which shear away weak ties and lead to a community of the initiated. The fact that the only answer to the charge of solipsism that has been developed centres around multiple occupancy is, in a sense, a concession of defeat. In isolating multiple membership as the only palliative to single-context interactions, cyber-theorists have conceded the ground that virtual communities are essentially single interest based.

The tendency of virtual communities towards singularity and homogeneity has profound implications for how we can understand information diffusion. If we accept Dewey's proposition on community as communication, then the transfer of information is highlighted as a key element of social cohesion. Studies of the dynamics of information flow through groups have highlighted the importance of community leaders (Lazarsfeld *et al.* 1968), intimacy (Erbe 1962) and weak ties (Granovetter 1973) in the movement of information through communities. Thus William Erbe's study of information flow (Erbe 1962) found that the key factors affecting information diffusion were the level of intimacy within a group, considered as the continuity of interactions within it, and the number of group members. According to Erbe's study, information diffusion occurs better in environments where there are a large number of medium-sized groups who meet regularly over a sustained period, for it is in such environments that the members may generate the intimacy required to pool information, and in which the convergence of social circles, the individual contacts of the members, may allow new information to be obtained. The work of Lazarsfeld and Katz, on the other hand, demonstrates the role of community leaders and hierarchies within these groups. Typically, they found, media content's influence is refracted through the politics of group norms, with opinion leaders possessing disproportionate influence on the uptake, and flow, of information. It is thus to the dynamics of hierarchies that we now turn.

Non/hierarchical power in online communities

As we have seen in Chapter 5, discussions of power in relation to online life most often focus on the 'digital divide' as the core question. Approaches to power which derive from models of social inclusion and exclusion hold as a tacit assumption that power is an attribute of inclusion and that the included are characterized by a certain equality of power. Partly as a result of this conception, and partly as a result of the dominant methodological commitments of sociologists of internet community, questions of power *within* online communities are less often discussed.

This oversight is compounded by the utopian nature of much of internet discourse. In focusing on the internet's potential to realize a democratic public sphere, accounts consistently downplay both the level of online conflict and the extent to which the technologies of, and practices around, the internet produce stratification. Community is used more often in the warmly approving sense noted by Williams (1961) than in a strictly sociological one. Thus Douglas Schuler (1996) saw online communities as convivial spaces of support rather than environments of interaction. A moderated claim for communities being 'inherently anti-hierarchical' is put forward by Jordan (1999a) who argues that that offline hierarchies cannot be effectively translated into online communities.

However, the evidence that is available strongly belies the conception of communities as anti-hierarchical. Early research on internet communities, most often focused on the now largely extinct proto-communities and groups known as MUDS,[1] depicts a bizarre social world halfway between *Lord of the Flies* and *Reservoir Dogs*. This is a world populated by 'gods' and 'wizards' who may turn people into barnyard animals as punishment for transgressions (Reid 1999), a world in which public shaming and torture are the only methods of control. 'Hierarchies are maintained through the careful attention to the trappings of power, power which, like medieval kingship, owes its legitimacy to the favor of the gods' (Reid 1999: 119). Community/MUD leaders are thus styled as temperamental gods, who may delete a user's hard work or exile the character at a whim. In this respect social power is developed through shameless self-aggrandizement and ingratiating oneself with the leader.

Multi-user domains, and their variants (MOOs and MUSHs – multi-user object-oriented and multi-user shared habitat), respectively, are now a rarity online but the remnants of this 'dungeons and dragons' approach to social order can still be seen in modern goal-orientated communities. Cooper and Harrison's (2001) account of life in an illegal MP3 exchange community shows clearly the importance of currying favour as a means of gaining social capital, the use of harsh and peremptory punishments as a means of social control, and the extraordinary personal power of the leader. Cooper and Harrison's account offers a vision of online community as a competitive space, where users struggle to maintain their position in the face of relentless demands to prove their worth. Social order is maintained through threats of having their accounts deleted and being denied access. 'In a social ecology based on data and access to it, taking someone's passwords and deleting all their data is,' the authors argue, 'practically speaking, akin to social death' (Cooper and Harrison 2001: 86).

These glimpses into online community are, of course, anecdotal and the objection could be raised that these are both anachronistic and unrepresentative. However, there are reasons to suppose that whereas the fantasy role-playing model of community has gone the way of the dinosaur, its fossilized remains still have a structuring role to play. The norms and practices of high-speed textual interaction still structure our use of electronic spaces, and thus the same social imperatives apply. As Putnam argues, the 'poverty of social cues in computer-mediated communication inhibits interpersonal collaboration and trust' (2000: 176). The lack of visual and verbal cues which enable the reader to narrow the indexical range of an utterance up the stakes in conflict management in online communities. DuVal Smith (1999) points out the perils of rapidly composed purely textual communication as the high possibility that users will take offence at a poorly worded response or feel that they are being ignored by an out of sequence one. The conditions of interaction in online communities appear to produce a high likelihood of hostility. Moreover, this hostility is more likely to become more severe rather than less. Whilst Carnevale and Probst (1997) contended that the internet has potential to unite people as a means of resolving offline conflicts, the development of the technology to date gives reason to suppose the opposite. Carnevale and Probst saw cross-cutting relationships as core to de-escalation of conflict. The involvement of third parties to disputes is a universally accepted means for resolution. However, the authors point out that third parties are most effective in this role when they themselves belong to multiple groups and have overlapping group membership with many others, thus fulfilling a requirement for homophily whilst maintaining distance from intra-group prejudices. That the internet tends to act as a centripetal force, separating communities out into largely homogenous groups which are strongly differentiated, militates against this dynamic.

Thus ethnographic accounts of life in online communities consistently show that power is central to their operation. The nature of this power, however, is essentially disciplinary. As Jordan (1999a) and Reid (1999) both point out, in a space where other cues to social status are problematic, the only forms of visible power are the use of highly loaded symbols. The internet is here a dramaturgical space where power, in order to be effective, must be enacted and performed. Social control can only be founded on ritualistic disciplining, online shaming and persona torturing in an arena where the lack of a physical site on which to visit punishment combines with a greater need to impose discipline owing to the greater level of social antagonism.

However, to accept this version at face value would be to cut off discussion at precisely the point where it becomes sociologically interesting. To understand power online as solely a function of kingly authority over small domains is to miss the point. The question then becomes, on what basis is such authority grounded? An easy answer is that the technologies themselves allow power to become invested in an individual or clique far more than they allow distributed power. The granting of administrator privileges to particular individuals is the basis of their ability to act in the future. This is an instance of what Jordan has referred to as 'technopower'. For Jordan technopower is a distinctive form of social power that relates mainly to online life. 'The difference between online and offline is that online social forms are constituted fundamentally, if not totally, from technopowers. The fundamental importance of realizing that cyberspace is informational space is that it means technopower is dominant in online societies' (Jordan 1999b). For Jordan, information:

> is endless in cyberspace and creates an abstract need for control of information that will never be satisfied. The direction of technopower in cyberspace is toward greater elaboration of technological tools to more people who have less ability to understand the nature of those tools. Control of the possibilities for life in cyberspace is delivered, through this

spiral, to those with expertise in the increasingly complex software and hardware needed to constitute the tools that allow individual users to create lives and societies.

(Jordan 1999b)

Technopower is therefore not something that relates to a particular community or group, but to the social whole of cyberspace. Technopower controls the means of information gathering and connection between people and as a result constitutes the very space of cyberspace. As Stone (1991) points out, the evolution of ranking within communities, in which some have the powers of moderators or administrators, was itself a response to the need to impose social order after early communities were almost destroyed by anti-social behaviour and spamming. The communities' response to these threats was to introduce a hierarchy as a means of self-defence.

Therefore communities develop hierarchies out of a need to control resources: in Jordan's case the development of greater technical tools to manage information which shifts power out to technical expertise; in Stone's the need to protect a given community from spam. This control of resources has become more entrenched in internet culture, from the macro level (see Part Four for discussion) to the micro or individual level. Thus amongst the file sharers studied by Cooper and Harrison (2001), those who enjoyed the highest profile, i.e. had the greatest 'cultural capital', were those that were best able to upload music at the moment of its release. This was taken as an index of the quality of that supplier's connections and, concomitantly, sites with good suppliers moved quickly through the hierarchy of sites. However, such status could be lost at the throw of a die, for the sites were constantly engaged in a running battle to secure exclusives. Power within a virtual community, then, is inherently a process, rather than an accomplishment. It is something that is in constant need of maintenance rather than a resource on which the individual can draw. In this sense, community hierarchies are inherently tied to control of resources not only within, but between groups. As a result we need to shift the frame of research from intra-group dynamics to inter-group dynamics in order to make progress on understanding the nature of online community. This raises the question of how groups are maintained as distinct entities, to which we now turn.

Forms of solidarity

The sense of online community that emerged from the above discussion is a highly pessimistic one. Online communities appear as single-stranded and context-specific groups whose interactions are fraught with tension. The rapidly shifting political winds of power relations seem more reminiscent of a feudal court than of a modern agora and the sense of peril that emerges from them is palpable. Given that electronic communities appear riven by status and conflict, atomized and unstable, how is it then that these communities do stay together and show a degree of cohesion? Why do people stay and commit to them? How can we account for the fact that the web has not disintegrated into atomized communities of one?

In trying to address this question, sociologists have most often fallen back on an attempt to uncover the overt motives and intentions of the participators. In so doing we have developed an understanding of participation which is based in the psychological satisfactions afforded by the practice of participation. However, as argued in the Introduction to this book, this is an unstable basis for further enquiry, uncovering only end results. The core question, as Bourdieu *et al.* (1990) argue, is not what satisfactions are derived from behaviours, but why certain behaviours produce certain satisfactions at all. Why then do people derive satisfaction from participation in online communities?

The first response concerns the idea of a loss of community. People join online communities in order to compensate for their lack of solidarity elsewhere. The sense that online community emerges as a palliative to civic erosion, discussed above, providing a refuge from the ills of modernity, is one that privileges a reading of community as a rational and goal-orientated space. Communities, in this account, exist to address specific social problems, either the lack of other spaces for political action, or the lack of affective spaces within offline communities. They are modelled as serving fundamental needs which are pre-constituted, such as a need for participation or a need for acceptance or companionship. The problem with such an approach is not difficult then to uncover. The supposition that people have a need for social behaviours which exists apart from their means of satisfaction involves us in a fundamental teleology. Even when we reduce the concept to a more specific goal, e.g. political action, the idea that people go online in search of an unrealized ideal may be valid, and from this perspective certainly explains the high dropout rate in virtual communities, but this does not explain why those who remain online do so if their experiences do not live up to their expectations and hopes. Therefore examining community in relation to psychological satisfactions will not get us far. Rather, we need to consider how group solidarity is created and maintained in this environment. What, then, are the architectures of solidarity in cyberspace?

In the first instance academics have isolated the central role of collective symbols. Whilst many commentators have argued that the dramaturgical nature of the internet enforces a greater reliance on symbols, the power of collective symbols is recognized as a fundamental aspect of the development of group solidarity in all communities. Alluquere Stone cites Anslem Strauss in this context:

> we may say that every group develops its own system of significant symbols which are held in common by its members and around which group activities are organized. Insofar as members act towards and with reference to each other, they take each other's perspectives towards their own actions and thus interpret and assess that activity in communal terms. Group membership is thus a symbolic, not a physical, matter.
>
> (Stone 1996: 87)

The collective symbols of the online community, as noted above, include FAQs, group-specific terminology and abbreviations, and common linguistic and symbolic resources. For example, Nancy Baym points to the development of group-specific acronyms such as IOAS (it's only a soap) on R.A.T.S (Baym 1998: 53). However these, whilst serving to identify the initiated from the outsiders, probably do not serve as a form of solidarity in the sense that Strauss meant. Common symbols create solidarity only where they are used for a more cohesive purpose than mere tribal identification, which is what appears to be being invoked in the case of online community. Members act with reference to each other *through* the symbols, and not solely with reference to the symbols themselves in Strauss's account. Moreover, the very fact of drawing upon common symbolic resources presupposes exactly what it purports to explain, for how can community be generated by collective symbols prior to those symbols being endowed with meaning? As Mead argued, 'Gestures become significant symbols when they implicitly arouse in the individual making them the same response which they explicitly arouse, or are supposed to arouse, in other individuals ... to whom they are addressed' (Mead 1927, cited in Scott 1995: 103). Symbols then are symbolic *for* someone, meaningful only within a social context and thus cannot be the cause of that context.

The second key feature in the development of online solidarity is the question of reciprocity. Early attempts to understand the internet as an exaggerated form of computer-supported cooperative work enshrined the question of reciprocity at the heart of sociological attempts to understand online group activities. For early commentators it was clear that the internet was likely to support only specific reciprocity, which is to say contract-like relations between individuals or small groups to return a favour. The likelihood of a more generalized reciprocity emerging was regarded as low. However, in some respects the net has confounded these early pessimistic visions. To use the example of file-sharing communities, in Cooper and Harrison's description of the different social roles occupied by members of audio pirate communities, members are often found posting audio files for the benefit of 'leeches', members who do not post files themselves but lurk online awaiting a chance to download others' files. Although Cooper and Harrison also note that members act as 'traders', offering their goods only in direct exchange for other files, the community of file sharers could not survive without some goods being given away free in this way. Thus individuals who may be traders or 'couriers' in another context turn 'leech' feeders in order to advance communal interest (Cooper and Harrison 2001). It is also clear from ethnographic accounts that such 'gifts' are not directly solicited or demanded and thus it appears that a norm of generalized reciprocity is in operation. This could be used to support the vision of the internet as a utopian space, the pure social bond which early theorists hoped would emerge.

However this evidence is questionable. Peter Kollock (1999) and Butler *et al*. (forthcoming) dispute the idea that such apparently unselfish acts are communally orientated. Rather, they argue, these acts do provide intangible benefits for the givers. Butler *et al*. understand these benefits as divided into four main categories: informational, gaining information otherwise not available; social, gaining social interaction and a sense of camaraderie; visibility, becoming better known perhaps in a work-related field; and altruistic, the residual category as far as they are concerned. For Kollock (1999) the possibility of future reciprocation and the benefit to one's reputation is key to understanding people's motivations to give 'goods' away for free. Wellman (1997) also sees the imperative of self-creation as a core factor in generating diffuse reciprocity in online communities. All these authors therefore concur on at least the point that one of the primary motivations is self-promotion/creation. People offer help and advice in order to support their self-presentation as experts in a particular field. The need to create and maintain a self in an online community acts as a powerful spur, requiring that we offer our 'goods' for free in order to build recognition and participate in the reputation hierarchies of online life. In recent years this unstated social norm has come to be 'translated' into a technical one. Many sites, particularly those which centre on the distribution of 'goods', whether file sharing or informational, have developed complex systems of 'ratios' and 'karma points' in which individuals gain points for each transaction they perform. Thus, on file-sharing sites such as BitTorrent, each user has a ratio of files uploaded to files downloaded. In the event that the user 'selfishly' downloads but does not allow other members in the peer-to-peer network to download from them, that user's account will automatically be suspended. In this sense the injunction to 'play fair' and offer 'goods' to the community at large is shifted out to the technologies which enable the transaction in the first place.

What this flags up is the increasingly central role played by what are referred to as reputation systems. Reputation systems can be understood as a form of social capital in so far as accumulated reputation acts as a source of power both within and between communities. Ciffolilli's (2003) ethnography of Wikipedia, a community centred around the development of the online encyclopedia of the same name, identifies reputation as the key factor in status and power within the community. Administrator privileges are granted to individuals on the basis of their reputation within the community and, therefore, technical power can be achieved only through long-term investment in the community. Such forms of power cannot easily be transferred from one community to another. The same would be true of the reputation systems of leading private sales sites such as Amazon Marketplace and eBay. However, Cooper and Harrison's study (2001) of audio pirates suggests that in some fields promotion within one community may allow a given individual to improve their position or simply to enter other communities of file sharers. Their research found that occupying a core position in one group of file-sharers allowed an individual to 'get a foot in the door' in other higher-status groups. However, it is equally clear that an ability to capitalize upon this position was only useful in gaining entry and thereafter a position in the complex social rankings of the audio pirates was down to the individual's own initiative. Of course, reputation is inherently unstable as a source of social power, subject to challenge and only effective in so far as it can repeatedly be demonstrated to be valid.

Conclusion

The above discussion has highlighted the extent to which internet community studies draw upon an inheritance from social network conceptions of community. Rather than seeking community in locality, as organized around a space whether virtual or otherwise, or solidarity, network approaches see community as an emergent property of social ties. As Wellman and his co-authors put it: 'Community, like love, is where you find it' (Wellman *et al.* 1988: 130). The central methodological commitment of social network analysis is, therefore, to the proposition that communities do not enjoy an independent existence above the ties that form and create them, they do not have enduring or constraining features. In this sense internet community studies tend to understand community not as fostering a sense of identity, but as formed around and through identity and voluntary linkages. Whilst, on the one hand, this emphasizes questions such as how communities stay together, how and under what circumstances they are formed and what types of governance emerge within them, this approach systematically removes from the frame other possible readings. Thus it would make little sense in a social network approach to pose questions such as the impact of bureaucratization, urbanization or centralization on communities since the community is not an entity that can be victimized or affected on this level. As this is translated into internet community studies it makes little sense to examine how changing legal or political environments impact on communities. Certainly studies of internet community do not tend to foreground issues such as solidarity or the divisions of roles and labour. Rather the social is understood to consist mainly in the subjective orientations of actors. This understanding of community ultimately reduces it to identity and subsumes the question of the social into that of the individual. Following this, the main focus of sociological attention has shifted to the way self is developed online, which is the subject matter of the next chapter.

Note

1. Multi-user domains (MUDs) are similar to chat rooms in so far as all users are engaged in real-time interaction, but differ in so far as they operate as a virtual environment, complete with geographical features. Users can move around in this virtual space, interact with other users and construct their own props, environments and characteristics. For a more detailed discussion see Turkle (1995).

9 Online identity

The question of the nature and formation of the online self is central to sociological enquiry into the social impact of the internet. From the beginning, theorists have been fascinated by the question of how we develop a persona, and interact with each other in an environment as devoid of social cues as the early internet. Investigation into the area has taken its cue from the cybercultural and postmodern discourses associated with writers such as Mark Poster, Alluquere Stone and Sherry Turkle. For these authors, cyberspace, as it was then commonly called, is understood as fragmenting and reconstituting identity. The subjectivity of the online citizen was seen in terms of the postmodern project of self-realization, a realization which is seen to operate free from the constraints imposed by offline social order. This chapter introduces and examines cybercultural theories around identity formation, and argues that they are deeply flawed, both in epistemological and empirical terms.

The most often cited study of postmodern online identity is that of Sherry Turkle, whose study of early MUD users (see note p. 119) has become a landmark text. For Turkle the 'subjective computer' differs radically from other technologies. This is in so far as people use computer and online 'tools' in search of new experiences which will *change* their ways of thinking rather than simply as a tool to do a predetermined job (see discussion in Part Four; Turkle 1995: 26). As a result cyberspace is, for Turkle, a self-consciously reflexive space, an arena where 'you are who you pretend to be' (1995: 192) and where the self is the sum of these mythologies distributed over the net as a whole. In this account, then, the online self is multiple, transitory and always in the process of redevelopment. The end result of this process is the development of a global 'melting pot' self. The core idea is that as we develop and express multiple characters, drawing on latent aspects of our personality and 'projecting' them into coherent personas, we come more and more to 'live in each other's brains'. Thus she argues: 'With our relationships spread across the globe and our knowledge of other cultures relativizing our attitudes and depriving us of any norm ... Individual notions of self vanish' (Turkle 1995: 257). The cyber self that develops is not, then, the solipsistic, informational hermit feared by some writers on internet community, but an all-embracing global self whose consciousness of difference is more attuned through embracing and inhabiting that difference.

The second commonly cited position is that of Mark Poster, whose argument, whilst in agreement with Turkle's on some points, is a little different. Poster also understands online identity as constructed online, rather than a pre-constituted essence that we bring with us when we log in. However, he takes his cue from literary post-structuralism rather than the psychoanalytic postmodernism of Turkle. Poster thus rejects the voluntarism of Turkle's account, instead seeing the net and the citizen as mutually constructed and constructing. Drawing on Foucault, Poster argues that the 'individual is not a natural being, is not a being centred in consciousness, but is actually given shape in the interactions that occur in language and in action' (Poster 1995b). Therefore online 'internet discourse constitutes the subject as the subject fashions him or herself ... individuals construct their identities ... in relation to ongoing dialogues, not as acts of pure consciousness' (Poster 1995c: 211). For both authors, however, there are certain shared commitments. In both Poster's and Turkle's work, identity is synonymous with subjectivity, and with a rejection and reconstitution of a prior coherent self. For our purposes here, there are two main problems with this. The first is the extent to which it maps onto the empirical forms of the internet. The second is that it is theoretically dubious and epistemologically contradictory. I will deal with each of these in turn.

The theory of reality: postmodern selves online

The first line of objection to the postmodern conception of the self in online environments relates to the extent to which the internet actually requires or causes the deconstruction of the self into multiplicity. The empirical warrants for the claim that it does in the work of both Poster and Turkle are their studies of early uptake internet users. Thus both authors draw on experiences of MUD users and virtual reality environment players whom they saw as characteristic of the early internet experience. Whether this is historically accurate or not, it is clear that these practices are no longer truly relevant to the modern internet. Over the past few years studies have consistently shown differences in the uses of the internet from those emphasized in cybercultural accounts. As Castells points out, '[r]ole-playing and identity-building as the basis of on-line interaction are a tiny proportion of Internet-based sociability, and this kind of practice seems to be heavily concentrated amongst teenagers' (2001: 118). The outdatedness of MUDs as an exemplar of internet use in action is clear when we consider that the metaphor of 'virtual reality' is now far less often invoked in relation to the internet and has been substituted by that of the database. Indeed, the major trend in internet use appears to move directly away from the postmodern identity play observed by Poster and Turkle, and towards the opposite, but equally postmodern, dynamic of hyper-identity.

The theme of hyper-identity comes to the fore in so far as it is inherently tied to the internet's functionality as a 'social network'. Stable identities are required in order for the network to operate. There are, of course, structural and technical reasons why the internet should emphasize stable identity. Consider for example the centrality of trust online. Since the early days of the internet's popularity, its darker side has been just as mythologized as its positive potential. In particular, fears and popular concerns centred on the probability that the internet could come to act as a conduit for conmen and fraudsters. Early on, then, the problem of trust online came to be a central preoccupation. Identity has been a core principle in organizing a response to this on the part of commercial internet concerns. Resnick *et al.* (2000) point to the significance of 'reputation systems' as a means of overcoming lack of consumer confidence in online auction concerns such as eBay. Such is the effectiveness of reputation systems that they are now common on commercial sites, e.g. Amazon, subscription services such as expert advice sites, consumer review sites, and popular services such as iTunes. Reputation systems, Resnick *et al.* explain, work by casting the 'shadow of the future' into the present. In an arena where it is possible to walk away from entangling commitments, there is little prohibition against individuals cheating customers or selling shoddy or defective goods in the knowledge that there is little likelihood of retribution. The problem is of the same order as the free-rider problem in cooperative work. Where there is lack of accountability, there is no benefit in producing a good service, but financial imperatives provide an incentive to poor service such as deceit or cutting corners. Reputation systems, developed around software capable of collecting and distributing feedback from previous customers, act to introduce account-ability, by ensuring that shoddy products or cheating practices will continue to dog the conman/woman and compromise future sales, whilst positive feedback provides for future sales. Thus reputation systems act both as a means of social control and as a powerful incentive for the development and maintenance of a particular type of identity. In the discussion above, I highlighted the way that less formal reputation systems act as a means of stratification within online communities. In this context the necessity to develop reputation also acts as a spur to the development of identity.

Second, there is the question of the nature of production itself. If we accept the idea that the web's interactivity makes it inherently a productive medium, in which there are no clear boundaries between producers and consumers (see discussion in Chapter 6), we must still be aware that the fact of producing content at all presupposes an audience (Burnett and Marshall 2003: 120–1). In order to gain and keep an audience, individuals have in some sense to engage in or orientate to marketing strategies for their own sites, and identity is a core principle of this. In order to attract an audience, or to act as a seed of community, the self we present online must be intelligible to this audience, and this requires a certain coherence. In essence, in order to achieve online visibility we must produce ourselves as an easily recognizable 'brand' of person. Consider the case of weblogs, or 'blogs'. A blog is a form of online diary, to which others can post comments (see Blood 2002). Blogs can take the form of more or less anything: random thoughts, project notes, commentary on current events, or whatever content the blogger decides to use. The key point with blogs is that they are a public forum. If we do not wish

for an audience then there is little reason to keep a blog. However,
gain a public profile for a blog, the blogger needs to become kr
certain kind of content provider. In so densely packed an info
space, a blogger needs to have a theme in order to be identifi
potential audience. This needs to be a consistent theme so that readers will
return to that blog to read updates and so on.

Moreover the kinds of identity we develop must be readily recognizable
not only to our projected audience but also to others within our peers. In so
far as self-presentation is based on the production of personal sites, e.g. home
pages, personal weblogs and so forth, and further in so far as personal sites are
composed from heteroglossic formats, a bricolage of and links to other found
and produced materials, then the self is constructed from linkages. These
linkages, as Turkle herself points out, locate identity within the network.

> On the Web, the idiom for constructing a 'home' identity is to assemble a
> home page of virtual objects that correspond to one's interests. One
> constructs a home page by composing or 'pasting' on it words, images, and
> sounds, and by making connections between it and other sites on the
> Internet or the Web ... one's identity emerges from whom one knows,
> one's associations and connections.
>
> (Turkle 1995: 258)

For Turkle this means that one's identity will remain in flux, as a product of
network connections, friendships and memberships of different interest
groups.

However, this conclusion does not necessarily follow and, indeed, the
majority of research evidence on group dynamics does not support it. In fact,
research has usually found that the direction of cause is the opposite: self-
presentation does not follow association, but association self-presentation. In
order to generate a social circle, or the connections necessary to develop an
online presence, we must already have a clear sense of self. As Burnett and
Marshall put it, '[i]f the success of a web site is related to its capacity to attract
other users, one of the critical avenues for that success is how well the site is
linked to other sites' (2003: 76). Separate research by Papacharissi (2002) and
Smith (1998, cited in Burnett and Marshall 2003: 69) confirms the central role
of feedback and linking up mechanisms in personal home pages, including
the use of invitations to email and guestbooks, as well as site hit counters. As
Waskul and Douglass argue:

> the fact that participants present meaningful identities in the on-line
> context confirms the environment as inherently social – a context in
> which participants interpret interaction as perceived by others. That is, in
> order to have an identity bestowed on oneself, it is necessary to be in a
> context in which one can identify with others and be identified.
>
> (Waskul and Douglass 1997: 378)

Moreover this sense of self becomes more rarefied as we amplify it. As Cass
Sunstein points out, the dynamics of group membership online tend to
produce specialization, polarization and greater in-group effects. In psychological studies, where anonymity and group identity are both emphasized in

laboratory experiments, individuals are found to move towards more extreme opinion positions than they originally held (Sunstein 2001: 71–2). Extrapolating group effects from opinion to self-construction we can easily see how the internet, by linking individuals with similar interests, can equally allow greater polarization and extremity. Taking a relatively trivial example to illustrate this, a person may be a *Star Trek* fan in real life, but they are very unlikely to start conversing in Klingon or discussing the properties of warp cores in mixed company. At a *Star Trek* convention, perhaps, this would be a normal way to behave. However, even extreme *Star Trek* fans spend little time at conventions in proportion to the time they spend at work, with family or doing domestic chores. Their fandom therefore occupies a discrete status in their lives, a status moderated by the knowledge that few others share their interests to the same extent. In an online group, however, everyone will be more or less fanatical about the Klingon language, the Cardassians and the possibilities of a warp core breach. Behaviour that offline would be moderated can come to appear more generalized, and therefore more legitimate. Moreover, given the distribution of *Trek* fans in the overall population, a meeting offline would be likely to include fans of *Deep Space Nine* as well as those of the *Next Generation* or original series. Online this would be less likely (see above) and thus there is little reason to learn to tolerate and accommodate even this, from an outsider's perspective, minute level of difference. If this is confined to television fan communities then it is interesting, but unlikely to have great consequences for non-participants. However, Susan Douglas and Meredith Michaels have pointed to a less trivial example in their discussion of forums for stay-at-home mothers (SAHMs) in the USA. Here they observed the fragmentation of support groups into Christian SAHMs, homeschooling SAHMs, black SAHMs, and so on (2004: 314–16). Where the potential exists to link up those who are widely geographically distributed, it appears that there is little incentive to join up with those of differing opinions and, as a result, personal choices in lifestyle or particular opinion and belief come to be amplified into identities, which then go on to act as a structure for a more diffuse range of interactions and choices.

Finally, some critics have noted that the internet acts as a voyeuristic space, in the sense that more and more of the self must be revealed in order to achieve online visibility and validation. In order to produce an 'audience-effect the personal web site must reveal more and must transgress the public display into the private and intimate to achieve its sought after audience' (Burnett and Marshall 2003: 79). In order to differentiate one's personal page from the mass of other personal pages the author must be prepared to grant the audience more and more intimate perspectives on his or her life and this in turn locks the author into a quasi-pornographic logic of visibility, making available more aspects of his or her self to their audience. In an inherently theatrical space, an online presence depends on making visible, on enacting the self for an audience, and thus we come to 'play act' our own personas. In this sense we move from inhabiting identity to performing it, enabled by the low cost and low user requirements of web technologies.

In a more general sense this voyeuristic enactment can be seen as part of a wider trajectory in modern life. For Jon Dovey the prevalence of personal home pages, webcams, online public access photo albums and so forth is part of a wider trend epitomized by reality television shows, paparazzi journalism and the development of entertainment industries devoted to behind-the-scenes views of celebrities. Dovey understands these trends as tied to a postmodern collapse. Subjectivity, and the personal, is the 'only remaining response to a chaotic, senseless, out of control world in which the kind of objectivity demanded by grand narratives is no longer possible' (cited in Yesil 2001). For others this is linked to the rise of celebrity culture and the yearning for participation in a culture where public visibility and fame are the only valid indexes of status. It is the hope of enjoying our 15 minutes that drives people to participate in this revelatory culture. For Marxist-inspired authors visibility culture is tied to the collapse between the public and private. Bunting, for example, notes that:

> One of the most curious phenomena of the last fifteen to twenty years has been the publicising of what was once regarded as strictly private. So, television programmes are now devoted to the minute details of couples' sex lives, neighbours and disputes, and people are prepared to reveal all to chat shows and the tabloids. Our culture has become compulsively self-revelatory and voyeuristic. This publicisation of the private life is the corollary of the privatisation of public life which has dominated political debate for two decades. As privatisation has removed many activities from the public sphere . . . the personal has moved in to fill up the space . . . The result of these twin processes has been a transformation of the terms and understandings which form the national conversation . . . The primary beneficiary of these parallel processes has been capitalism.
>
> (Bunting 2001)

In these accounts the internet is simply one of a bundle of media technologies which are locked into the processes of individualization characteristic of late capitalism.

However, it is immediately apparent that this presents a theoretical conflict. If self-realization is, as postmodernists have argued, a refuge from the meaninglessness of a world without meta-narrative, then it is difficult to understand how this fits alongside the equally postmodern celebration of identity play as self-annihilation. One cannot simultaneously hold that people take refuge in and flee from the same thing. This brings us on to the second set of problems with cybercultural views of identity, namely the extent to which they depend on contrary and incompatible epistemologies.

The reality of theory

The second problem is that of contradictions within the framework itself. The idea foregrounded in cybercultural accounts is that of the self as synonymous with the viewpoint of the actors and this derives from classic psychoanalytical positions. In Turkle's account the self and individual identity are positioned, at their most basic, as a product of the internal life of the individual. As Frank Furedi explains, the conception of the psychotherapeutic self is one in which:

the private search for identity should be seen above all as an attempt to find meaning in a world where the self relation to wider communities and networks is already tenuous. The ambiguous and fluid relationship of the self to external points of reference is the outcome of the individualising imperative of late modernity ... [an imperative which] ... legitimises the estrangement of people from each other. 'Be yourself' has become both a cultural obligation and a desired state of self enlightenment.

(Furedi 2004a: 146)

Thus, in the language of the psychoanalytically inspired cybercultural accounts, self is synonymous with subjectivity, represented through the language of emotionalism and a therapeutic vocabulary. From this perspective, self-realization is the primary goal of the subject, a realization that becomes synonymous with enlightenment and autonomy.

Moreover, the autonomous self of psychoanalysis is positioned as the wellspring of association: 'self autonomy is represented as the precondition for forging relationships' (Furedi 2004a: 146). It is through the development of ourselves as autonomous self-aware beings that we form links with a wider community and make meaningful and rewarding connections. This, of course, is the basis of the classic transference pattern in psychoanalysis. However, these ideas are applied selectively by Turkle, who wants to argue for self-realization as the core purpose of online life and for the fluid relationship to external referents as the crux of self-realization, but also to reject the idea of the realized self as the basis of community, seeing instead community as the basis for the self, an inversion of the psychoanalytical position.

Whilst these commitments are core to the cybercultural approach, they present a logical paradox. Chia-Yi Lee expresses the problem particularly well:

If fluid subjectivity in total disintegration is a virtue welcomed in cyberspace, the subject who takes part in any activities of virtual communities would hardly achieve any identity. How can a group of fragmented, fluid, disintegrated subjects perform identification to reach a possible identity? At best, what they can work out is only an identity of non-identity. If a communal identity is possible to achieve out of subjectivity, then this subjectivity will never be totally fluid and disintegrated. Thus the subjectivity–identity relation in this postmodernist context is no more than an oxymoron, an aporia.

(Lee 1996)

If we enter cyberspace as *tabula rasae* then we must posit interaction and community as the basis of self, but we cannot posit either interaction or community without prior identity. Cybercultural theory's contradictions rest on the resolution of the origins of identity in so far as it maintains a commitment to the idea of self as both interactionally developed and as an internal voluntaristic state. In this respect the basis of the cybercultural approach is incoherent and contrary.

The second serious problem with the conceptions of self promulgated by cyberculture theories is the remove between them and the academic mainstream. Although authors such as Turkle and Poster would see this remove as a strength, arguing that their theories are novel responses to a novel technology, the problem is the extent to which they substantiate this claim to novelty by fiat, by simply ignoring (in this case a very substantial body of) prior theory. What is at stake here is not disciplinary ascendancy, the validity of the psychoanalytical view versus the sociological one, but rather the manner in which cybercultural theorists have selectively operationalized the theories available to them, both within *and* between disciplines. The chief claims of cybercultural theories to novelty are, first, the claim of self multiplicity and, second, the claim that there is a radical difference between self-identity online and offline. Let us look at these in turn.

The first claim, of multiplicity, quite apart from the empirical evidence discussed (see above), is in any case sociologically dubious. Turkle queries whether in a world of multiple decentred selves any primacy can be granted to the original. Thus she cites approvingly one respondent who questions 'why grant such superior status to the self that has the body when the selves that don't have bodies are able to have different kinds of experiences?' (Turkle 1995: 14). From a sociological point of view we do not need to go far for an answer to this. Marx's famous dictum that 'life is not determined by consciousness but consciousness by life' (Marx and Engels 1970) should suffice to reveal the problems with this. As Wynn and Katz point out, only one of these multiple selves possesses autonomy.

> They exist as artefacts of that being that types them in. Therefore they cannot be claimed to have equality, because the being can easily continue without these 'selves'. They, on the other hand, will discontinue without the basis of the person in the body, because as programs they lack the situated intelligence to even pretend to be 'someone'.
>
> (Wyan and Katz 1997: 305)

Put another way, only one of the selves is engaged in the productive order that maintains the body on which all depend.

The second point, that of radical discontinuity between internet and offline life, is expressed well by Turkle in the introduction to *Life on the Screen*:

> From scientists trying to create artificial life to children 'morphing' through a series of virtual personae, we shall see evidence of fundamental shifts in the way we create and experience human identity. But it is on the Internet that our confrontations with technology as it collides with our sense of human identity are fresh, even raw.
>
> (Turkle 1995: 10)

The problem here is that the claim to novelty is the claim that in 'real life' we have traditional, singular, monolithic and private identities. As Wynn and Katz point out, this flies in the face of the majority of sociological theorizing, in which the self is not a transcendent unity but constructed through interaction with others. In this context the authors cite Simmel, Schlegof, Berger and Luckmann, and Schutz as exemplifying a tradition of seeing the self as developed in relation to groups (Wynn and Katz 1997: 300–1). We could equally add to the list Durkheim, for whom the normlessness implied by lack of identity had rather less liberatory consequences, a point raised by the authors in a different context (Wynn and Katz 1997: 299).

The interactionist tradition of sociology, then, has always seen the self as process. This is not, of course, to say that cybercultural theory and interactionism has much the same outlook. However, this has not prevented theorists from drawing upon interactionist frameworks in an attempt to bolster their observations on the nature of online identity, and this is particularly the case in studies which emphasize parallels between online identity and Goffman's work on the self as performance. This borrowing does not at first glance appear that problematic and certainly students who are unfamiliar with Goffmanian sociology would not see that much conflict between the notion of self as an actor and interaction as a dramaturgical performance and the cybercultural 'playful' self. The differences, however, could hardly be more profound.

In the first instance, as Wynn and Katz point out, Goffman is not making claims about the *self* so much as about *self-presentation*:

> the notion of self-presentation outlined by Goffman in which interactants collaborate to facilitate the respective images of self that each party tacitly attempts to project. Goffman calls this 'face': not 'self' but self-*presentation*. His theory is premised not on an elusive definition of selfhood per se but on the image of self that social participants put forth as viable means of negotiating normal social life.
>
> (Wynn and Katz 1997: 301)

'Self', argues Goffman, 'is not an entity half concealed behind events, but a changeable formula for managing oneself during them' (1974: 573). It is 'a code that makes sense out of . . . the individual's activities and provides a basis for organizing them' (Goffman 1971: 366). This is a far cry from the psychoanalytical self as a state of enlightenment and thus the two accounts cannot be used additively in the sense that internet theories have used them.

Second, and following on from this, academics studying online identity have read Goffman as an analyst of self-presentation management. For Patricia Wallace, Goffman was 'the father of impression management theory, believed that everybody uses tactics to present themselves in whatever light they think appropriate for the context. Your motives are key' (1999: 28). In understanding Goffman as concerned with the 'spin doctoring' of the self, work on interactionism and online identity tends to overemphasize the strategic or manipulative elements of interaction in Goffman's account. This is not entirely unfair, as Goffman certainly devoted a large amount of his published works to this theme, however it is to miss the main thrust of his argument. Explicitly, Goffman (1969: 231–40) emphasizes these elements as an heuristic for analysis, a way of observing rather than a statement on a way of being. Goffman is not primarily concerned with the way we manipulate the appearances of an essential self. What he is concerned with is the general rules that underpin interaction and foreground issues of ritual and conformity to social norms. For Goffman rituals of self-presentation are not voluntary in the sense that cybercultural theories would understand them to be. The array of possible forms of presentation are strategies, certainly, but they are generated by a normative order. Thus the social is primary over the strategy, forming and organizing it.

To explain this in more detail, we can consider Goffman's treatment of 'identity' and 'self' in one of his most prominent works, *Stigma* (1968). Goffman describes three potential social groups, organized according to the extent of control over an 'informational domain of the self' that they can be said to have. The first group, 'normals', have nothing to hide, the third are the 'discredited', those whose stigma is impossible to hide and who are therefore unable to exercise public control over their image, which is to say they have lost control of an informational domain of the self. The middle group are the liminal case, the 'discreditable', those who are potentially able to belong to either group. The discreditable are those 'with a secret' who can nonetheless 'pass' as 'normal' provided they can retain control of their presentation. In order to do so they must be able to control both the 'expressions given', which are voluntary self-presentations, and 'expressions given off', the involuntary symbols and signs that we attempt to manage in order to convince others of the validity of our presentations (Goffman 1969: 16).

There are two respects in which this typography illustrates the primacy of the social. First, the salience of expressions given off is greater to the discreditable than to the 'normals' for whom they are enacting their performance. In real life we do not seek to discredit people for the most part. Rather, we tend to take them at face value *unless there is reason to suppose a discrepancy*. Therefore the discreditable will pay more attention to the expressions given off and accord them a greater status than the normals. What this demonstrates is the normative order underpinning these interactions in the first place, namely that as a society we extend a general trust to people in the absence of reasons to disbelieve them. The 'default setting' of social interaction is trust, not distrust. Thus, although I have been a lecturer for years, no student has yet asked to see my PhD. It would be irrational and unreasonable to ask a bus driver for his licence and resolutely refuse to believe he is able to drive a bus. Only if I asked a student 'Who's Durkheim?', or our bus driver careered madly off the road, would we begin to question whether the apparent facts were real. In terms of online interactions this is significant in so far as it relates back to discussions of trust and anonymity. Although the internet offers greater potential for people to hide the 'discreditable', to 'pass' as something they are not, there is no reason to suppose this represents a fundamental distinction from offline life, since belief is the norm from which disbelief deviates. In any meaningful relationship between actors, the internet affords enough intimacy to dissolve attempts to control 'expressions given off'. Only in causal interactions could an individual successfully 'pass' and if this is the substance of the relationships we view online then they are, sociologically at least, irrelevant. What this does then is to refer us back to the notion of a normative order, that society comprises people, that people have roles, that these roles are real and constraining, and so on.

Second, the example of stigmatic identities returns us to the social in another respect, in so far as it demonstrates the primacy of the normative order in distributing potential identities. Everyone is potentially discreditable in some circumstances and some context. I may look normal in appearance, but be subject to instant social disgrace if I try to cut a dash on the dance floor. A local beauty queen's claim to gorgeousness may be beyond dispute in her home town, but in a national contest she may appear only ordinarily good looking. The normative order here relates to knowing *what* identities we are required to conceal as much as knowing *how* to go about concealing them. It may be cute or idiosyncratic to admit to being a chocoholic, but not an alcoholic, and certainly not a heroin addict. Thus the rituals we perform when enacting self are not games or playful constructions in the sense that cyberculture would understand them to be. They are real-life manifestations of, and reactions to, the fundamental social order, with deadly serious consequences.

Moreover, the repertoire of available presentations and circumstances under which they are to be used are socially defined. Cross-dressers use socially defined codes for 'doing' femininity or masculinity. Using Turkle's example we might present ourselves online as a 'rabbit of unspecified gender [called] Carrott' (Turkle 1995: 13) but to do so we will have to use social codes on 'doing' rabbit. The roles we might choose to play are equally socially defined. We might, as in the famous case of 'Joan' (Turkle 1995: 228–30; O'Brien 1999: 88–9) role-play a wheelchair-bound lesbian psychotherapist, but we are unlikely to choose to role-play a persistent paedophile or a herpes sufferer. Thus what Goffman's work flags up for us is the enabling and constraining nature of the moral order and of the self. Without a moral order there can be no creativity because there are no benchmarks or nodes through which it can develop.

That developing a 'self' or a 'face' presupposes a shared moral background is significant in so far as it returns to the starting position of sociology, namely that agreements as to particular types of interaction or forms of representation are always more fragile than the social bedrock on which they sit. This was the point raised by Durkheim in his discussion of contract theory:

> the contract is not sufficient by itself, but is only possible because of the regulation of contracts, which is of social origin. This is implicit, firstly because the function of contract is less to create new rules than to diversify pre-established rules in particular cases; secondly, because it has not, and cannot have, any power to bind save under certain conditions that need to be defined. If in principle society confers upon it a power of obligation it is because generally the agreement of individual wills is sufficient to ensure ... harmonious collaboration between the diffused social functions.
> (Durkheim 1984: 162)

The voluntary contracts into which we enter are meaningless without the definition of social obligations which underpin them. Likewise, the particular forms of social interaction and the self-images we enter into are meaningless and impossible without a shared social framework in which they can be understood. Thus it is not that identity can be understood as a retreat from meaninglessness, but that apparent meaninglessness conceals meaning if social order is present.

What this flags up is that attempts to reconcile community and identity are fundamentally flawed. In the first instance, in taking their cue from understandings of the self in literary and cultural theory, where the self is understood as the means of operation of power on the individual, cybercultural theories have miscast the relationship between the two. In such accounts, the compliant self is seen as structured through and produced by power: its casting off, though a practical impossibility, is cast as a liberation from the shackles of power (Wynn and Katz 1997). However, as the discussion of Goffman's work shows, the celebration of the overthrow of the moral order implied by the rejection of stable self by cybercultural theorists over-emphasizes constraint and ignores the enabling nature of social norms. Moreover, the analysis of the work of Goffman shows clearly that there is no reason to regard these two entities as separate to begin with. Internet community may foreground identity as a more pressing question, but any serious examination of identity resolves back into community eventually as both concepts are framed and organized by the moral order.

Conclusion *to* Part Three

These chapters have examined the social organization of cyberspace in relation to the themes of identity and community, the way self is developed online and the way we organize ourselves and coordinate action and opinion on the internet. The questions posed in relation to the internet and community were, as we have seen, foregrounded by the gradual transformation of emphasis in community studies from communities as environments to communities as voluntary associations which are primarily affective in nature. This is paralleled by an increasing emphasis on self-identity as equally voluntaristic. As Bunting (2001) has noted: 'Personal identity has been recast, primarily in terms of emotional need, and delinked from concepts such as class, creed or nationality.'

The rhetorical force of the overlap between these therapized notions of the individual as a self-determining autonomous being whose only point of reference is his or her emotional needs (Furedi 2004a), and the libertarian ideology of the internet, accounts in large measure for the popularity of the cybercultural approach to the internet as social space. However, this discourse of self as need, and need as transcending time and space, is far more general in scope, finding its points of enunciation in multiple arenas of academic, political, policy and popular debate. The understanding of globalization as a moral force rather than an economic one, the extent to which debates about identity have been re-categorized as debates about lifestyle, the individualization of social problems into discourses of choice and inclusion, all recapitulate and entrench these individualized notions of the self. Thus, although theorists have seen the internet as requiring changes in emphasis, these changes were already well established in academic discourse before the internet became a topic of scholarly debate and argument.

However, similarly to these other arenas, viewing the electronic sphere as one which liberates the individual from the obligations of community and bonds of identity underestimates the collective and external nature of the social order. In so doing we run the risk of constructing online sociality as 'fantastic and unreal rather than practical, effective and socially constructed' (Wynn and Katz 1997: 300). In order to recover a sociological perspective on online identity, we need to rediscover and retain sociology's understanding of social facts as much enabling as constraining and draw back from the debates over form to uncover the underlying structures on which they depend. Without this concern sociologists of the internet run the risk of recapitulating an emergent conceptualization of both self and community as merely locational axes of consumption.

Many theorists have flagged up the problem that in viewing the internet as a space, sociologists have failed to take into consideration the extent to which it is now a commercial space in which the logics of promotion and consumption organize and order all social dynamics, including those of community and the self. The internet, it is argued, promotes and entrenches 'attentional economics' (Thorngate 1997: 296–7), competition for audience attention and time, at the heart of social relations. It is this that produces the hyper-voyeurism observed in relation to home pages and blogs. However, it is important to note that if the commercial web has truly colonized the internet as a whole, then the way we express identity online must also be related back to the dynamics of commercialism. As Wellman and Gulia point out, social interaction online is something of a buyer's market, with supply exceeding demand, which produces greater specialization: 'the market metaphor of shopping around for support in specialised ties is even more exaggerated than in real life. Indeed the architecture of computer networks promotes market-like situations' (1999: 186).

More significantly perhaps this market metaphor acts to constrain the available options within a commercially produced typology. Burnett and Marshall point out that the web's identity as a commercial space, as it precedes the individual's participation in particular arenas, acts as a brake on the imagination of the user, which is applied at point of entry. In order to learn to use the web, they argue, people need to choose between and conform to certain predetermined categories. Thus services such as AOL and Yahoo! enjoin the user to set preferences which serve to construct a controlled space of information or, as the authors put it, a 'simplified circuit of information'. This 'safer, suburban, family construction of the Web' (Burnett and Marshall 2003: 30) is likely to characterize people's use of the web thereafter, for once we enter into these predetermined categories, the routine flow of information to us is that which fits with these initial categories. This is the substance behind Lockard's dismissive claim that the whole idea of internet communities is nothing more than 'Mutually supporting participatory consumption' (1997: 224).

Thus the clash between ideologies of the individual versus the collective is far more than merely a 'dry' academic debate. For some theorists this is as much a political position as it is a theoretical one. It is a striking feature of scholarship around the internet that the most politicized arenas of debate are neither around media, nor sociality, but in relation to a topic long considered rather dry and conventional, namely the sociology of technology, to which we now turn.

Part **Four**
The **internet** *as a* **technology**

Introduction *to* **Part Four**

The sociology of technology is a rather Balkanized area of the discipline, one which is largely cut off from other streams of influence within sociology. In part this can be attributed, as Feenberg has argued, to the strongly idealist tenor of Western philosophy (Feenberg 1999: 1), a tendency to laud the cultural achievements of society rather than the technicals and therefore to treat technology as a simple means to cultural ends. Critiquing this instrumentalism has involved attempts to 'reintegrate' technology and culture in order to access these discourses of worthiness and substantiate technology's importance in understanding the social order. It is this attempt to reconcile the social and the technological that gives this area of debate its particular character. Perspectives in the sociology of technology have become solidified around the axes of one particular debate, that of the causal status of technology as a category of social 'things'. This is in contrast to most other areas of sociological theory which are governed by multiple problematics. In this chapter I will be arguing that the advent of the internet acts as a spur towards new theory which fundamentally alters both the position and the nature of sociologies of technology. In so doing it moves its concerns from the margins to centre stage in sociological debate, at the same time as it decentres and occludes the technological/social determinism which has been the axial principle of research in the field.

For sociologists of technology, any technology raises certain issues, and the internet is no exception. Where do technological innovations come from? How are they developed? How did the internet come to take the form that it does? What factors affect its diffusion and uptake within society, and what consequences follow from these patterns of adoption? How far can users of the technology affect its subsequent development, how much flexibility of use is apparent and what factors constrain or enable flexibility of use? How far does this technology constrain people to behave in certain ways towards it? These questions are a prelude to, or a subset of issues directed at, answering a larger question with wider implications, namely how far does the insertion of this new technology alter the nature of the social world? How fair is it to attribute social change to technologies?

To view the internet as a technology is to view it fundamentally as a thing, an artefact with more or less fixed properties which can be used in certain ways. Technologies are tools, instruments by means of which people achieve other goals than the mere use of the technology. Thus unlike a view of the internet as a public space, where 'mere' use of the space and visibility within it are goals in their own right, understanding the internet as a technology involves looking beyond it, through it, in order to appreciate the social goals realized by its use and forms. Or so the story goes. Recent research and theoretical innovation in the sociology of technology over the past few decades has been directed away from this conception of technology. As I will shortly be going on to illustrate, the sociology of technology has shifted focus profoundly away from an instrumental view of technology and towards a more sociological conception which downplays or disavows a substantialization of technology into a 'thing', and instead deconstructs technics into social processes. In actor-network theory (ANT), the social construction of technology (SCOT), critical social theory such as the works of Feenberg and authors drawing on Bourdieu, and in cultural studies approaches to technology, the same refrain emerges. Technologies are understood as crystallizations of social processes, neither separate nor separable from human practice. This rewriting of received wisdom on the subject has led to the charge of technological determinism fast becoming an intellectual term of abuse, which in turn has led to rereadings of classical theorists in an attempt to rescue them from the stain of attributing inappropriate agency (Weber 2005).

This trajectory of intellectual development, however, is not much in evidence in sociological studies of the internet as a technology. It is significant that the theorists to whom academics first turned in the early blush of enthusiasm over the internet were as far from this trajectory as it is possible to get. The first question with which this part of the book must therefore deal is an explanation of this extraordinary occurrence. In order to do so, I will first outline the main theories of technological process and development and the points of contrast between them.

However, the story of the internet as a technology does not end with 'prêt-à-porter' theorizing. In attempting to understand the internet as a technology, theorists from a wide range of academic positions have been forced to consider whether communications technologies can be understood in the same theoretical light as other more instrumental technologies. Chapter 11 is devoted to an examination of theories of technology which take this communicative problematic as their central point of departure. This chapter considers the role of information society theorists, autonomist Marxism, and the reconfigured position of actor-network theory within the sociology of technology.

10 Sociologies *of* technology

In the Introduction to this part I characterized the field of studies of technology as organized around the issue of the potential autonomy of technology and the extent to which it can be regarded as having the status of an agent. This issue has emerged as a fulcrum of debate within sociology of technology (SOT) as a result of the sustained effort directed at socializing 'the technology question'. This chapter introduces the main theoretical approaches to understanding technologies, offering an overview of the field as a whole, before moving on to an analysis of the reasons why some theories have achieved wider currency in relation to the internet than others. We begin with the notion of technological determinism.

Technological determinism

The idea of technology as an autonomous force, something that in itself creates certain effects is technological determinism and in the current intellectual climate much frowned upon: 'To label someone a technological determinist is to condemn him or her as thoughtless and uncritical' (Barney 2000: 35). Such blanket condemnation is, however, unhelpful and masks the range of thought within perspectives that take technology as a starting point. As Raymond Williams points out, an awareness of the limitations of deterministic stances 'can depress us into a vague and indifferent state in which no necessary factors ... can be admitted to exist'. Williams suggests that it is 'a kind of madness' if we are simply determined not to be deterministic (Williams 1981, cited in Chandler 1995). The three schools of thought most often criticized in the attack on determinism are Marxist, substantivist and Medium Theory approaches. Although each of these approaches *to some extent* posits a determining or causal role to technologies, the mechanism through which technologies are said to affect social processes, the means by which they become powerful enough to reconfigure social reality, is very different in each case.

The Marxist perspective is the most frequently invoked position in discussions of determinism. Until recently it was widely accepted that Marx had isolated technology as the primary independent variable in the transformation of the social order. The now standard line on Marx was that taken by Langdon Winner (1978). For Winner, Marx's argument goes thus: Marx's 'man' has never been free, people do not establish their conditions of existence through personal choice; the nature of the individual depends crucially on the material conditions of production. For Marx the material conditions of production can be divided into the forces of production and the relations of production. It is this combination that is decisive. Winner argues that in Marx '[t]he mode of production of material life determines[1] the general character of the social, political and spiritual processes of life' (1978: 51). However, for Marx, it is the forces of production that play the key determining role, for they are the means by which the relations of production are organized. Winner does concede that at times Marx portrays the process as a circular one, citing Marx's statement in *The Poverty of Philosophy* that: 'As the concentration of instruments develops, the division of labour develops also, and *vice versa*. This is why every big mechanical invention is followed by a greater division of labour, and each increase in the division of labour gives rise in turn to new mechanical inventions' (Marx 1963, cited in Winner 1978: 80). However, for Winner, this concession is not important for '*in most cases* Marx seems to be saying that there is a one-way influence between the forces and relations of production' (Winner 1978: 80, emphasis added). Thus, for Winner, Marx's argument is clearly of the most deterministic sort.

For subsequent readers, however, Marx's position is less clear. Sociologists of technology have taken the most relevant snippet of Marx to be his now quoted to the point of nonsense assertion that: 'In acquiring new productive forces men change their mode of production; and in changing their mode of production, in changing the way of making a living, they change all their social relations. The hand mill gives you the feudal lord; the steam-mill, society with the industrial capitalist' (Marx and Engels 1963). This seems to substantiate the case well enough. Marx is arguing that the form of technology determines the form of society. This quote has, however, been rendered into a form of mantra, used by determinists in support of their position, and against determinism by those who are keen to point out its crudity. Our familiarity with the quote as a result of its all too frequent and out-of-context quotation makes it difficult to read against the grain of standard interpretations. For other theorists who have done just that, though, a rather different sense of Marx's allegiances in the non-determinism/determinism debate has emerged. The issue focuses on how the new productive forces are 'acquired'. 'In the end,' Winner argues, 'the relations of production [in Marx] consist of all organized relationships in society' (1978: 80). In the end, argue revisionists, so do the forces of production. The 'acquiring' of new technologies is in itself a social process and the technologies themselves, far from being an independent variable, are the fetishised product of class conflict which emerge in the form, and at the time, that they do, not in order to provide a 'hinge factor' for eager political economists, but as an expression and concretization of that conflict as it is experienced at that time. It is to this that Marx referred when he argued that

every productive force is an acquired force, the product of former activity.
The productive forces are ... the result of practical human energy, but this
energy is itself conditioned by the circumstances in which men find
themselves, by the productive forces already acquired, by the social form
which exists before they do.

(Marx 1963: 181)

Thus technologies do not, as Winner appears to be implying, appear by
happenstance in order to be subsumed by the dominant interest, but emerge
from human action and the class struggle.

Of course whilst such a reading is less deterministic, shifting agency from
the technology to the forms of social conflict, it is scarcely less pessimistic. To
understand technology as a 'strategy of societal power' (Dyer-Witheford 1999:
53) is to reject its determining value as an object but is also to focus through it
onto the all too concrete social relations of which it is composed. As Noble
argues, technology's 'social effects follow from social causes that brought it
into being; behind the technology that affects social relations lie the very
same social relations. Little wonder, then, that the technology usually tends
to reinforce rather than subvert those relations' (cited in Dyer-Witheford
1999: 52). Technology is a strategy of social power, extending the influence of
dominant interests through the 'necrotic tyranny of dead labour'. It is the
inescapable nature of the preservation of class interest through technology
that gives history its form. As Marx puts it: 'Because of the simple fact that
every succeeding generation finds itself in possession of the productive forces
acquired by the previous generation, which serves it as the raw materials for
new production, a coherence arises in human history' (1963: 181).

Unfortunately the technology-as-domination school accepts the same
premise and therefore falls into the same trap as those keen to use Marx for
the end of support or of ridicule, namely ending the story of technology at
the point of adoption. Marx himself, characteristically, has a great deal more
to say. For Winner, Marx's argument means that 'the sociotechnical context
into which we are born must simply be accepted as given' (Winner 1978: 83).
For Noble, as for other theorists in what Dyer-Witheford has termed the
technology-as-domination school, 'the essence of the technology question
today' is that 'there is a war on but only one side is armed' (cited in Dyer-
Witheford 1999: 53). However, being outgunned has never prevented
struggle, especially where the stakes are as high as those attributed to the
technology war. The key point for recent theorists is that traditional readings
of Marx overemphasize the power of the ruling class to effect the changes it
desires. The history of technology, they argue, may be understood as the
history of the attempt to solidify and retain class interests, but that can only
be effective if it takes account of 'the possibility that capital's labouring
subjects may find real use values, even subversive ones, for the new
technologies' (Dyer-Witheford 1999: 54). For new theorists such as Hardt
and Negri, the process of technological development is driven not by the
interests of the ruling class but by their response to the resistance of those
they seek to oppress. The distinction between these approaches, and their
implications for understanding the development and dynamics of the
internet is an issue to which we will return below. For the present it is

sufficient to note that in refocusing attention on the class struggle, rather than the class triumph, new interpreters of Marx move the focus of attention in technology from its attributes to the process of the fetishization of these attributes. In so doing they move the analysis closer to the ground usually occupied by the second school of thought we will consider here, substantivism.

✳Substantivism

Whereas traditional readings of Marx understand the power of technology as power over action and social structure, the substantivist position, by contrast, locates this purported autonomy at the level of the lifeworld, the arena of social life in which meanings are produced. The substantivist tradition develops out of the works of Habermas and of Heidegger. Within this perspective, individual technologies may have a variety of uses and have, therefore, a neutral character, but this is largely irrelevant. For the substantivists there are two main issues: first, that technology in general enforces a way of being in the world (Barney 2004: 38), a certain mindset, and, second, that technologies themselves organize the way we perceive the world.

First, then, modernity is characterized by a certain relation to technology. As Ellul puts it, the 'technical phenomenon' has become the defining feature of what it is to be modern (Ellul 1964: 6) and thus the way we live our lives in modern society is closely tied up with 'technical rationality' and a way of thinking which privileges technical solutions to almost every problem. The very fact of this linkage of means and ends means, for the phenomenology of technology, that technological development unfolds apart from human agency as an autonomous process. As Feenberg (1999) points out, this, coupled with an understanding that technology is biased towards domination and social inequality, makes for a very pessimistic view of the process. However, the means by which technologies reorder the world are not the formal properties of the technologies themselves, but the abdication of human responsibility for them. The sense that technology is an unstoppable force or a sufficient explanation for change in its right is at the root of technology's power; it is not technologies themselves but the norms of practice around them that render them compelling (Bimber 1994: 81–3). Thus Ellul's predictions are prefaced by the caveat that this situation will occur '[i]f man does not pull himself together and assert himself' (cited in McGinn 1991: 73).

This abdication occurs at both micro and macro levels. On the level of everyday life we have all experienced situations where technological operations are regarded as sufficient cause for a particular set of actions. The way that the technology works is appealed to as reason enough to act in certain ways – for example, when we give information to operatives at call centres, there is a prescribed order of information required that the computer cannot work without. On the macro level, to which Ellul's analysis is directed, the problem appears more as a form of technological and economic arms race.

Thus we are familiar with arguments around technology where competition is invoked as the key variable initiating change. If Japan is using high-tech production methods and as a result can offer goods in the market at a lower price than the USA, the USA must adopt, and improve upon, the technologies. If children are better educated as a result of access to the internet, then failing to invest in a universal roll-out of network access to schools will prove a national disadvantage. In Ellul's work this competitive principle becomes generalized and diffuse in so far as the whole trajectory of Western economic development is organized around the pursuit of innovation, with research and development institutionalized in large companies and the education sector of most Western countries. As a result the process of technological adoption, reciprocal adoption, development, refinement and re-adoption is a constant movement which assumes a logic of its own, quite apart from any benefit or otherwise the individual technologies and improvements may have.

Medium Theory

The second part of the argument is that technologies themselves organize human perception. As Don Ihde puts it: 'Technologies organize, select and focus the environment through various transformational structures' (Ihde 1979, cited in Chandler 1995). It is this latter point that is taken up and expanded in Medium Theory. Medium Theory comes up through the works of what has come to be termed the Toronto school or Canadian sociology as it is advanced in the works of Harold Innis and Marshall McLuhan. Although McLuhan is more widely known, Innis's contribution has been regarded by many scholars as foundational, since it was in Innis's work that much of the conceptual work that McLuhan would later draw on was developed.

For Harold Innis, a Canadian historian, the key issue with technologies was the way in which they organize time and space. Technologies instantiate the relations of time and space within a given culture at a given time and provide us with a means of reading off the forms of social organization of that society. Innis differentiates between two types of media, *time* extending and *space* extending (Innis 1986). In traditional societies the way of preserving information is through time. The common media are clay or stone, highly durable and likely to survive over time, but not very portable. In such a society knowledge is likely to be 'eternal' truth, rather than more disposable information. It is likely to remain in one place and this presupposes and requires a high degree of geographical centralization, a physical location in which knowledge is deposited. It is likely that societies which are dependent on durable media will also have strongly conservative tendencies with a reasonable expectation that truths that hold today will also hold for subsequent generations. Thus the core issue of social integration resolves into intergenerational integration, the continuation of the society over time. For modern societies such media are impractical. In the modern world, knowledge is not timeless truth. Social integration is achieved spatially and media are required to be portable and capable of being transported. Media are therefore 'action at a distance' where distance is considered as space, rather than the traditional society's action at distance over the future. Thus Innis argues that 'Materials that emphasize time favour decentralization and hierarchical types of institutions while those that emphasize space favour centralization and systems of government less hierarchical in character' (1986: 5). For Innis, then, portable 'space-biased' media are associated with the modern commercial and administrative society, whereas durable 'time-biased' media are more common in traditional hierarchical societies. Innis is not, of course, arguing that each form of society develops or uses only forms of media which correspond to these axes of space and time, but rather that the balance of media within the society, whether space- or time-biased media are dominant, is inclined towards the relevant pole. Innis, however, does not expand his claims beyond the observation of a correlation between the forms of social order and the forms of media.

Marshall McLuhan's work, however, makes much bolder claims, specifying not only correlation, but also causation. McLuhan argues that media act directly on the senses of the individual and are a necessary and sufficient cause of the social changes which correlate to them. For McLuhan a media is anything that extends one of the human senses or faculties. This ranges from a hammer (an extension of the arm) to speech ('Speech is utterance, or more precisely *outering*, of all our senses at once' – McLuhan 1995: 240) and onwards to communications technologies. The message, on the other hand, is the change of scale or pace or pattern that a new invention or innovation 'introduces into human affairs' (McLuhan 1964: 8). Thus the point for McLuhan is not to demonstrate that media have 'effects' but to read from the effects to the media itself. The direction of cause is already assumed. The model that McLuhan has in mind, then, is that media act on human cognition and through this on society, where society is understood as an aggregate of the experiences of the individuals. Thus, in *The Gutenberg Galaxy*, McLuhan (1962) argues that print creates the habit of linear thought, through introducing a separation between the word and the deed, obliterating the instantaneous nature of information transmission. Thus the written word created the modern person, the solitary rational and reflective individual which is the basis of modern society. This is achieved in so far as each medium constitutes a disruption in the balance of the senses. In primitive (unmediated) societies all the senses are in balance and are tied in directly in every encounter. In the printing age this ratio of senses is out of balance, and the eye, the observing organ which does not participate but which reflects on life as on a scene, is dominant. The technology of the printing press cemented and solidified this change. 'The printing press hit ... like a 100-megaton H bomb ... The new medium of linear, uniform, repeatable type reproduced information in unlimited quantities and at hitherto-impossible speeds, thus assuring the eye a position of total predominance in man's sensorium' (McLuhan 1995: 243).

McLuhan's work has, of course, been heavily criticized for exactly this deterministic bias and, although it is not my intention here to rehearse these criticisms in depth, three core criticisms are relevant in so far as they bear on the adoption of McLuhan as the philosopher of the internet age. First, there is the question of where *technology* actually figures in McLuhan's account. McLuhan's definition of a medium as an extension of the senses involves a critical slippage between the 'medium' which he uses in the arts-based sense, as in the 'medium' of sculpture or paint, and technology or technique. This allows a second slippage, namely that between technology-media and use. As Williams argues, the 'physical fact of instant transmission as a technical possibility, has been raised uncritically to a social fact' (2003: 131). This conceptual slippage between technology, use and media layers neatly onto the slippages in the way that the internet is talked about, between technology, media and social form, and acts as a warrant to circumvent discussion of the different properties of each with the consequences I discussed in the Introduction to this book.

Second, this slippage, as Williams argues, further means that the medium has to be understood as a 'thing' rather than a practice. In McLuhan all practices are subsumed by psychic functions which serve to dissolve intentions. Since McLuhan is directing his analysis to the level of the 'general individual', a generalized human organism the alteration of which can provide the basis for understanding the properties of media and whose experience is the aggregate experience, then intention is irrelevant and when intention falls away then it also becomes unnecessary to discuss content. In this way, all 'media operations are in effect desocialised; they are simply physical events in an abstracted sensorium, and are distinguishable only by their variable sense ratios' (Williams 2003: 130). This is a significant construction in so far as it paves the way for the kinds of quantitative and mathematical models which have begun to dominate the discussion of the internet (see discussion in Part One).

Thus it is precisely the features of McLuhan's account that from the point of view of the modern sociology of technology are fundamental flaws, that make McLuhanism as a perspective so attractive to theorists of the internet as a technology. McLuhan's commitment to a uniformity of characteristics between media and technology warrants the disregard of the different nature of the experiences of those who define themselves as audience-producers as against those whose use of the internet is the use of a tool. It allows a further desocialization of the internet into its manifest features and architecture. This substantiates the construction of the internet as an egalitarian space, where egalitarian is read off as lacking a structure of roles and different subject positions, for it privileges the technical facts of the internet over the social arrangements which develop around and through those facts. As we will see later, the technical fact of an occlusion between the roles of consumer and producer has become the fulcrum of attempts to exert control over cyberspace.

Finally, McLuhanism warrants the utopian strand of theorizing around the internet by rendering invisible the operation of power within the field. The internet truly appears as a bright global village in McLuhan's flat world of uniform effects and occluded agency. McLuhan's determinism, then, circumvents the whole question of the political power relations around the internet. These problems were anticipated by Raymond Williams, who argues:

If the effect of the medium is the same, whoever controls or uses it, and whatever apparent content he may try to insert, then we can forget ordinary political and cultural argument and let the technology run itself. It is hardly surprising that this conclusion has been welcomed by the 'media-men' of the existing institutions. It gives the gloss of avant-garde theory to the crudest versions of their existing interest and practices, and assigns all their critics to pre-electronic irrelevance.

(Williams 2003: 131)

This then is a concrete example of the operation of what Bourdieu has termed the force of the 'pre-constructed' or 'prenotions' (Bourdieu *et al.* 1991: 13–15) operating within an academic discipline. In theoretically bolstering the utopian and levelling claims made in relation to the internet, the McLuhanite strand directs the academic imagination to questions of agency in a way that privileges technical features and therefore solutions.

As noted above, however, although the McLuhanite problematic has achieved wide currency in cyber-theory, it, along with technological determinism more generally, has fared less well in the field as a whole. The major direction of the sociology of technology has been towards positions which emphasize the social nature of technology, to which we now turn.

Social constructionism

Social constructivist approaches have developed in response to and away from the central premises of both material and substantivist determinism. For constructivists, technology's 'effects' can neither be read off from its form or from a logic of efficiency or other technical discourse. Rather, technologies need to be understood as possibilities that congeal in particular socially determined circumstances. As Feenberg explains:

Constructivists argue that many paths lead out from the first forms of new technology. Some are well trodden while others are quickly deserted ... there are always viable technical alternatives that might have been developed in place of the successful one. The difference lies not so much in the superior efficiency of the successful designs, as in a variety of local circumstances that differentiate otherwise comparable artefacts. Like other institutions, artefacts succeed where they find support in the social environment.

(Feenberg 1999: 10)

Thus, for constructivism, the emphasis is not on the technology and its properties but rather on the forms of technical action that particular 'things' embody and the ways in which these actions are established. As Langdon Winner writes: 'The things we call "technologies" are ways of building order in our world. Many technical devices and systems are important in ordering human activity' (Winner 1980: 30). As such constructivism is concerned to understand how different designs come to embody and act for certain influential groups. The example most frequently cited is Pinch and Bijker's (1987) explanation of the development of the safety bicycle. In the beginning two competing designs, the high front wheel 'penny farthing' cycle and the equal wheeled safety bicycle, were both manufactured and in circulation. The fact that the modern bicycle is the safety bicycle and the penny farthing is a museum curio is, they argue, down to the presence of a variety of actors in the scene and the dynamics of their interactions. The fact that women cyclists had particular problems with the high wheeler (i.e. it was seen as a potential affront to modesty, there were safety concerns at a time when women were understood as more fragile than men) is used to good advantage in cementing a definition of the cycle which excludes the high wheeler. Once a successful conversion has been performed – that is to say, once a definition of a technology is fully in place – then all subsequent examples of this particular technology must conform to the 'code' laid down. Thus in order for a particular bicycle to be regarded as an *acceptable* bicycle, it must have this orientation to safety. A non-safety bicycle is no longer an *alternative* bicycle, it is instead an *inadequate* bicycle. The high wheeler, although it could have emerged as the 'more' adequate bicycle if the code that had been triumphant had been speed or sport, is therefore not an adequate bicycle when the code dictates safety. The key point to take from this, then, is that it is a direct contradiction of the substantivist position and a particular blow for the stance taken by Ellul. The example of the bicycle clearly demonstrates that 'efficiency' is not an external property that can be brought to bear on the decision to develop technology or to adopt an available design, but is instead co-created along with the technology itself.

In constructionism, then, the objects themselves, technologies, texts, nature, are devoid of meaning in their own right. Meaning, and from meaning practice, is a social process that attends the development and uptake of the object. Thus these perspectives are socially deterministic in so far as only the social has any power. Between the two poles of social and technological determinism, however, lies our final perspective, actor-network theory, which rejects both positions.

Actor-network theory – radical relationality

The other approaches considered here take as their starting point that people and objects have given attributes, whether inherent or constructed, and are thereby distinct from each other. It is this distinctive identity that allows things and actors to enter into relation with each other. Actor-network theory (ANT) rejects this. For ANT the key methodological commitment is to what John Law calls radical relationality: '[n]othing that enters into relations has fixed significance or attributes in and of itself. Instead the attributes of any particular element in the system, any particular node in the network, are entirely defined in relation to other elements in the system, to other nodes in the network' (Law 2000: 4). For ANT, then, nothing is ontologically special, or sociologically different, whether that be technologies, people, social settings or power relations. In ANT 'the nabobs of this world are powerful ... But ... they are no different in kind sociologically to the wretched of the earth ...

Napoleons are no different in kind to small-time hustlers, and IBMs to whelk stalls' (Law 1992: 1–2).

Actor-network theory is discussed as a perspective in greater detail in Part One and I do not want to recapitulate that discussion here so much as to draw attention to some features of ANT that particularly bear on technology studies. Although ANT is not unitary as a perspective, as evidenced by the often bewildering array of terminology in circulation within the field, some generalizations can be drawn. First, there is the role of heterogeneous networks. For ANT the social is nothing other than 'patterned networks of heterogeneous materials'. Any given social situation or artefact is not only a product of a process of 'engineering' these materials into a particular form, but also composed of these materials. Thus, to use an everyday example, having a drink with a friend in a pub is an interaction formed by two or more people, alcoholic and non-alcoholic beverages, glasses, furniture, a location, the entrepreneurial spirit of the bar owner, the bar tender, money, and so on. Moreover, each of these elements are themselves network effects: money, for example, is an effect of the actions of chancellors, world banks, social custom around ownership and also around exchange, metals, paper and inks, machines for manufacturing coins and notes, and so on. Any social situation then, or any object, is for ANT composed of these elements and none is decisive in forming the nature of the encounter *in itself.* This is not, however, to say that in particular social situations some element of the network does not become determining, some technology which requires that people act in certain ways towards it, or some individual person who becomes more of a Napoleon than a wretch, but that this is, first, an effect of the network and, second, an empirical question which needs to be demonstrated in each particular circumstance in relation to each network component. The power of a technology or a Napoleon is not necessarily transferable from one network to another.

Such a perspective is analytically too cumbersome for everyday life, and in terms of practical activity we tend to refer to networks as single actors. Although we are aware that our computers are assemblages of bits and pieces of technologies, software and human interactions, viruses, codes, emails, text documents, etc., it does not prevent us from exclaiming that the 'computer' does not work. Likewise, we may be aware that our bank is composed of people, and computers, and software, and money, and papers, pens, offices, phone lines, and so on, but in real life we will mostly blame 'the bank' if our direct debits do not go out on time. Why is this? Actor-network theory explains it in terms of 'punctualization' and 'resourcing', the processes by which networks become actors through simplification. When a particular network pattern is frequently performed it is 'punctualized', the network disappears from view to be replaced with the action itself or an apparent single author of the action.

This punctualization thereafter acts as a resource for further conversions, what Latour refers to as 'translations', which is when a particular network effect comes to stand for the network as a whole, and a particular definition of the object or social situation comes to be 'locked in' (2005: 108). Actor-network theory has been particularly interested in exploring what makes some attempted translations more successful than others, and in particular what network effects produce 'durability', the universalizing of the translation that is necessary if it is to be a success. It is in respect of the central role of durability that ANT is ideally positioned to occupy an important place in communications theory and sociologies of communications, for, of the four dimensions of durability which Law identifies, the two most significant are those that are tied to communications media of some form. For ANT a stable network is held together by stable materials, thus the greater the longevity of the materials of the network, the greater the scope of the network as a whole. This would seem to be a mere recapitulation of Innis's position were it not for the fact that, as Law further points out, the durability of materials is itself a network effect, as well as resource from which networks can be constructed (1992: 6).

Universalizing a network also requires mobility, a means by which that network or network effect can act at a distance, and this secondary dimension thus emphasizes the role of materials and processes of communication over space. Of course, it would be over-egging the pudding to understand mobility effects as entirely grounded in the means of communication over distance, and Law moderates this apparent media-centrism with an equal emphasis on what Latour has called 'centres of translation'. As Latour explains, a 'translation' is 'a relation that does not transport causality but induces two mediators into coexisting. If some causality appears to be transported in a predictable and routine way, then it's the proof that other mediators have been put in place to render such a displacement smooth and predictable' (2005: 108). Centres of translation are stable arenas whether physical, intellectual or institutional, which have achieved sufficient enrolment, or acceptance, to have a particularly compelling claim to achieve this displacement reliably. Centres of translation are powerful resources in the struggle to establish one network or network effect as dominant, although of course, for ANT, the centre of translation is itself an effect of network processes. Thus government statistical offices may be a centre of translation for particular constructions of social problems, but only in so far as they themselves are an effect of other networks such as bureaucracy, literacy, the state, empiricism, statistical knowledge, and so on.

In the age of the internet, the actor-network approach to technology has come more to the fore in the discipline. In part, as Chapter 1 one argues, this comes about as a result of a misidentification of actor networks and technical networks as covering the same ground. However, ANT's potential is not exhausted by this. The challenge for the sociology of technology in relation to the internet is to examine how far theories of technology can be applied to *communications* technologies, which may involve a qualitative shift in emphasis (Rogers 1986). Communications technologies are a liminal case, crossing social arenas. If we consider Habermas's typology of social actions, and the central division of communicative and instrumental action, this can more easily be seen. Technologies are discursively tied in our society to instrumental and rational ends. However, communicative technologies occupy a different position, in so far as they straddle this divide; they are both orientated to instrumental ends and the end of human understanding and cultural meaning. The next chapter considers how emergent perspectives in the sociology of technology bring to the fore themes and methods in the sociology of technology that have previously been latent and can be used to better account for communications technologies.

Note

1. Marx himself uses the term 'conditions' rather than 'determines' (Marx 1970: Preface).

11 *The* **sociology** *of* **technology** *and the* **internet: emergent perspectives**

The previous chapter outlined the range of theories within the field of technology studies in sociology and illustrated the reasons why internet theorists have adopted technological theories which are at such a remove from the intellectual zeitgeist in SOT studies. In concluding the previous chapter I considered the distinction between technologies and communicative technologies. This chapter examines this issue in more detail, looking at theories of technology which emphasize specifically communicative elements. These theories are drawn from the margins of sociology and, as a result, are seldom emphasized in more textbook-based accounts of the internet and new media. However, it is my contention here that they can offer a means of decentring an increasingly stale structuring dichotomy between technologies and agency which has led to the Balkanization of SOT as a subject area. I begin with an outline of an application of actor-network theory.

Actor-networks and technologies

One of the chief objections to using ANT is its unwieldiness. The methodological challenge presented by employing constructionist methodologies is not to be understated and ANT is a particularly high-investment method. It could be argued that the internet, as a vast system of linkages, nodes and networks, is not readily amenable to actor-network analysis. However, this argument itself makes little sense from a constructionist point of view. That we understand the internet as a 'thing', however complex, is a construction, in ANT terms a network effect in itself. The primary question which ANT would foreground would be, how does the internet come to be a thing in the first place? It is here perhaps that we can see the greatest utility for ANT in so far as the actor-network point of view is a way of disintegrating the object and rendering it ontologically strange, allowing us to gain analytical purchase on what makes it what it is. This point is raised by Castells, who regards constructivism as a particularly useful position in this context: 'The internet is a particularly malleable technology, susceptible of being deeply modified by its social practice, and leading to a whole range of potential social outcomes – to be discovered by experience and not proclaimed beforehand' (Castells 2001: 5). In the same sense ANT is particularly useful for uncovering processes at work because the internet is not yet formed, not yet translated, and thus these processes are readily visible. Thus ANT highlights as a *topic* what other theories of technology use as a *resource*, namely the simultaneous complexity and singularity of the internet. The question becomes, how does the internet come to be singular?

The easiest approach to understanding this phenomenon from an ANT perspective is through the use of an example, and I will here take the case of intellectual property rights. Intellectual property is a pivotal issue for the internet at the moment. In Part Two I pointed to the role of the web as a means of distributing cultural goods. Here I argued that the dominance of the commercial centre of the web, and the creation of the centre as a commercial space, was premised on the use of the internet to distribute existing content by large-scale media concerns in the early days of the web's development. The fact of being first on the scene with existing content provides a significant advantage to these concerns in achieving dominance within this new sphere. The leveraging of brand-name recognition, tapping into existing mass media agendas of interest and concern, and so on, all allow larger-scale commercial media providers to become major players in the online arena.

However the use of the internet as a medium of distribution is a double-edged sword. As Vaidhyanathan explains, 'the digital moment has ... collapsed the distinctions among three formerly distinct processes: gaining access to a work; using a work; and copying a work' (2004: 152–3). The ease with which informational products can be copied and distributed is increased by distribution over the internet in so far as each 'use' is also a 'copy' of the product, for the file accessed is downloaded to the terminal. Companies attempting to use electronic distribution to create or further a 'just-in-time' or 'content-on-demand' model of sales have run into the problem that it is equally easy for others to provide free of charge what they wish to sell for profit. Of course, the widespread copying of cultural goods was not invented with the internet. Copying of audio music tapes and compact discs was seen as a key problem for the record industry in the 1980s and 1990s, for example. However, the opportunity for mass copying for profit that the internet provides is new. For this reason the question of intellectual property rights has come to be a central area of contention.

The problem, to oversimplify greatly, is the circumstances under which existing laws can be applied to the situation. Vaidhyanathan points out that the existing body of law

> was designed to regulate only copying. It was not supposed to regulate one's rights to read or share. But now that the distinctions among accessing, using, and copying have collapsed, copyright policy makers have found themselves faced with what seems to be a difficult choice: either relinquish some control over copying or expand copyright to regulate access and use.
>
> (Vaidhyanathan 2004: 152–3)

Laurence Lessig (2001, 2004) explains the situation similarly as the collapse of boundaries. Whereas use of content was not regulated before, the fact that use or reception, unlike broadcasting, creates an actual additional copy of a given product means that the scope of the law is increased to include use. When we buy a book we are free to read it as many times as we like, quote from it, burn it, resell it. What we are not free to do is create another copy and sell that. It is the creation of another copy that extends the power of law into use, creating a dilemma for policy makers and producers.

However, such legalistic and technical models tend rather to view the internet as fate. When legal scholars discuss the issue of intellectual property it is from the point of view of a problem that must be solved. Thus when Lessig speaks of the 'accidental feature of copyright law that triggers its application upon there being a copy' (2004: 144) and the fact that 'before the internet, reading did not trigger the application of copyright law' (2004: 145), what seems to be invoked is the idea of an alien technology which has somehow to be absorbed into existing social arrangements. It is in this sense that we can talk of the internet's 'impact' on the legal arrangements which govern its use. However, in viewing the matter in this light we are already accepting as given features which ANT would regard as worth investigating. Thus the fact that the web works by making a copy is not an accidental attribute of the web but a designed feature. The fact that these technical features further imply a particular value judgement, i.e. that because the internet makes a copy copyright law must be applied, also goes without question in this account. This is odd because there are plenty of laws and statutes that exist uneasily in the annals of law which are not applied to current circumstances. There are plenty of anachronistic laws. It is a matter of urban legend in Britain, for example, that an Englishman in Chester may kill a Welshman found in the city walls after midnight, provided he uses a bow and arrow. This does not necessarily mean that it is legal in the current sense to do so. Likewise one UK city is still officially at war with the Soviet Union. Examples like these are not illustrative of the idiosyncrasies of the British so much as they point to the fact that law is *law in use*. The anachronistic and irrelevant elements tend simply to fall into obscurity and exist only as curiosities. When we recover a previously disregarded law from obsolescence, or allow a law to become obsolete it is not because the law demands it, but because actors achieve it. Thus understanding the debate over intellectual property as primarily a matter of updating law cuts off debate at precisely the point it becomes interesting. How, then, does the internet come to be an entity to which law can be applied?

From an ANT perspective intellectual copyright can be understood as a centre of translation. Centres of translation function to 'trace' a network, mobilizing and coordinating relationships within it and directing action towards network goals (see above for discussion). Consider, for example, the case of technical permissions. Lessig (2004) has argued that the most important 'effect' of electronic delivery on copyright law is to change the emphasis from law to control. He cites the example of the technical permissions granted to users of electronic copies, in this case an eBook reader. The software used to read and present eBooks grants permissions, for example the permission to print or copy a given number of text selections in a given period or to have the book read aloud to you. These 'permissions' are, from Lessig's point of view, euphemisms for 'controls': it is not that if you violate the permissions you will be punished, but that it is not possible to violate these permissions, the code of the software will not allow it (Lessig 2004: 151–2). In this sense, technologies like these involve a shift from law to code, from contract to control.

The bypassing of the law (contract) in favour of control (technology) considered from a constructionist point of view is a fairly clear example of the 'shifting out' of a function from law to technology, from people to things. The network of intellectual copyright shifts out policing of its rules from people to code. In so doing, however, as Lessig further points out, the network's scope is increased (2004: 139), which is another way of saying that further heterogeneous elements are enrolled into it. Books and cultural works which were previously not included under the remit of copyright law can be become included or re-included. Thus the re-presentation of works whose copyright protection has elapsed, books whose authors have been dead for a long enough period to mean that their works pass into the public domain, can technically be reincorporated into the network, benefiting from the same technical protection as new works by living authors by virtue of the code. Thus Lessig cites the example of an eBook of *Alice's Adventures in Wonderland*, a work which, although in the public domain, is subject to controls over copying and reading aloud through the code of the eBook (2004: 152). Whilst this appears to be an 'accidental effect' of technical affordances, in reality it is a 'network effect' of network affordances. The enrolment of software, and software producers, comes about through the need to protect intellectual property but in so doing alters, and coincidently enlarges, the scope of the term 'intellectual property', from the legally enforceable to the technically regulable.

This is characteristic of the dynamic as a whole; each alliance that is made is an alliance not with one element, but with a network of elements. With the likelihood of intellectual property infractions being met with punishment being perceived as low, companies have been forced into 'show trials' of individual miscreants which are hoped to then deter others. This, however, involves a new group of agencies in the policing and detection of this crime. Thus the regulation of offences enrols, albeit unwillingly, internet service providers, universities and workplaces that provide internet access in so far as the shifting out of responsibility for policing to them positions them as actors within the network. This also involves the interweaving of legal standards of proof and evidence into the complex network as a structuring element. When we broaden the canvas, we can clearly see that regulation of a global medium is of little practical import when conducted on a national scale. International regulation, however, requires international agreements to be reached, and with them the means of enforcement. From this the network expands further to include international agencies, such as the World Trade Organization. Moreover, a greater range of actors becomes incorporated in the logic of intellectual property protection. Software producers must anticipate and react to the activities of those who will seek to circumvent the controls they put in place, and this in turn enrols hackers as part of the problematic. Thus whereas hackers once figured in public discourse as *Matrix*-style war gamers hacking government secrets (Chandler 1996) they are positioned within this network, admittedly as the 'enemy', in the role of pirates and ruthless businessmen. Finally, the need and ability to regulate use brings together distributors of content online into an alliance. The need to protect online content from the activities of hackers and crackers creates a common purpose for purveyors of music, film, books, art, graphic designs, typesetters, database writers, web designers, and indeed any artist in any medium. This sets up a set of equivalencies. All content is content, all information is information. The point at which law becomes applied is no longer to individual cases of property and products but to an abstract entity which includes more than the sum of the original definitions.

In this sense, then, intellectual copyright acts to create a network of networks. The legal debates can be understood not as a first principle from which action to regulate the internet proceeds, but as part of an ongoing and not yet complete or 'black-boxed' process of arranging the parts. In the process, though, the *technical* fact of connection made possible by the internet is raised to a *social* fact, the *capacity* to link up the world becomes a *necessity* to link up the world. What this means for the way we understand the internet as a technology is that it disorders our common sense of the order of procession. Whereas we understand the internet as a particular entity to which another entity, the law, can be applied, when considered from an ANT perspective, this is inappropriate. The internet may have the capacity to link people to people and institutions to institutions, but the desire to police a new arena for cultural goods (itself a contingent definition of the internet (see Part Three)) is what creates the 'will to connection'. Likewise, whereas globalization and the shrinking technological world of the internet is understood as an precondition of intellectual property, from an ANT perspective it is an outcome of those processes.

As we have seen, then, an ANT perspective gives a way around the determinism implied by seeing the internet's or the law's capacities as primary in fuelling social change. From the perspective of ANT the internet becomes a 'thing' through these processes of regulation and use. However, whilst a case can be made for seeing intellectual property as one centre of translation, the problem with leaving the story at this point is that ANT does not give us reasons for regarding any centre as particularly important. As a method it provides tools of description or re-description but not any particular warrant for using them in concrete cases.

Thus in order to develop the analysis further it is necessary to situate the concern for intellectual property in context. The actor-network approach, as I have pointed out elsewhere (see Chapter 1), analytically depends on a network being formed in opposition to other competing networks. Alliances created by intellectual property as a locus of concern or centre of translation have been taken up and analysed in detail in autonomist critique of communications technologies. Although clearly actor-network theory and Marxian autonomism share very different views of the social, they are not as widely distributed on the theoretical spectrum as might be imagined.

Both approaches see power not as a pre-given attribute but as created through action. Both understand the social as inherently heterogeneous in so far as autonomism departs from traditional interpretations of Marx which emphasized personnel – the labouring and bourgeois classes – focusing instead on capital as the embodiment of two contradictory impulses, those towards heterogeneity and those towards control. This heterogeneity is premised on conflicts within capital which, crucially, for autonomists never resolve themselves. Thus in a sense autonomism goes further than ANT, for whilst ANT understands networks as eventually achieving a stability, for autonomism this resolution never comes. The remainder of this chapter will be given over to an exploration of the contribution of this perspective to understanding communications technologies, expanding upon the issue of intellectual property as an exemplar.

Autonomism and the information society

As Nick Dyer-Witheford has pointed out, this key development in thinking about the status of communications technologies in sociological theorizing comes about as a reaction to what are termed 'information society' theses. The 1950s and 1960s saw the rise of instrumentalist theories which posited the arrival of a new form of social configured around the production and dissemination of information. The chief proponents of this viewpoint, Daniel Bell (1973), Peter Drucker (1969) and their popularizers, have come to be known as the first wave of information society theorists, the first to recognize that new information technologies occupied a potentially unique position in history. For information society (IS) theorists, new information technologies provided the material basis for the rise of a new kind of economy, the knowledge economy, which would lead to the end of both labour and capital as the main sources of production. In the wake of the knowledge economy, Bell, for example, foresaw the rise of a professional class, and the reshaping of the working class as a result of the automation of manual labour and the rise in living standards it produced. Bell's work was followed by a number of more populist accounts, of which Alvin's Toffler's *The Third Wave* (1980) and John Naisbitt's *Megatrends* (1982) have proved durable. Although these analyses were based on an extrapolation from the apparent trajectory of economic development in the USA, itself informed by rivalry with Japan, where investment in information technology (IT) and high-tech production had formed the basis of state policy, the core of the IS argument is that the new economy was global in scope. New information technologies not only implied a new ideological formation, but further allowed for integration at the level of the nation state by eroding ideological difference or by promoting conditions in which ideology is no longer the most relevant axis of tension in the modern world (Bell 1973; Fukuyama 1992).

This latter thesis, known as the end of ideology thesis, developed in part as a response to the perception that the information society meant the 'death of Marxism' and a resolution of the chief axis of tension in post-war politics. For many mid-twentieth-century intellectuals, post-war affluence and calm in the

West suggested that society had reached a pinnacle of development. Generalized affluence, collective bargaining and the rise of the welfare state in the industrial West combined with a new renaissance of knowledge on the back of large-scale government investment in education and new scientific breakthroughs which resulted from wartime investment in technological research. Liberal capitalism came to be understood as the apex of human development to which other 'underdeveloped' societies would aspire and to which estate they would eventually succeed. As a result, neither international nor national conflicts would abide long. For these theorists, Marxism as a revolutionary force was dead because the object and process of its struggle, class and class interest, was vanquished in favour of a flat plane of power. However, as Dyer-Witheford explains:

> Few social theories have ... had the misfortune to have been so swiftly discredited as the 'end of ideology' thesis. Within a matter of years the appearance of peaceful, passionless capitalist stability was spectacularly contradicted by the upsurge of domestic and international dissent in the late 1960s and early 1970s. Industrial society – the unsurpassable pinnacle of modernity, prosperity and technological advance – went into paroxysm, its military machine stalled in the jungles of Vietnam; its urban ghettos burning through successive summers, its huge automobile factories paralysed by labour conflict; its university campuses in rebellion, its culture subverted by the music, drugs, and politics of youth revolt.
>
> (Dyer-Witheford 1999: 17)

The attempt to explain how and why the perceived promise of the new era had not materialized led theorists such as Bell to revise their earlier prognoses. For Bell and his counterparts these symptoms of malaise could be explained as the birth pains of the new world order, a post-industrial society whose axiom was information and knowledge (Dyer-Witheford 1999: 17). The new information industries provided the foundation for the preservation of the new affluent classless society. In the writings of Bell, and more notably of Toffler, an information society meant the obsolescence of class. As information became the means of production so all workers would share equally in the ownership of it, in so far as each worker owned and contributed his or her own information. The ease with which goods could be disseminated allowed for a general reduction of prices, in turn allowing greater levels of participatory consumption. As information industries do not require the physical attendance of a mass workforce, so work would be shifted out to the home, and small artisanal communities would become the norm. As a result, the level of social integration would increase, people would no longer be gathered in mass ghettos but would live in smaller *Gemeinschaft*-type communities. As a further corollary, endemic social problems would become less widespread. The rise in participatory consumption and higher standards of living would result in a fall in crime. Greater emphasis on education as a means of developing the informational infrastructure would mean greater investment in children, who as a result would be better socialized.

From the point of view of Marxism, this transformation reads as a form of 'Marxism against Marx' (Dyer-Witheford 1999: 26), in so far as changes in the economic-technological base are regarded as setting the form of life within that society. Moreover, as I pointed out in the Introduction to this book, this is a form of anti-Marxist socialism in which socialist dreams and promises are realized through the changing forms of capital.

The reaction to this position came, unsurprisingly, largely from Marxian-inspired writers who were keen to analyse the dynamics of this new labour. Beginning with Braverman's analysis of the 'degradation of labour' (1974) under capital, and moving on through the work of David Noble (1986) into the effects of computerization and Zuboff's analysis of work in the age of 'smart machines' (1988), the idea that this new style of information work brings about a qualitative shift away from exploitation and towards equality has been extensively criticized. In their writings, the utopian visions of information work put forward by the information society theorists come to appear thin indeed. A second strand of critique, inspired by the work of the Frankfurt school, has been equally influential, if equally disheartening in conclusions. The picture that emerges from the critique of the culture industries is a relentlessly bleak vision of cultural domination in which the information/cultural industries are pivotal in the subordination of the social to the imperatives of capital. In the work of Schiller (1996), Mosco (1989), Webster and Robins (1986), Robins and Webster (1999) and Garnham (1979), large-scale information merchants act to restrict the supply of information, disseminate corporate propaganda, and promote false needs which can only be satisfied through consumption and form the basis of cultural domination by the commercial ethos.

However, the problem with such accounts as these is that they tend merely to depict the dynamics of information production as a continuation of the prior social order by other means. As this translates into more mainstream discourse, it appears as an injunction to dispense with social privilege. Rifkin, for example, argues that:

> We are being swept up into a powerful new technology revolution that offers the promise of a great social transformation, unlike any in history. The new high-technology revolution could mean fewer hours of work and greater benefits for millions. For the first time in modern history, large numbers of people could be liberated from long hours of labour in the formal marketplace, to be free to pursue leisure-time activities. The same technological forces could, however, just as easily lead to growing unemployment and a global depression.
>
> (Rifkin 1995: 13)

For Rifkin, the latter possibility is an outgrowth of the unequal distribution of benefits around the globe. For as long as this inequality remains, the gains of the information society cannot be realized. This understanding, that the gains are concrete but currently not in evidence, is made more explicit by Perelman, who argues 'the existence of classes conflicts with the requirements of an information age. In other words, as long as we permit the existing class structure to remain in place, we will never be able to enjoy the promise of an information age' (1998: 33). For traditional Marxian theorists, then, class deforms the new social order of information. Class appears either as the helpless product of economic forces, blown 'hither and yon' by changes in the base, or as a hangover from the past, a desiccated ghost which haunts its own wake.

Autonomism takes a rather different line, offering an until recently controversial reading of Marx in which labour, rather than capital, is the active subject. For autonomists, labour is the creative force of history, a force which capital attempts to incorporate through successive compositions of the productive activity. For capital, its dependence on labour as the source of creativity and development drives it to attempt to domesticate labour, and to emancipate the machinery of capital from it. As Dyer-Witheford notes:

> In *Capital* Marx had observed that the initial impetus for capital's intensifying use of industrial machinery came from proletarian move-ments' demanding the shortening of the working day. Building on this, the autonomists argued that capital does not unfold according to a self contained logic, spinning technologies and organizations out of its own body. Rather, it is driven by the need to forestall, co-opt, and defeat the 'other' that is simultaneously indispensable and inimical to its existence.
> (Dyer-Witheford 1999: 66–7)

Capital's need to control production/human activity is here figured as the driving force of innovation and of capital's development. The nature of capital is understood to be expansion and change; it is not a static institution, but a configuration of 'power in motion'. However, the incorporation of labour can only ever be partial, as capital requires its creativity in order to function, a creativity that is lost when labour becomes fully incorporated. This central contradiction of capital, the need to expand and domesticate whilst preserving labour, has greater implications as we move into the modern globalized, electronic era. Capital in its network form, as discussed in Chapter 2, opens out onto the new spaces that it subsumes, not as a colonizing or annexing force, something that imposes its own forms on the new spaces, but as one that includes them, a 'benevolent welcoming of difference' within the context of expansion (Terranova 2004: 62).

Thus, to recap, the central premises of the autonomist approach are, first, the understanding that capital is reactive to labour, not vice versa; second, a decoupling of capital as a totality, an institution with needs, which autonomism accepts in so far as it views capital as a logic of practice, from the idea of capital as a monolithic and enduring form which relates to this institution, which is rejected; third, an understanding that capital's existence is predicated on expansion, which is not a new reading of Marx; but, fourth, that this expansion takes the form of incorporation of difference, and reconstitution of the labouring class, which is a different emphasis.

Autonomism could have remained an obscure rereading of Marx, known and used only by Marxist scholars, had it not been for the apparent fit between its predictions and premises and our current attempts to understand the dynamics of the globalizing world. The case of autonomism deftly demonstrates the power of Victor Hugo's 'idea whose time has come'. The core development in autonomist thinking that brings about this fit is the emphasis placed on the notion of the socialized worker and the social factory, particularly as popularized in the work of Hardt and Negri. For these authors, capital's inherent need to expand has caused it to breach the boundaries of the physical factory, spreading out to form a wider 'factory without walls', which encompasses all aspects of social and communal life. In the social factory, all arenas are subjugated to the logic of capital, namely productivity and profit generation. Schooling aims to make a productive subject, classes are oriented to acquiring work skills, or to socializing children into useful consumers; the modern family, as Mariarosa Dalla Costa and Selma James (1975) noted, is orientated to the reproduction of labour power through the physical reproduction of workers; likewise the family and the home is the core site of consumption, and children are produced as consuming subjects rather than productive ones, until they are of an age to take their place as workers. The logic of capital is therefore to annihilate distinctions between work as productive, and work as consumptive activity. As Negri puts it, 'productive labour is now that which produces society' (cited in Dyer-Witheford 1999: 81). The expansion of the social factory, however, also serves to equally generalize opposition to capital. The conflict between the logic of capital and the practices of the 'multitude' (see p. 43) is refracted into a multiplicity of points. 'Contestation snakes through homes, schools, universities, hospitals and the media … In the newly socialized space of capital … each apparently independent location replicates the fundamental antagonism that informs the entire structure – capital's insistence that time-life be subordinated to profit' (Dyer-Witheford 1999: 82).

This new understanding of the operation of capital has, in the past couple of decades, made a significant impact on a variety of intellectual fields, both within and without the academy. Italian autonomism and particularly Hardt and Negri's work on empire and the nature of the multitude has been brought to centre stage through its adoption within the discourse of the anti-globalization movements of the late twentieth and early twenty-first centuries. Within the academy, and especially in social and political science, there has been a marked shift from the use of postmodern theorists, especially Baudrillard, to an embrace of the ideas of critical psychiatrists Giles Deleuze and Felix Guattari, whose work is linked into the autonomist tradition. Sociology is beginning to awaken to the possibilities of the approach, and in particular theorists of media and technologies have found a rich vein of new concepts to manage the emergent fields of globalization and media, and the dynamics of information in the new media age.

For our purposes, one of the key elements of this account is the role of communications and media in the social factory. According to Negri, the complexity of the social factory, the fact that, unlike the original factory, it is no longer tied to a physically accessible location; the broad-ranging nature and constantly shifting character of the struggle; and the core problem for capital that the means of production resides in a place not accessible to enclosure – the heads of the workers – places communication and information centre stage in the newly configured conflict between capital's logic and the multitude. For Negri, 'communication is to the socialized worker as the wage relation was to the mass worker' (Negri 1989: 118), the core site of strategic struggle to defend practice against the incursion of capital. Hardt and Negri argue that in a society characterized by the factory without walls, communicative skills are a prerequisite of everyday life, in addition to being the means of generating profit (2000: 289–94). Whereas traditional Marxian analysts have understood information and media as being essentially a one-way flow of propaganda from corporate capital to the consumer, autonomism sees the dynamics of information as far more diffuse and, of course, this diffuseness develops out of the reaction and counter-reactions within capital. Fordism, the attempt to control labour through standardization, automation and concentration of labour in geographically distinct sites, can be understood as a reaction to militant labour, an attempt to incorporate and domesticate labour through de-skilling and recomposition of human *action* as micro-divisions of *activity*. However, this recomposition of the working class reconstitutes class militancy in the form of the mass union. This in turn creates a greater potential for unions to act as a single unit with unitary interests, as a consequence of the affinity between labour in various locations and industries. Attempts to pre-empt this led to Keynesianism and the collective contract, which in turn increases the price of labour in Western societies (see Dyer-Witheford 1999). As a result, capital flees to the less expensive areas of the globe, and Western labour is in turn reconfigured as a service class. In the process, labour in the West has been recomposed as a communicative, coordinating class. Its strength and skills reside in its manipulation of symbolic data, skills which can be harnessed to the interests of capital or, the autonomists argue, double-back to confront and challenge capital. Thus capital's attempts to assert control and incorporate all activity within its frames of reference are mirrored by potential forms of resistance.

The modern 'information society' then, for autonomists, is a product of capital's ongoing war with labour, a war in which, contra Noble, both sides are armed. Communication and information are the current terrain and resources of this guerrilla warfare, a terrain selected by the outcome of previous bitter engagements. Capital's imperative at this time is thus to constrain information within its own channels and to control the nature and forms of cooperation and communication. Whereas traditional Marxian models would understand this need to control information as a means of bridling radicalism, for autonomism no such conspiratorial implications can be drawn. Capital's attempts to control information are not related to the content of communication (propaganda, agitprop, intelligence, counter-intelligence, and so on) but to its value. Jodi Dean (2004) explains this particularly well. In a society in which communication has come to behave as an economic form in itself, there is a concomitant transformation in its nature:

> Messages are contributions to circulating content – not actions to elicit responses. Differently put, the exchange value of messages overtakes their use value … Uncoupled from contexts of action and application – as on the Web or in print and broadcast media – the message is simply part of a circulating data stream. Its particular content is irrelevant. Who sent it is irrelevant. Who receives it is irrelevant … Any particular contribution remains secondary to the fact of circulation.

> (Dean 2004: 273–4)

The logic of capital as the extraction of value and information is the new source of value. Thus, argues Negri, capital attempts to control information in the interests of generating profit:

> Capital must ... appropriate communication. It must expropriate the community and superimpose itself on the autonomous capability of manufacturing knowledge, reducing such knowledge to the mere means of every undertaking of the socialised worker. This is the form which expropriation takes in advanced capitalism.
>
> (Negri 1989: 116)

The key imperative, therefore, is to constrain and enclose the means of production, through the enclosure of the means of *intellectual* production. For Porat, 'information is data that have been sorted and communicated' (cited in Perelman 1998: 18). For Negri, information is expropriated communication, the inert product of communication and the means of extracting value from human mutuality and cooperation. Such a bleak vision, wherein our very attempts to relate to each other are advanced only in so far as they form a reserve of profit for capital is, however, only half the story. As Dyer-Witheford (1999) points out, the irony of the development of the internet is that an era regarded as the epitome of free-market capital saw the growth and development of the first mass media born out of state-sponsored research and developed as a result of voluntary cooperation and self-organization. The internet here figures as an example of unharnessed creativity, an open space within capital which forms an arena potentially oppositional to it. This is not merely that the internet can be used effectively as a source of resistance to capital – acting as a medium of communication to coordinate and intensify radical opposition – but further that the mere fact of such unregulated mutual endeavours and the possibility of the creation of knowledge outside the channels controlled by and in the interest of capital represents a challenge to it.

Of course such a challenge is unlikely to go unanswered. For Shoshana Zuboff, an 'information economy requires ... a new social contract derived from a new moral vision' (Zuboff 1993, cited in Perelman 1998: 132). This new social vision very quickly emerged. In 1994 the publication of 'Cyberspace and the American dream: a Magna Carta for the knowledge age' offered the outlines of such a contract. For the authors, including Ester Dyson, George Gilder and Alvin Toffler, cyberspace represented 'the central event of the 20th century ... the overthrow of matter ... a bioelectronic frontier [where] exploration can be civilization's truest, highest calling' (cited in Dyer-Witheford 1999: 34). The recommendations of the group were that the information infrastructure should be owned by an unregulated private monopoly, tax breaks should be established for information-orientated companies and the federal government regulation structure should be dismantled, a recommendation that was realized in the 1996 telecommunications bill (Dyer-Witheford 1999: 34–5). The core to the development of cyberspace was, they argued, firm support for intellectual property rights. Since that time we have, autonomists would argue, seen progressive attempts at enclosure and appropriation of the internet as a resource. Beginning with moral panics over internet pornography, fraud and cyber crime (Cavanagh 2002) and moving on through fears over the use of the internet by terrorists, the public have been enjoined to applaud the gradual and progressive establishment of control over the formerly free arenas of the internet. However, the establishment of control over the internet requires a great deal more than recruitment of the public will and it is in this context that autonomism emphasizes the strategic importance of intellectual copyright. It is this arena in which it is argued the real battle for control of communication will be waged, and battle is joined on the basis of attempts to extend, and resistance to, enclosure of information.

Thus the autonomist contribution to understanding the internet as a technology is to foreground the question of control not as a reaction to the development of the technology, as though the internet appeared and then had to be controlled, as in determinist positions, nor as a fait accompli in a progressive subjugation of labour as traditional Marxian positions would hold. Rather, from the perspective of autonomy, the battle for control over the internet is a counter-reaction to a reaction to a counter-reaction. As Terranova (2004) has pointed out, although the mythology of the internet gives us the legend of its development as a strategic response to the possibility of nuclear war, creating robust communication systems which could operate despite heavy infrastructural damage, the 'problem' in reality was that of finding ways to link up geographically and institutionally disparate groups. This problem was created in the first instance by the attempt to control and institutionally locate knowledge within rival commercial concerns (Stallman and Gay 2002). In a world where expertise is distributed and duplicated within different institutions, where each individual commercial concern requires an expert who does a particular function, the need to link up personnel comes to the fore. In order to assume an employment world where the internet is of any particular use, we have already to presume this distribution of expertise and the lack of professional commonality between workers located in the same physical space that is at the bottom of attempts by professionals to link up with their peers. We must also further posit institutional barriers to cooperation to which the technology is a solution. That the internet has achieved such rapid uptake is testament to the pervasiveness of this model of work. Thus the internet at its inception can be understood more appropriately as a social response to a social problem, but one which is framed by capital as a structuring structure.

In this chapter we have looked at the avenues opened up by attempts to understand the internet as a communications technology. It has been my argument that perspectives from the network sociologies provide for a renewal of the field through decentring the stale dichotomies of causality that have so far been their axis. The impact of the internet on theorizing around technology has been to bring down *some* of the barriers separating different approaches in the discipline by forcing us to recognize the mutually implicating nature of the debates. In attempting to theorize an already social communications technology, we move away from the questions of determinism and towards a view of technology as an arena where strategies of social power are contested and played out. As a result, the field of the sociology of technology has come to the fore in sociology's attempts to theorize the political and social impact of the internet.

References

Abbott, A. (1997) Of time and space: the contemporary relevance of the Chicago school, *Social Forces*, 75(4): 1149–82.

Agamben, G. (1993) *The Coming Community*, trans. M. Hardt. Minneapolis, MN: University of Minnesota Press.

Agger, B. (2004) *Speeding Up Fast Capitalism: Cultures, Jobs, Families, Schools, Bodies.* Boulder, CO: Paradigm.

Aldridge, M. (1998) The tentative hell raisers: identity and mythology in contemporary UK press journalism, *Media, Culture and Society*, 20(1): 109–27.

Anderson, B. (1991) *Imagined Communities: Reflections on the Origin and Spread of Nationalism*, 2nd edn. London: Verso.

Aspden, P. and Katz, J.E. (1997) A nation of strangers, *Communications of the ACM*, 40: 81–6.

Barabasi, A.-L. (2003) *Linked: How Everything is Connected to Everything Else and What it Means for Business, Science, and Everyday Life.* New York: Plume/Penguin.

Barber, B. (1995) *Jihad vs McWorld.* New York: Ballantine.

Barney, D. (2000) *Prometheus Wired: The Hope for Democracy in the Age of Network Technology.* Vancouver: University of British Columbia.

Barney, D. (2004) *The Network Society.* Cambridge: Polity.

Bayly, C.A. (2004) *The Birth of the Modern World, 1780–1914: Global Connections and Comparisons.* Oxford: Blackwell.

Baym, N. (1997) Interpreting soap operas and creating community: inside an electronic fan culture, in S. Kiesler (ed.) *Culture of the Internet.* Mahwah, NJ: Lawrence Erlbaum Associates.

Baym, N. (1998) The emergence of on-line community, in S. Jones (ed.) *Cybersociety 2.0: Revisiting Computer-Mediated Communication and Community.* London: Sage.

Beck, U. (1992) *Risk Society: Towards a New Modernity*, trans. M. Ritter. London: Sage.

Bell, C. and Newby, H. (1971) *Community Studies: An Introduction to the Sociology of the Local Community.* London: Allen and Unwin.

Bell, D. (1973) *The Coming of Post-Industrial Society.* New York: Basic Books.

Bimber, B. (1994) Three faces of technological determinism, in M.R. Smith and L. Marx (eds) *Does Technology Drive History: The Dilemma of Technological Determinism.* Cambridge, MA, and London: MIT Press.

Blood, R. (2002) *We've Got Blog: How Weblogs Are Changing Our Culture.* Cambridge, MA: Perseus.

Bourdieu, P. (1984) *Distinction: A Social Critique of the Judgement of Taste*, trans. R. Nice. London: Routledge. (First published Les Editions de Minuit, Paris, 1979.)

Bourdieu, P., Boltanski, L., Castel, R., Chamboredon, J.-C. and Schnapper, D. (1990) *Photography: A Middle Brow Art*, trans. S. Whiteside. Cambridge: Polity.

Bourdieu, P., Camboredon, J.-C., Passerson, J.-C. (1991) *The Craft of Sociology: Epistemological Preliminaries*, trans. R. Nice, ed. B. Krais. Berlin and New York: Walter de Gruyter. (First published Ecole des Hautes Etudes en Sciences Sociales, Paris, 1968.)

Braverman, H. (1974) *Labor and Monopoly Capital: The Degradation of Work in the Twentieth Century*. New York and London: Monthly Review Press.

Briggs, A. and Burke, P. (2002) *A Social History of the Media: From Gutenberg to the Internet*. Cambridge: Polity/Blackwell.

Bunting, M. (2001) From socialism to Starbucks: the decline of politics and the consumption of our inner self, *Renewal*, 9(2–3): 23–32, www.renewal.org.uk/issues/2001/summer/feature3.asp (accessed 29 Nov. 2006).

Burke, K. (1945) *A Grammar of Motives*. New York: Prentice-Hall.

Burkhalter, B. (1999) Reading race online: discovering racial identity in Usenet discussions, in M.A. Smith and P. Kollock (eds) *Communities in Cyberspace*. London: Routledge.

Burnett, R. and Marshall, P.D. (2003) *Web Theory: An Introduction*. London: Routledge.

Burrows, R. (2005) Sociological amnesia in an age of informational capitalism: a response to Frank Webster, *Information Communication and Society*, 8(4): 464–70.

Burrows, R. and Ellison, N. (2004) Sorting places out? The social politics of neighbourhood informatization, *Information, Communication and Society*, 7(3): 321–36.

Butler, B., Sproull, L., Kiesler, S. and Kraut, R. (forthcoming) Community effort in online groups: who does the work and why?, in S. Weisband and L. Atwater (eds) *Leadership at a Distance*. Mahwah, NJ: Laurence Erlbaum Associates. Also available at www.cs.cmu.edu/~kiesler/publications/publications.html.

Calcutt, A. (1999) *White Noise: An A–Z of the Contradictions in Cyberculture*. London: Macmillan.

Callon, M. (1986) Some elements of a sociology of translation: domestication of the scallops and the fishermen of St Brieuc Bay, in J. Law (ed.) *Power, Action and Belief: A New Sociology of Knowledge*. London: Routledge and Kegan Paul.

Carnevale, P. and Probst, T. (1997) Conflict on the internet, in S. Kiesler (ed.) *Culture of the Internet*. Mahwah, NJ: Laurence Erlbaum Associates.

Case, D.O. (2002) *Looking for Information: A Survey of Research on Information Seeking, Needs, and Behaviour*. London and New York: Academic Press/Elsevier.

Castells, M. (1996) *The Rise of the Network Society*. Oxford: Blackwell.

Castells, M. (1997) *The Power of Identity*. Oxford: Blackwell.

Castells, M. (2000) *The Rise of the Network Society*, 2nd edn. Oxford: Blackwell.

Castells, M. (2001) *The Internet Galaxy: Reflections on the Internet, Business and Society*. Oxford: Oxford University Press.

Cavanagh, A. (2002) Journalists' representations of the internet: the limits of moral panic theories. Unpublished PhD thesis, Department of Sociology, University of Manchester.

Chandler, A. (1996) The changing definition and image of hackers, *International Journal of the Sociology of Law*, 24(2): 229–51.

Chandler, D. (1995) *Technological Determinism*, www.aber.ac.uk/media/Documents/tecdet/tdet13.html (accessed 30 Nov. 2006).

Ciffolilli, A. (2003) Phantom authority, self-selective recruitment and retention of members in virtual communities: the case of Wikipedia, *First Monday*, 8(12), www.firstmonday.org/issuer/issue8_12/ciffolilli/ (accessed 30 Nov. 2006).

Cole, J.I., Suman, M., Schram, P. *et al.* (2004) Surveying the digital future: ten years, ten trends, www.digitalcenter.org (accessed 2 Aug. 2006).

Conboy, M. (2004) *Journalism: A Critical History*. London: Sage.

Connery, B.A. (1997) IMHO: authority and egalitarian rhetoric in the virtual coffee-house, in D. Porter (ed.) *Internet Culture*. London: Routledge.

Cooper, J. and Harrison, D. (2001) The social organisation of audio piracy on the internet, *Media, Culture and Society*, 23(1): 71–89.

Critcher, C. (2003) *Moral Panics and the Media*. Buckingham: Open University Press.

Crossley, N. (2002) *Making Sense of Social Movements*. Buckingham: Open University Press.

Curran, J. (1991) Mass media and democracy: a reappraisal, in J. Curran and M. Gurevitch (eds) *Mass Media and Society*. London: Edward Arnold.

Curran, J. and Seaton, J. (1981) *Power without Responsibility*. London: Fontana.

Dalla Costa, M. and James, S. (1975) *The Power of Women and the Subversion of the Community*. Bristol: Falling Wall Press.

Day, J.C., Janus, A. and Davis, J. (2005) Computer and internet use in the United States: 2003, www.census.gov/prod/2005pubs/p23-208.pdf (accessed 2 Aug. 2006).

Dean, J. (2004) The networked empire: communicative capitalism and the hope for politics, in P. Passavant and J. Dean (eds) *Empire's New Clothes: Reading Hardt and Negri*. London: Routledge.

Debord, G. (1994) *The Society of the Spectacle*. New York: Zone Books. (First published 1967.)

Delanty, G. (2003) *Community*. London: Routledge.

Deleuze, G. (1994) *Difference and Repetition*, trans. P. Patton. London: Athlone.

Deleuze, G. and Guattari, F. (1988) *A Thousand Plateaus: Capitalism and Schizophrenia*, trans. and ed. B. Massumi. London: Athlone Press. (First published Les Editions de Minuit, 1987.)

Deleuze, G. and Guattari, F. (2004) *Anti-Oedipus: Capitalism and Schizophrenia*, trans R. Hurley, M. Seem and H. Lane, Preface by M. Foucault. London: Continuum. (First published Les Editions de Minuit, 1972.)

Doheny-Farina, S. (1996) *The Wired Neighbourhood*. London: Yale University Press.

Douglas, S.J. and Michaels, M.W. (2004) *The Mommy Myth: The Idealization of Motherhood and How it has Undermined All Women*. New York: Free Press.

Dreyfus, H. (2001) *On the Internet*. London: Routledge.

Drucker, P. (1969) *The Age of Discontinuity: Guidelines to our Changing Society*. London: Heinemann.

DuVal Smith, A. (1999) Problems of conflict management in virtual communities, in M.A. Smith and P. Kollock (eds) *Communities in Cyberspace*. London: Routledge.

Durkheim, E. (1952) *Suicide: A Study in Sociology*, trans J.A. Spaulding and G. Simpson, ed. G. Simpson. London: Routledge and Kegan Paul. (First published 1897.)

Durkheim, E. (1984) *The Division of Labour in Society*, trans. W.D. Halls. Basingstoke: Macmillan. (First published 1893.)

Dyer-Witheford, N. (1999) *Cybermarx: Cycles and Circuits of Struggle in High-Technology Capitalism*. Urbana and Chicago, IL: Illinois University Press.

Ellul, J. (1964) *The Technological Society*, trans. J. Wilkinson, ed. R.K. Merton. New York: Vintage/Random House.

Erbe, W. (1962) Gregariousness, group membership and the flow of information, *American Journal of Sociology*, 67(5): 502–16.

Ericson, R., Baranek, P. and Chan, J. (1987) *Visualising Deviance: A Study of News Organisation*. Milton Keynes: Open University Press.

Ess, C. (1996) Thoughts on the I-way: philosophy and the emergence of CMC, in C. Ess (ed.) *Philosophical Perspectives on Computer-Mediated Communication*. Albany, NY: State University of New York Press.

Feenberg, A. (1999) *Questioning Technology*. London: Routledge.

Fenton, N., Bryman, A. and Deacon, D. (1998) *Mediating Social Science*. London: Sage.

Fischer, C.S. (1992) *America Calling: A Social History of the Telephone to 1940.* Berkeley, CA, and Oxford: University of California Press.

Fiske, J. (1996) Opening the hallway: some remarks on the fertility of Stuart Hall's contribution to critical theory, in D. Morley and K.-H. Chen (eds) *Stuart Hall: Critical Dialogues in Cultural Studies.* London: Routledge.

Flew, T. (2005) *New Media: An Introduction.* Oxford: Oxford University Press.

Florida, R.L (2004) *The Rise of the Creative Class: And How it's Transforming Work, Leisure, Community and Everyday Life.* New York: Basic Books.

Foster, D., (1997) Community and identity in the electronic village, in D. Porter (ed.) *Internet Culture.* London: Routledge.

Foucault, M. (1971) *Madness and Civilisation,* trans. R. Howard. London: Tavistock.

Foucault, M. (1977) *Discipline and Punish: The Birth of the Prison.* London: Penguin. (First published Editions Gallimard, 1975.)

Foucault, M. (1994) *Essential Worlds of Foucault 1954–1984 Vol 3: Power,* ed. J.D. Faubion. London: Penguin.

Fox, S. (2005) Digital divisions report of the Pew Internet and American Life Project, www.pewinternet.org/pdfs/PIP_Digital_Divisions_Oct_5_2005.pdf (accessed 1 Aug. 2006).

Fraser, N. (1992) Rethinking the public sphere, in C. Calhoun (ed.) *Habermas and the Public Sphere.* Cambridge, MA, and London: MIT Press.

Fukuyama, F. (1992) *The End of History and the Last Man.* London: Penguin.

Furedi, F. (2004a) *Therapy Culture: Creating Vulnerability in an Uncertain Age.* London: Routledge.

Furedi, F. (2004b) *Where Have All the Intellectuals Gone?* London: Continuum.

Furedi, F. (2005) *The Politics of Fear.* London: Continuum.

Gane, N. (2005) An information age without technology: a response to Webster, *Information, Communication and Society,* 8(4): 471–6.

Gans, H. (1979) *Deciding What's News: A Study of CBS Evening News, NBC Nightly News, Newsweek, and Time.* New York: Pantheon.

Garnham, N. (1979) Contribution to a political economy of mass communication, *Media Culture and Society,* 1(2): 123–46.

Gates, B., Myhrvold, N. and Rinearson, P. (1996) *The Road Ahead.* London: Penguin.

Gauntlett, D. (2000) Web studies: a user guide, in D. Gauntlett (ed.) *Web.Studies: Rewiring Media Studies for the Digital Age.* New York: Hodder Arnold.

Gauntlett, D. (2004) Web studies: what's new, in D. Gauntlett and R. Horsley (eds) *Web.Studies,* 2nd edn. London: Arnold.

Giddens, A. (1991) *Modernity and Self-Identity: Self and Society in the Late Modern Age.* Cambridge: Polity.

Gieber, H. (1964) News is what newspapermen make it, in H. Tumber (ed.) *News: A Reader.* Oxford: Oxford University Press.

Goffman, E. (1968) *Stigma: Notes on the Management of Spoiled Identity.* London: Pelican/Penguin. (First published Prentice-Hall, New Jersey, USA, 1963.)

Goffman, E. (1969) *The Presentation of Self in Everyday Life.* Harmondsworth: Penguin. (First published 1959.)

Goffman, E. (1971) *Relations in Public: Microstudies of the Public Order.* Harmondsworth: Penguin.

Goffman, E. (1974) *Frame Analysis: An Essay on the Organization of Experience.* New York: Harper and Row.

Golding, P. (1998) Worldwide wedge; division and contradiction in the global information infrastructure, in D. Thussu (ed.) *Electronic Empires: Global Media and Local Resistance.* New York: Arnold.

Golding, P. and Middleton, S. (1979) Making claims: news media and the welfare state, *Media, Culture and Society,* 1(1): 5–21.

Gouldner, A.W. (1985) *Against Fragmentation: The Origins of Marxism and the Sociology of Intellectuals*. Oxford: Oxford University Press.

Granovetter, M. (1973) The strength of weak ties, *American Journal of Sociology*, 78(6): 1360–80.

Granovetter, M. (1974) *Getting a Job*. Cambridge, MA: Harvard University Press.

Habermas, J. (1989) *The Structural Transformation of the Public Sphere: An Inquiry into a Category of Bourgois Society*, trans. T. Burger. Cambridge: Polity. (First published Herman Luchterhand Verlag, 1962.)

Hampton, M. (2001) Understanding media: theories of the press in Britain 1850–1914, *Media, Culture and Society*, 23(2): 213–31.

Hardt, M. and Negri, A. (2000) *Empire*. Cambridge, MA, and London: Harvard University Press.

Hardt, M. and Negri, A. (2004) *Multitude: War and Democracy in the Age of Empire*. New York: Penguin Press.

Hawthorne, S. and Klein, R. (1999) *Cyberfeminism: Connectivity, Critique and Creativity*, Melbourne: Spinifex.

Hayles, N.K. (1999) *How We Became Posthuman: Virtual Bodies in Cybernetics, Literature, and Informatics*. Chicago, IL: University of Chicago Press.

Haythornwaite, C. (2002) Strong, weak and latent ties and the impact of new media *The Information Society*, 18(5): 385–401.

He, Z. and Zhu, J. (2002) The ecology of online newspapers: the case of China, *Media, Culture and Society*, 24(1): 121–37.

Herman, E.S. (1998) Privatising public space, in D. Thussu (ed.) *Electronic Empires: Global Media and Local Resistance*. New York: Arnold.

Herring, S. (1996) Posting in a different voice: gender and ethics in CMC, in C. Ess (ed.) *Philosophical Perspectives on Computer-Mediated Communication*. Albany, NY: State University of New York Press.

Hesmondhalgh, D. (2006) Bourdieu, the media and cultural production, *Media Culture and Society*, 28(2): 211–31.

Hicks, C.R. (1998) Places in the net: experiencing cyberspace, *Cultural Dynamics*, 10(1): 49–70.

Hobsbawm, E. (1975) *The Age of Capital 1848–75*. London: Weidenfeld and Nicolson.

Holmes, D. (2005) *Communication Theory: Media, Technology and Society*. London: Sage.

Innis, H. (1986) *Empire and Communications*. Victoria and Toronto: Press Porcepic. (First published Oxford, Oxford University Press, 1950.)

Islam, N. (1988) Defining intellectuals and their social location in a peripheral society, in B.M. Chowdhury and S.Z. Sadeque (eds) *Bangladesh: Social Structure and Development*. Dhaka: Bangladesh Sociological Association. Also available at www.bangladeshsociology.org/myweb21.

Jordan, T. (1999a) *Cyberpower: The Culture and Politics of the Internet and Cyberspace*. London: Routledge.

Jordan, T. (1999b) Cyberpower and the meaning of online activism, *Cybersociology*, i. 5, www.cybersociology.com/files/5_timjordan_cyberpower.html (accessed 29 Nov. 2006).

Kamenka, E. (1982) *Community as a Social Ideal*. London: Edward Arnold.

Katz, J. (1997) Birth of a digital nation, www.wired.com/wired/5.04/netizen_pr.html (accessed 30 Aug. 2006).

Kolko, B. and Reid, E. (1998) Dissolution and fragmentation: problems in on-line communities, in S. Jones (ed.) *Cybersociety 2.0: Revisiting Computer-Mediated Communication and Community*. London: Sage.

Kollock, P. (1999) The economies of online cooperation: gifts and public goods in cyberspace, in M.A. Smith and P. Kollock (eds) *Communities in Cyberspace*. London: Routledge.

Kornhauser, W. (1959) *The Politics of Mass Society*. London and Glencoe, IL: Free Press.

Kraut, R. and Keisler, S. (2003) The social impact of internet use, *Psychological Science Agenda*, 16(3): 8–10.

Kraut, R., Patterson, M., Lundmark, V., Kiesler, S., Mukhopadhyay, T. and Scherlis, W. (1998) Internet paradox: a social technology that reduces social involvement and psychological well-being? *American Psychologist*, 53(9): 1017–31.

Kroker, A. and Weinstein, M. (1994) *Data Trash: The Theory of the Virtual Class*. Montreal: New World Perspectives.

Kuhn, T.A. (1962) *The Structure of Scientific Revolutions*. Chicago, IL: Chicago University Press.

Laclau, E. (2004) Can immanence explain social struggles?, in P. Passavant and J. Dean (eds) *Empire's New Clothes: Reading Hardt and Negri*. London: Routledge.

Lash, S. (2002) *Critique of Information*. London: Sage.

Latour, B. (1986) The powers of association, in J. Law (ed.) *Power, Action and Belief: A New Sociology of Knowledge*. London: Routledge and Kegan Paul.

Latour, B. (2004) On using ANT for studying information systems: a (somewhat) Socratic dialogue, in C. Avgerou, C. Ciborra and F. Land (eds) *The Social Study of Information and Communication Technology: Innovation, Actors and Contexts*. Oxford: Oxford University Press.

Latour, B. (2005) *Reassembling the Social: An Introduction to Actor-Network Theory*. Oxford: Oxford University Press.

Law, J. (1992) Notes on the theory of the actor-network: ordering, strategy and heterogeneity, www.comp.lancs.ac.uk/sociology/papers/Law-Notes-on-ANT.pdf (accessed 22 Aug. 2006).

Law, J. (2000) Networks, relations, cyborgs: on the social study of technology, www.lancs.ac.uk/fss/sociology/papers/law-networks-relations-cyborgs.pdf (accessed 22 Aug. 2006).

Lazarsfeld, P.F., Berelson, B. and Gaudet, H. (1968) *The People's Choice: How the Voter Makes Up His Mind in a Presidential Campaign*, 3rd edn. New York: Columbia University Press.

Lee, C.-Y. (1996) Thinking cyber-subjectivity: ideology and the subject, www.isoc.org/inet96/proceedings/e3/e3_4.htm (accessed 30 Aug. 2006).

Lessig, L. (2002) *The Future of Ideas: The Fate of the Commons in a Connected World*. New York: Vintage/Random House.

Lessig, L. (2004) *Free Culture: How Big Media Uses Technology and the Law to Lock Down Culture and Control Creativity*. New York: Penguin.

Lewis, D.M. (2003) Online news: a new genre, in J. Aitchison and D.M. Lewis (eds) *New Media and Language*. London: Routledge.

Lloyd, L., Kauldud, P. and Skiena, S. (2006) Newspapers vs blogs: who gets the scoop? Paper presented to the AAAI Spring Symposium on Computational Approaches to Analyzing Weblogs (AAAI-CAAW), Palo Alto, CA, March. Also available at algorithm.cs.sunysb.edu/lloyd/blog_paper.pdf (accessed 21 Aug. 2006).

Lukes, S. (1968) Methodological individualism reconsidered, *British Journal of Sociology*, 19(2): 119–29.

Lockard, J. (1997) Progressive politics, electronic individualism and the myth of virtual community in D. Porter (ed.) *Internet Culture*. London: Routledge.

Lopez, J. (2003) *Society and its Metaphors: Language, Social Theory and Social Structure*. London: Continuum.

Lyotard, J.-F. (1984) *The Postmodern Condition: A Report on Knowledge*, trans G. Bennington and B. Massumi. Manchester: Manchester University Press. (First published Les Editions de Minuit, 1979.)

Maasen, S. and Weingart, P. (2000) *Metaphor and the Dynamics of Knowledge*. London: Routledge.

Marx, K. (1963) *Selected Writings in Sociology and Social Philosophy*, trans. T.B. Bottomore, eds T.B. Bottomore and M. Rubel. London: Penguin.

Marx, K. (1970) *A Contribution to the Critique of Political Economy*, trans. S.W. Ryazanskaya, ed. Maurice Dobb. New York: International Publishers. (First published 1859.)

Marx, K. and Engels, F. (1963) *The Poverty of Philosophy*. New York: International Publishers. (First published 1847.)

Marx, K. and Engels, F. (1970) *The German Ideology*. London: Lawrence and Wishart. (First published 1846.)

Massumi, B. (1993) *A User's Guide to Capitalism and Schizophrenia: Deviations from Deleuze and Guattari*. Cambridge, MA: MIT Press.

McChesney, R.W. (1998) Media convergence and globalisation, in D. Thussu (ed.) *Electronic Empires: Global Media and Local Resistance*. New York: Arnold.

McGinn, R.E. (1991) *Science, Technology*, and Society. London: Prentice-Hall.

McGuigan, J. (1998) What price the public sphere, in D. Thussu (ed.) *Electronic Empires: Global Media and Local Resistance*. New York: Arnold.

McLuhan, M. (1962) *The Gutenberg Galaxy: The Making of Typographic Man*. Toronto and London: University of Toronto Press.

McLuhan, M. (1964) *Understanding Media: The Extensions of Man*. New York: McGraw-Hill.

McLuhan, M. (1995) Playboy interview, in (eds) *Essential McLuhan*, E. McLuhan and F. Zingrone. London: Routledge.

McQuail, D. (2000) *McQuail's Mass Communication Theory*, 4th edn. London: Sage.

Meyer, P. (2004) *The Vanishing Newspaper: Saving Journalism in the Information Age*. Columbia, MO: University of Missouri Press.

Miller, D. and Slater, D. (2000) *The Internet: An Ethnographic Approach*. Oxford: Berg.

Mills, C.W. (2000) *The Sociological Imagination*. Oxford: Oxford University Press. (First published Oxford University Press, New York, 1959.)

Mitchell, C. (1974) Social networks, *Annual Review of Anthropology*, 3: 279–99.

Monteiro, E. (2004) Actor network theory and cultural aspects of interpretative studies, in C. Avgerou, C. Ciborra and F. Land (eds) *The Social Study of Information and Communication Technology: Innovation, Actors and Contexts*. Oxford: Oxford University Press.

Morgan, G. (1997) *Images of Organization*. London: Sage.

Mosco, V. (1989) *The Pay-per Society: Computers and Communication in the Information Age*. Toronto: Garamond Press.

Nadel, S. (1957) *The Theory of Social Structure*. London: Cohen and West.

Naisbitt, J. (1982) *Megatrends*. New York: Warner Books.

Negri, A. (1989) *The Politics of Subversion: A Manifesto for the Twenty-First Century*. Cambridge: Polity.

Nie, N.H. and Erbing, L. (2002) Internet and society: a preliminary report, *IT&Society*, 1(1): 275–83.

Noble, D. (1986) *Forces of Production: A Social History of Industrial Automation*. Oxford: Oxford University Press.

O'Brien, J. (1999) Writing in the body: gender (re)production in online interaction, in M.A. Smith and P. Kollock (eds) *Communities in Cyberspace*. London: Routledge.

Ornebring, H. and Jonsson, A.M. (2004) Tabloid journalism and the public sphere: a historical perspective on tabloid journalism, *Journalism Studies*, 5(3): 283–95.

Papacharissi, Z. (2002) The presentation of self in virtual life: characteristics of personal home pages, *Journalism and Mass Communication Quarterly*, 79(3): 643–60.

Park, R. (1923) The natural history of the newspaper, *American Journal of Sociology*, 29(3): 273–89.

Perelman, M. (1998) *Class Warfare in the Information Age*. New York: St Martin's Press.

Pinch, T.J. and Bijker, W.E. (1987) The social construction of facts and artifacts, in W.E. Bijker, T.P. Hughes and T.J. Pinch (eds) *The Social Construction of Technological Systems: New Directions in the Sociology and History of Technology*. Cambridge, MA: MIT Press.

Plant, S. (1997) *Zeros + Ones: Digital Women + the New Technoculture*. London: Fourth Estate.

Poster, M. (1995a) *The Second Media Age*. London: Polity.

Poster, M. (1995b) Communication and the constitution of the self: an interview with Mark Poster, 14.8.1995, reproduced in Poster, M. (2001) *The Information Subject*. Amsterdam: OPA.

Poster, M. (1995c) Cyberdemocracy: internet and the public sphere, reproduced in Porter, D. (1997) *Internet Culture*. London: Routledge.

Poster, M. (1998) Virtual ethnicity: tribal identity in an age of global communications, in S. Jones (ed.) *Cybersociety 2.0: Revisiting Computer-Mediated Communication and Community*. London: Sage.

Poulantzas, N. (1978) *Classes in Contemporary Capitalism*, trans. D. Fernbach. London: Verso.

Preece, J. (2000) *Online Communities: Supporting Sociability, Designing Usability*. Chichester: John Wiley and Sons.

Putnam, R.G. (2000) *Bowling Alone: The Collapse and Revival of American Community*. London: Simon and Schuster.

Radcliffe-Brown, A.R. (1940) On social structure, *Journal of the Royal Anthropological Society of Great Britain and Ireland*, 70, reproduced in S. Leinhardt (ed.) (1977) *Social Networks: A Developing Paradigm*. New York and London: Academic Press.

Rafaeli, S. (1988) Interactivity: from new media to communication, *Sage Annual Review of Communication Research: Advancing Communication Science*, 16: 110–34.

Reid, E. (1999) Hierarchy and power: social control in cyberspace, in M.A. Smith and P. Kollock (eds) *Communities in Cyberspace*. London: Routledge.

Resnick, P., Zeckhauser, R., Friedman, E. and Kuwabara, K. (2000) Reputation systems, *Communications of the ACM*, 43(12): 45–8.

Rheingold, H. (1994) *The Virtual Community: Surfing the Internet*. London: Minerva.

Rifkin, J. (1995) *The End of Work: The Decline of the Global Labor Force and the Dawn of the Post-Market Era*. New York: Tarcher/Putnam.

Robins, K. and Webster, F. (1999) *Times of the Technoculture: From the Information Society to the Virtual Life*. London: Routledge.

Roe, P. (2003) That-which-new-media-studies-will-become, *Fibreculture*, 2, journal. fibreculture.org/issue2/issue2_roe.html (accessed 30 Aug. 2006).

Rogers, E. (1986) *Communication Technology: the New Media in Society*. New York: Free Press.

Rose, N. (1991) *Governing the Soul: The Shaping of the Private Self*. London: Routledge.

Ross, A. (1999) *The Celebration Chronicles: Life, Liberty and the Pursuit of Property Values in Disney's New Town*. New York: Ballatine Books.

Schiller, H. (1996) *Information Inequality: The Deepening Social Crisis in America*. London: Routledge.

Schuler, D. (1996) *New Community Networks: Wired for Change*. New York: ACM Press.

Scott, J. (1995) *Sociological Theory: Contemporary Debates*. Cheltenham: Edward Elgar.

Scott, J. (2000) *Social Network Analysis: A Handbook*. London: Sage.

Slouka, M. (1995) *The War of the Worlds: Cyberspace and the High-Tech Assault on Reality*. London: Abacus.

Schudson, M. (1978) *Discovering the News: A Social History of American Newspapers*. New York: Basic Books/Perseus.

Shannon, C. and Weaver, W. (1963) *The Mathematical Theory of Communication*. Urbana, IL: University of Illinois Press. (First published 1949.)

Shapiro, K. (2004) The myth of the multitude, in P. Passavant and J. Dean (eds) *Empire's New Clothes: Reading Hardt and Negri*. London: Routledge.

Slevin, J. (2000) *The Internet and Society*. Cambridge: Polity.

Sparks, C. (1998) Is there a global public sphere, in D. Thussu (ed.) *Electronic Empires: Global Media and Local Resistance*. New York: Arnold.

Stallman, R. (2002) *Free Software, Free Society: Selected Essays of Richard M. Stallman*, ed. J. Gay, intro. L. Lessig. Boston, MA: Free Software Foundation.

Sterne, J. (2003) Bourdieu: technique and technology, *Cultural Studies*, 17(3/4): 367–89.

Stone, A. (1991) Will the real body please stand up? Boundary stories about virtual cultures, in M. Benedikt (ed.) *Cyberspace: First Steps*. Cambridge, MA: MIT Press.

Stone, A. (1996) *The War of Desire and Technology at the Close of the Mechanical Age*. Cambridge, MA: MIT Press.

Sunstein, C. (2001) *Republic.com*. Oxford: Princeton University Press.

Tannen, D. (1999) *The Argument Culture: Changing the Way We Argue*. London: Virago.

Taylor, P.M. (2000) The World Wide Web goes to war: Kosovo 1999 in D. Gauntlett (ed.) *Web.studies: Rewiring Media Studies for the Digital Age*. New York: Hodder Arnold.

Terranova, T. (2004) *Network Culture: Politics for the Information Age*. London: Pluto.

Thompson, J. (1995) *The Media and Modernity*. Cambridge: Polity.

Thorngate, W. (1997) More that we can know: the attentional economics of internet use, in S. Kiesler (ed.) *Culture of the Internet*. Mahwah, NJ: Lawrence Erlbaum Associates.

Toennies, F. (2001) *Community and Civil Society*, ed. J. Harris. Cambridge: Cambridge University Press. (First published 1887.)

Toffler, A. (1980) *The Third Wave*. New York: Bantam/Morrow.

Turkle, S. (1995) *Life on the Screen: Identity in the Age of the Internet*. London: Phoenix/ Orion.

Turner, B.S. (1999) *Classical Sociology*. London: Sage.

Urry, J. (2003) *Global Complexity*. Oxford: Polity.

Vaidhyanathan, S. (2004) *The Anarchist in the Library: How the Clash between Freedom and Control is Hacking the Real World and Crashing the System*. New York: Basic Books/ Perseus.

Wallace, P. (1999) *The Psychology of the Internet*. Cambridge: Cambridge University Press.

Wallerstein, I. (2004) *World-Systems Analysis: An Introduction*. London: Duke University Press.

Waskul, D. and Douglass, M. (1997) Cyberself: the emergence of self in on-line chat, *Information Society*, 13: 375–97.

Watts, D. (2004) *Six Degrees: The Science of a Connected Age*. London: Vintage/Random House. (First published Heinemann, 2003.)

Weber, M. (2005) Remarks on technology and culture, *Theory, Culture and Society*, 22(4): 23–38.

Webster, F. (1995) *Theories of the Information Society*. London: Routledge.

Webster, F. (2005) Making sense of the information age: sociology and cultural studies, *Information Communication and Society*, 8(4): 439–58.

Webster, F. and Robins, K. (1986) *Information Technology: A Luddite Analysis*. Norwood, NJ: Ablex.

Wellman, B. (1997) An electronic group is virtually a social network, in S. Kiesler (ed.) *Culture of the Internet*. Mahwah, NJ: Lawrence Erlbaum Associates.

Wellman, B. and Gulia, M. (1999) Virtual communities as communities: net surfers don't ride alone, in M. Smith and P. Kollock (eds) *Communities in Cyberspace*. London: Routledge.

Wellman, B., Carrington, P. and Hall, A. (1988) Networks as personal communities, in B. Wellman and S.D. Berkowitz (eds) *Social Structures: A Network Approach*. Cambridge: Cambridge University Press.

Wernick, A. (1991) *Promotional Culture: Advertising, Ideology and Symbolic Expression.* London: Sage.

White, H., McConnell, E., Clipp, E. *et al.* (1999) Surfing the net in later life: a review of the literature and pilot study of computer use and quality of life, *Journal of Applied Gerontology*, 18(3): 358–78.

Whyte, J. (2003) *Bad Thoughts.* London: Corvo.

Wiggins, R.W. (2001) The effects of September 11th on the leading search engine, *First Monday*, 6(10), http://firstmonday.org/issues/issue6_10/wiggins/index.html (accessed 30 Aug. 2006).

Wilhelm, A.G. (2000) *Democracy in the Digital Age: Challenges to Political Life in Cyberspace.* New York: Routledge.

Williams, K. (1998) *Get Me A Murder A Day: A History of Mass Communication in Britain.* London: Hodder/Arnold.

Williams, R. (1961) *The Long Revolution.* New York: Colombia University Press.

Williams, R. (1981) *Culture.* London: Fontana.

Williams, R. (2003) *Television: Technology and Cultural Form*, 2nd edn. London: Routledge. (First published Fontana, London, 1974).

Winner, L. (1978) *Autonomous Technology: Technics-out-of-Control as a Theme in Political Thought.* Cambridge, MA: MIT Press.

Winner, L. (1980) Do artifacts have politics?, reproduced in D. MacKenzie and J. Wajcman (eds) (1985) *The Social Shaping of Technology.* Milton Keynes: Open University Press.

Wirth, L. (1938) Urbanism as a way of life, *American Journal of Sociology*, 44(1): 1–24.

Wittgenstein, L. (1980) *Culture and Value*, eds G.H. von Wright and H. Nyman. Oxford: Blackwell.

Wynn, E. and Katz, J.E. (1997) Hyperbole over cyberspace: self-presentation and social boundaries in internet home pages and discourse, *Information Society*, 13: 297–327.

Yesil, B. (2001) Reel pleasures: exploring the historical roots of media voyeurism and exhibitionism, *Counterblast: e-Journal of Culture and Communication*, 1(1), www.nyu.edu/pubs/counterblast/archive.htm (accessed 30 Nov. 2006).

Yoon, S.-H. (1996) Power online: a poststructuralist perspective on computer-mediated communication, in C. Ess (ed.) *Philosophical Perspectives on Computer-Mediated Communication.* Albany, NY: State University of New York Press.

Zuboff, S. (1988) *In the Age of the Smart Machine: The Future of Work and Power.* Oxford: Heinemann Professional.

Index